AFRICAN AMERICANS AND AFRICA

AFRICAN AMERICANS AND AFRICA

A New History

NEMATA AMELIA IBITAYO BLYDEN

Yale

UNIVERSITY PRESS

New Haven and London

Published with assistance from the income of the Frederick John
Kingsbury Memorial Fund and with assistance from the foundation
established in memory of Philip Hamilton McMillan of the
Class of 1894, Yale College.

Yale University Press books may be purchased in quantity for
educational, business, or promotional use. For information,
please e-mail sales.press@yale.edu (U.S. office) or sales@yaleup.co.uk
(U.K. office).

Set in Janson type by IDS Infotech Ltd., Chandigarh, India.
Printed in the United States of America.

Library of Congress Control Number: 2018961154
ISBN 978-0-300-19866-9 (hardcover : alk. paper)
ISBN 978-0-300-25852-3 (paperback)

A catalogue record for this book is available from the British Library.

10 9 8 7 6 5 4 3 2 1

For Edward and Amelia

Contents

Acknowledgments

THIS BOOK HAS BEEN a long time in the making, and it could not have happened without a lot of support along the way. First and foremost, without my parents I doubt I would have come up with the idea for this book. When my father left his home in the small city of Freetown, Sierra Leone, in the late 1940s, he could not have known the trajectory his life would take. Yet in many ways he was coming full circle, retracing the steps his ancestors from Tennessee and Virginia had taken two hundred years before. My "African" father was coming back to his "American" roots. His great-great-grandfather George Erskine had left the United States seeking freedom for his family in Africa. My mother's story too is born out of the enslavement of Africans in the United States. Her father's roots in the South (Georgia) and her mother's in the North (New York and Massachusetts) are part of the larger story of black Americans in the United States. That my mother should also have come full circle by marrying an "African" is testament to the links between African Americans and Africa in the last four hundred years. This book tells part of their story and is dedicated to the memory of my father, Edward Wilmot Blyden III, and in honor of my mother, Amelia Elizabeth Blyden (née Kendrick). It is to these two remarkable individuals that I owe the greatest debt. I have attained much, both personally and professionally, with their love and support.

There are many others to remember and to thank. I would like to extend a general acknowledgment to those who over the years have listened to me talk about the book. I want to thank the many students in my African Americans and Africa: Links in History course over the years. My students in Texas and Washington, DC, contributed to the ideas that have come to fruition in this book. Their questions, feedback, comments, and critical inquiry of the material challenged me in useful ways. In particular, I thank the first group at the University of Texas at Dallas, where I first taught the course in 1996. Their engagement and interest in the topic allowed me to conceive of the idea of a book. Thank you to Taaja El Shabazz and Amanda Lam, who took the course at George Washington University in 2015, and agreed to read the entire draft of the manuscript, providing useful feedback. Thanks to Nichole Smith, my graduate research assistant, for her valuable assistance during the last leg of this process. She proofread, worked tirelessly on my endnotes and bibliography, and helped with the nitty-gritty, time-consuming work of finding images and illustrations.

To my family, friends, and colleagues who encouraged me through different stages, listening to my ideas and reading parts of the manuscript, offering comments and suggestions, I say a profound thank-you. I owe an enormous debt of gratitude to my colleague Ed Berkowitz, who graciously offered to read the whole manuscript and offer his insightful suggestions. I thank the members of the DC area African American Studies Works-in-Progress seminar for their comments on one of my chapters. A special shout-out to my Kellari ladies, from whom I received tremendous support and encouragement at our "black girls" happy hours. The sisterhood we have formed is a great joy. A special thanks to Dr. Vanessa Gamble, friend and mentor, who has guided me as a big sister with advice, chastisement, and all-round support. Thanks to my editor Sarah Miller for taking me to the finish line. It was a long journey. I would like to thank also the anonymous readers who read the book at various stages. The George Washington University Facilitating Fund and the Columbian College of Arts and Science Facilitating Fund allowed me to do part of the research for this project. A special thanks to my siblings, Isa, Bai, Fenda, Cleo (Coker), Eluem (Cozin), and Eddie (Didi), for being great role models and offering their baby sister support and encouragement over the years. To my eldest brother, Tunde—my biggest role model in my teenage years—we still miss you.

My biggest thank-you, with much love, is to my husband, Christopher Bickersteth, and my children, Pearl, Ayinde, and Nalo. P.A.N., you have always taken pride in me and the work I do, taking it for granted that Mom can do anything. Most of all I thank you, Chris: my love, my champion, my better half. I could not ask for a more loving and supportive partner. You have stood beside me in all that I do in our years together, and this time was no different. Without you I could not do what I do.

AFRICAN AMERICANS AND AFRICA

INTRODUCTION

"I'm not African. I'm American."

Years after she met my father, my mother recalled a conversation they had at their first encounter.

"I hate to admit this, but I couldn't find Sierra Leone
on a map of the world."

Edward's eyes rolled upward and I feared he thought
me an illiterate.

"Why Miss Kendrick, you know nothing about Africa!"

"Very little," I said, sorry because this was where he
came from. "I've never really thought about my ignorance in this regard."

My mother went on to explain that she had learned "a few geographical aspects of Africa, and slave history," but where she grew
up, some American history was taught "in a derogatory light," and
she had been ashamed of her slave ancestry. Edward pointed out
that others besides Africans had been enslaved. In Massachusetts,
she said, "Negroes bear the weight of racial prejudice." As she told
her husband-to-be, "Learning about George Washington Carver
and other famous Negroes was easier."[1]

My parents met a few years after my mother, a newly minted
graduate of Boston University, had taken her first job, as a music

teacher at an elementary school in Atlantic City, New Jersey. Her
experiences, up to that point, had been largely limited to encounters with other native New Englanders, both white Americans and
other African Americans. One Sunday in 1950, a friend invited her
to church to hear the main speaker—"an African man." Introduced
to him after the service, she found the smartly dressed man in a
suit little different from the young men with whom she had grown
up. He spoke perfect English, invited her to play tennis, and
courted her. He also talked about his native Sierra Leone with
great passion. When she went home she looked for his country on
a map, without success.

In the 1950s black Americans knew little of Africa and its history. Representations of the continent were typically negative, and
those of African descent distanced themselves from associating
with it. As my mother wrote in her memoir years later, while living
in Sierra Leone, "I was one of two Negroes in my high school
class. And in my class at Boston University there had been only
three colored women. Neither school curriculum nor course of
studies related to the Negro experience—no Negro writers or
poets were studied, no music by African or Negro composers. This
lack of exposure coupled with the image of white society reflected
in advertising, newspapers, literature, shaped me immeasurably, in-
culcated an image of white society that actually de-emphasized the
value of American Negroes."

My mother was an "American Negro," the label used for black
Americans at that time. When they came to the United States, men
and women from Africa, like my father, also fell into this category.
Edward and Amelia would later marry, and the sheltered girl from
Worcester, Massachusetts, who "had never before ventured further
south than Williamsburg, Virginia, nor further north than Maine,"
would embark on a journey to Africa that would last several decades, producing seven children and a lifelong regard for the continent. In the nearly seventy years since my parents met, African
Americans have gained more knowledge about Africa. Increasingly,
some even identify with the continent as the land of their ancestors. Many more over the centuries have engaged with Africa in
myriad ways.

Edward and Amelia Blyden, c. 1950.
(From Blyden family private photographs. Courtesy of Amelia Blyden.)

In 1989, the Reverend Jesse Jackson called on black Americans to embrace the label "African American." The term had been in limited use among some black Americans, but as Isabel Wilkerson reported in the *New York Times*, it was now "gaining currency among many other blacks, who say its use is a sign that they are accepting their difficult past and resolving a long ambivalence toward Africa." In calling for the change, Jackson noted, "This is deeper than just name recognition. . . . Black tells you about skin color and what side of town you live on. African-American evokes discussion of the world." Others pushing for the change highlighted the connection to Africa the label signified. The continent loomed large in the

decision to embrace the term. These calls for a greater connection
to Africa also brought American blacks into solidarity with the
growing anti-apartheid movement of the late 1980s in South Africa
and "led to the search for a clearer group identity."[2]

Yet not all black Americans readily accepted the label. The call
for a name change sparked much discussion and debate. Some argued that they were Americans, not Africans. Prominent black
Americans such as tennis player Arthur Ashe embraced the term
but others, like comedian and actor Whoopi Goldberg, rejected
the label, pleading,

> Don't call me an African American. Please. It divides us as a
> nation and as a people, and it kinda pisses me off. It dimin-
> ishes everything I've accomplished and everything every
> other black person has accomplished on American soil. It
> means I'm not entitled to everything plain old regular
> Americans are entitled to. Every time you put something in
> front of the word "American," it strips it of its meaning.
> The Bill of Rights is my Bill of Rights, same as anyone
> else's. It's my flag. It's my Constitution. It doesn't talk about
> SOME people. It talks about ALL people—black, white, or-
> ange, brown. You. Me . . . no, I am not an African Ameri-
> can. I'm not from Africa. I'm from New York. My roots run
> a whole lot deeper than most of the people who don't have
> anything in front of the word "American." I can trace my
> family tree back to the Mayflower. We may not have been
> on it, but we were under it, and that counts too.[3]

Goldberg echoed sentiments expressed by the likes of Frederick Douglass, who, in 1894, dismissed calls by some of his contemporaries for
closer ties to Africa, proclaiming: "All this native land talk . . . is non-
sense. The native land of the American Negro is America. His bones,
his muscles, his sinews, are all American. His ancestors for two hundred and seventy years have lived and labored and died, on American
soil, and millions of his posterity have inherited Caucasian blood."[4]

This opposition to the use of *African American* notwithstanding, the term gained currency and soon after Jackson's call most
major newspapers, national organizations, and local associations

began using it. It is evident that "African American," often used interchangeably with "black," is here to stay, at least for now.

The debates over the 1989 name change were not the first of their kind. From the moment women and men of African descent were brought to the United States, what they called themselves would be a contested issue. Enslaved men and women, who were from a variety of communities and varying ethnicities, arrived with no notion of "Africa." They used their family, lineage, or clan names to claim an identity. In the United States they would become "African." But before that they were Igbos, Congo, Mandingo, Cromantee, and "Guinea Coast negroes," as recorded in the records of people involved in the slave trade. What they called themselves is largely lost to history. Africa was the landmass from which they had been taken, and it was a place outsiders had named.[5]

In the Americas, enslaved Africans were sometimes labeled by place of origin/capture or by ethnicity, but mainly by phenotype or the perceived color of their skin—black, or Negro. In 1619 John Rolfe's account of the "20 and odd Negroes" first brought to the fledgling Virginia colony referred to men and women probably taken from the region of the Kingdom of Kongo. While it is difficult to re-create how enslaved Africans referred to themselves, the most commonly used description in colonial America was "Negro," although slave owners often used terms associated with African geographical regions, such as Guinea, Congo, and Angola, or with ethnicities, such as Mandingo, Bambara, and Joloka. As slavery became entrenched, a process of perpetual enslavement and racialization of Africans resulted in emphasis on their color. In other words, their dark skin served to mark them as enslaved. The term *Negro* embraced both enslaved and free Africans in the United States, enduring into the era of emancipation and even into the twentieth century. In the late 1960s the term fell into disuse. Despite its persistence from the eighteenth to the twentieth century, black Americans, particularly those who were literate and educated, chose other labels to describe themselves.

As black Americans became literate in European languages and began to write about their experiences and histories, they chose how they would identify themselves in a variety of ways. Blacks in the North, petitioning for various rights and concessions in Northern states, frequently referred to themselves as "Africans." Enslaved at the age of seven, Phillis Wheatley grew up in the household of a Boston family, where she learned to read and write. She became one of black America's first poets. Her poem "On Being Brought from Africa to America" reflects on her life as a Christian woman and articulates her gratitude for what America had given her:

> 'Twas mercy brought me from my *Pagan* land,
> Taught my benighted soul to understand
> That there's a God, that there's a *Saviour* too.[6]

Yet even as Wheatley rejoiced in her adoption of the Christian religion, she embraced the label African. Another poem, "To S.M., a Young African Painter, on Seeing His Works," celebrated a young black artist. Though choosing not to identify with Africa and glad for the "mercy" that had brought her to the United States, Wheatley nonetheless recognized her African ancestry.

In the eighteenth and early nineteenth centuries black Americans used the terms *Negro, African,* and occasionally *black* to describe themselves. In the South those enslaved on plantations often had little choice in what they would be called—they had identities ascribed to them. Privately, within the confines of slave quarters among other Africans, they no doubt chose their own labels. In those spaces they would almost certainly have assumed the names they were given at birth. In the North those who spoke and wrote publicly proudly embraced the label of *African* whether describing themselves or their institutions. Thus, in the eighteenth century Venture Smith's *A Narrative of the Life and Adventures of Venture, a Native of Africa: But Resident above Sixty Years in the United States of America* used the term *Africa* to indicate his heritage.[7]

Throughout the antebellum period, black Americans, fearing discrimination, found Africa looming in their imaginations. They constructed it as a homeland where the racial oppression they faced did not exist. Even those with fading memories and ties to the continent often embraced that heritage. As they sought inclusion and assimilation in the United States, many found that their African ancestry precluded incorporation into the larger society and looked for other ways to signify their place in the United States. In the

wake of efforts by the American Colonization Society (ACS) to encourage free blacks to emigrate to Liberia in 1820, the term *African*
was abandoned by many in favor of *colored*. As one scholar has
noted, "Displays of African culture fell into disrepute."[8] So it was
that in 1835 William Whipper, a black Philadelphian, recom-
mended that "colored" and "African" be abandoned, and that Americans of African ancestry try to assimilate more fully into American
society.[9] Though he received some support for abandoning the use
of racial designations, the use of "colored" persisted. Other terms,
such as *Anglo African* and *black*, were used occasionally, even into
the middle of the nineteenth century. In 1859 the *Weekly Anglo-African* newspaper and an accompanying magazine were published by
Robert and Thomas Hamilton to be a "press of our own."[10]

In the nineteenth century those who championed repatriation
to Africa continued to highlight their African background. Even
those who rejected the idea of a "return" identified with or embraced the term *African*. By the nineteenth century black Americans, now several generations removed from Africa, gradually
dropped that label from their institutions. Late in the nineteenth
century some embraced the "Afro American" label, as seen in the titles of organizations such as the National Afro American League
and the Baltimore Afro American. An early twentieth-century campaign resulted in the word *negro* being capitalized by the 1930s.
"Negro" continued to be used into the twentieth century.

W. E. B. Du Bois, whose life spanned almost a century and who,
throughout his life, encountered different labels describing black
Americans, responded to a letter from a young high school student
in 1928. Roland A. Barton objected to the use of "Negro," believing
it "a white man's word to make us feel inferior." He wondered why
even "natives of Africa" were called Negroes. Du Bois assured the
young man that a name change would not alter the condition of
blacks in America: "If men despise Negroes," he wrote, "they will
not despise them less if Negroes are called 'colored' or 'Afro Americans.'" Rather, he suggested that the conditions for blacks must be
changed: "*First*, to let the world know what there is fine and genuine about the Negro race. And *secondly*, to see that there is nothing
about that race which is worth contempt; your contempt, my contempt; or the contempt of the wide, wide world."[11] *Negro* became

the most accepted term until the 1960s when, at the height of the
Black Power movement, young Americans of African descent embraced the term *black*.

In 1967 the historian Lerone Bennett, writing in *Ebony* magazine,
widely read by black Americans, asked whether "Negro" should be
abandoned in favor of "Afro-American." Bennett explained the long
history of name changes in black history to the magazine's readers,
dating the rejection of "African" to the colonization era. As white
Americans, seeking to solve the free black problem, championed emigration, the "tentative efforts of Americans of African descent to define themselves in African terms" failed as blacks abandoned the term
in favor of "colored" or "free persons of color." As in 1989, the suggestion of a name change caused "bitter national controversy." Those
who advocated the change argued that Negro "perpetuates the mas-
ter-slave mentality," and that changing the name would "short circuit
the stereotyped thinking patterns that undergird the system of racism
in America." Indeed, in the late 1960s many organizations adopted
the label *Afro-American*. The Negro Teachers Association of New
York City, founded in 1964, became the African-American Teachers
Association. Black newspapers soon stopped using "Negro" because,
as one editor argued, "We are descendants of Africans and because we
are Americans." Young black nationalists preferred the term *black* for
"black brothers and sisters who are emancipating themselves."[12]

Those who argued against the change made the point that
using "Afro-American" would not change the power structure, urging that black Americans concentrate on more pressing concerns:
"A Negro by any other name, they say, would be as black and as
beautiful—and as segregated. The times, they add, are too crucial
for Negroes to dissipate their energy in fratricidal strife over
names."[13] In other words, as Du Bois had observed, addressing the
marginalized condition of black Americans was more critical than
what they were called. Yet others believed the two things were integrally related, and that it was important to understand the context, history, and politics of what they called themselves.

The many letters to the editor responding to Bennett's publication showed the diversity of opinion among black Americans regarding their preference. Some linked the terminology to larger
world issues, while others saw no need for a substitution that

would not engender significant change in their social, political, and economic condition. Similar debates and controversy followed Jackson's call. High-profile and ordinary black Americans alike weighed in. As in previous years, some disdained the attempts of black leaders to speak for them; others categorically declared they were too far removed from their African past to embrace the label African American. Still others argued that the label robbed them of their contribution to the United States.

In the late 1960s, at the height of the Black Power movement, and during periods of strong nationalist sentiments, black Americans took pride in identifying with their ancestry. As African nations gained independence from European colonizers, some African Americans chose to highlight their links to Africa. Likewise, in the late 1980s, some felt they were entitled to identify themselves however they wanted. The illustrious historian Mary Frances Berry perhaps best articulated the potential of using "African American" for building self-esteem, simply observing, "It's not going to make things worse."[14]

While "African American" is now widely accepted and used interchangeably with "black" by most Americans of African descent, the debate has resurfaced in the twenty-first century as black immigrants from Africa and the Caribbean settle in the United States. The issue has become complicated as continental Africans struggle with how to categorize themselves in a racial hierarchy that has historically relegated people of African descent to the bottom rungs. Some feel they are the "real" African Americans, but others eschew using the term because of its connection to slavery.

Recently, the actor Morgan Freeman, who since 1989 has asserted that he would not use the term *African American,* has reiterated, "I'm not African. I'm American." Freeman, who has eschewed the use of the term *black,* categorically claims his Americanness. Yet the actor was one of several black Americans who took part in a TV series hosted by Henry Louis Gates Jr. that traced his genealogical roots to Niger. Freeman, like many before him, recognizes and accepts his ancestry, but insists on his American roots and the contributions his ancestors made to building the United States. Charging those who persist in using the term *African American* with political correctness, he rejects attempts to foist the label on him.[15]

One label that has endured through the centuries has been "black." Although it describes little and does not specify a cultural or ethnic identity, it has the ability to encompass or embrace people of African descent under one big umbrella and allies them with other people "of color." Thus blacks descended from enslaved ancestors in the United States or the Caribbean as well as voluntary migrants from the continent have adopted this designation. Furthermore, the history of blacks in the United States has shown that regardless of what citizens with African ancestry choose to call themselves, they still face virulent racism, discrimination, and prejudice. In 1939 the sociologist Ira Reid explained: "Negro immigrants . . . do not possess many of the outward manifestations of the stranger that are common to European immigrants."[16] In other words, black immigrants are not easily identifiable as alien to American culture as other immigrant groups might be. Frequently mistaken for native-born black Americans, they are subject to the same treatment.

Black is a term many have embraced because it has helped to empower African-descended people in America. It has been appropriated at various times as a form of protest, a source of pride, and as an all-encompassing description for people of African descent worldwide. W. E. B. Du Bois used it in the title of his *Souls of Black Folk*, which examined the experiences of blacks in Africa and the United States. Richard Wright titled his travelogue about newly independent Ghana *Black Power*, presumably to indicate the triumph of the new African-led nation. More recently, the Black Lives Matter movement, founded by three black queer women— Patrisse Cullors, Alicia Garza, and Opal Tometi—has highlighted the utility of using the term *Black* (capitalized) to incorporate a wider, more global constituency: "We see ourselves as part of the global Black family, and we are aware of the different ways we are impacted or privileged as Black people who exist in different parts of the world." They have theorized about what it means to be black in the twenty-first century, recognizing that "African American" is too limited to encompass the various diaspora identities in the United States. *Black* continues to be used in the United States today as a descriptor for the country's population of African descent. In the long run, this label, frequently used in history to denigrate African-descended men and women, might endure.[17]

Despite disagreements and individual preferences, "African American" is now the most widely used label for phenotypically black citizens in the United States. Most organizations and groups and media outlets use it, as does the Census of the United States. As women and men of African descent immigrate to the United States, they might choose, as recent African immigrants have, to mark themselves as Nigerian Americans, Ghanaian Americans, or Sierra Leonean Americans. Some first-generation African immigrants use the phrase "Africans in America" to describe themselves. Regardless of what label they adopt, however, the larger society will persist in using "African American" to describe all those deemed black, until such time as a call for a change is made.

It is clear that a large part of the discussion surrounding what men and women of African descent call themselves is tied to their condition and historical moments. Changes in what members of this group call themselves are not arbitrary—they emerge out of specific situations in history. How Africa does or does not figure in these debates is often contingent on how marginalized members of the black population are (or feel), how white Americans perceive them, whether they believe that the path to assimilation is open to them and, more generally, whether identification with Africa helps or hinders them. For many African Americans, the descriptor they use is not seen to affect their place or status in American society. The embrace of a term that highlights their African heritage is more about pride in that ancestry than anything else. For others, highlighting their African roots is seen as a deliberate attempt to separate and serves to further marginalize them in the United States.

This book, as it explores African American links to Africa, will engage the question of how African American ideas, attitudes, perceptions, and opinions about Africa connect to what they called themselves historically. While not a textbook in the traditional sense, it tries to appeal to students, teachers, and general readers interested in the subject. The long relationship African Americans have had with the continent of their ancestors cannot be tackled in a single work. This book, therefore, cannot be exhaustive in its examination of African American engagement with Africa. Rather than being comprehensive in its coverage, it serves as an introduction and a gateway into the sometimes thorny connection between African Americans and Africa. I hope it will encourage those interested to delve more fully into aspects of these ties.

Because of the book's interpretive nature, much is left out, and the decision to include some historical moments and figures and not others may raise questions. Many people, ideas, and themes are omitted or neglected in this book. Why, some might ask, is James Baldwin not mentioned? Or Lorraine Hansberry, Madame C. J. Walker, Nannie Burroughs, and a host of other black Americans with thoughts on their ties to Africa? Why, they might wonder, is someone like Malcolm X mentioned only briefly? All these individuals (and there are many more) engaged with Africa in some way. Others will surely ask, "What of the Negritude movement? Why have you privileged the Anglophone world?" My response is that I could not do it all. What I have included is a reflection of what I know and what I believe best illustrates the ties between African Americans and Africa.

The book will consistently use the terms *black American* and *African American* to refer to the enslaved men and women brought forcibly to the United States, while designating those from the continent who came voluntarily as *continental Africans* or *indigenous Africans*. In an attempt to avoid objectifying the millions of men and women who were forcibly brought to the United States I avoid, as much as possible, using the term *slaves*, preferring the term *enslaved Africans* to denote the involuntary nature of their condition. Throughout this book the humanity of African and African-descended people will be foregrounded, as I attempt to present them as people with social lives and histories, both before and after their enslavement.[18]

The following chapters will illustrate the many ways African-descended men and women chose to engage and identify with, influence, and impact Africa over the centuries. Often prompted by changes occurring in the United States itself, the relationship with Africa has had ebbs and flows. The book makes a distinction among "identification," "engagement," and "interest" in Africa.

African Americans have never been a monolithic group. While some identified strongly with their African heritage, others recognized it as a discarded part of their past. Members of the latter group have, arguably, nevertheless always engaged with Africa in a variety of ways or been involved with issues relevant to that back-ground. Engagement implies recognition of ties to the continent and an interest in seeing Africa's uplift. Involvement implies an ac-tive attempt to connect with Africa, while identification could run the gamut from recognizing one's African ancestry to fully embrac-ing Africa as one's only homeland. Through the centuries some would express interest in the continent and its people even when they had no desire to engage with or become involved with it. Over the years many African Americans have influenced and im-pacted Africa and its people in a variety of ways. The long, tangled, and problematic relationship black Americans have had with the nation to which they were brought has bound them in various ways to Africa, whether in the seventeenth century or the twenty-first.

CHAPTER ONE

"What is Africa to me?"

In his 1925 poetry collection *Color* the poet Countee Cullen posed a question men and women of African descent have asked for centuries: "What is Africa to me?" From the moment they were forcibly enslaved and brought to the United States, African Americans have asked this question, and they continue to do so. How they answer has changed in the intervening years, but Africa, real and imagined, has been ever present in the consciousness of African Americans. Cullen's poem "Heritage" attempts to answer the question, illustrating some of the ambiguities and complexities in the relationship between African Americans and Africa. "Copper sun or scarlet sea / Jungle star or jungle track?" he wrote.

In Cullen's imaginings, prevailing Western stereotypes about the African continent abound: "goading massive jungle herds"; "great drums throbbing through the air"; "quaint outlandish heathen gods." The "Africa" in Cullen's reverie is clearly an imagined one: "Africa? A book one thumbs / Listlessly, till slumber comes."

> One three centuries removed
> From the scenes his fathers loved,
> Spicy grove, cinnamon tree,
> What is Africa to me?[1]

More than fifty years later, journalist Eddy Harris journeyed through Africa, coming to the conclusion that, although he was of African descent, he was not African but American. The portrait he painted was born out of his experience traveling through the continent:

> There are so many Africas that, like a river, you cannot step into the same Africa twice. There is Africa the cliché, Africa the postcard view. Africa is a Biafran baby with its belly distended from starvation. Africa is flies and illness everywhere, AIDS and malaria and green monkey disease. Africa is a tired old woman selling mangoes by the side of the road, a woman with a baby strapped to her back, a woman walking home with a basket on her head, her feet covered with dust, her back noble and strong but stooped a little from fatigue and from the years of carrying. Africa is music and song and endless patience. Africa is traditions that will not allow it to move forward. Africa is a tired old man waiting for the dirt walls of his ancient house to collapse. Africa is a six-thousand-year-old baby trying to find his legs. Africa is pain. Africa is joy in spite of the pain. Africa is enduring. Africa is the essence of mankind's ability to hunger for something better and the patience to wait for it. The traditions make movement slow, but they make the waiting easier. Africa is incredible generosity, Africa is selfish opportunism, Africa is contradiction. . . . Africa is the birth of mankind. Africa is the land of my ancestors. But Africa is not home. I hardly know this place at all.[2]

He, like Cullen, despite the many years in between their works, portrays the continent in illusory ways. At the heart of Cullen's reverie and Harris's rumination is the quest for an answer blacks in the United States have sought through the centuries. Generations after Cullen have responded differently to the question he posed. Having lost the concrete memories and tongues of their ancestors, they have embraced or rejected a universal "Africa" that has carried different meanings for them.

Growing up in New York, Cullen would have had little or no direct contact with African cultural practices, but Africa remained

Countee Cullen—in Central Park, New York City, June 20, 1941.
Photograph by Carl Van Vechten.
(Library of Congress, Prints and Photographs Division.
From Wikimedia Commons/Public Domain.)

in his consciousness. He may have met a few Africans, Christian and Westernized, yet Cullen recognized that even if mere imaginings connected him to his ancestral homeland, he nevertheless sprang from Africa's "loins." In this regard, Countee Cullen expressed the dreams of many African Americans.

While in the early twentieth century black Americans were beginning to learn more about Africa through encounters with continental Africans, the information they received was often incomplete and distorted. These images could be found in newspaper reports of "savage Africa," missionary tracts and their accounts of heathen natives, and in the writings of European explorers and colonizers. African Americans came to understand Africa through the prism of European and American whites. Although, as we shall see, elements of Africa remained in African American life and culture, after a time concrete knowledge about the continent eluded the many men and women whose ancestors had been wrested from their homelands. White Americans knew little of the continent whose people they enslaved beginning in the seventeenth century. Indeed, few had gotten beyond the coast into the interior.

Those brought to America tried to hold onto elements of their African past, but by the eighteenth century a generation of American-born Africans had emerged with little to no knowledge of their ancestral homeland. During this period, "memory and meditations on Africa were filtered through the creolized experiences of Africans who conceived themselves beyond the cultural and existential boundaries which their native land represented."[3] Depending on which region of the country they inhabited, eighteenth-century black Americans maintained varying degrees of kinship with Africa. Africans enslaved on southern plantations retained major elements of their cultures. In Northern states, although blacks shed many of their African ways, turning instead to Christianity and assimilation, they managed to hold onto some practices from the continent. Still, most American-born blacks were creolized in some way, and the "Africa" that most of them knew was mediated by their experience of enslavement, discrimination, and racism.[4]

Recent scholarship has alerted us to the continuing African American engagement with Africa. Even when black Americans

eschewed linking themselves to Africa, they recognized and identified it as part of their heritage. Earlier generations asking, "What is
Africa to me?" would have responded differently because of their
tangible ties to the continent. Enslaved Africans brought as captives
to the United States, with their direct and personal links to the continent, surely had a different vision, and version, of Africa. These African-born men and women had left loved ones behind. Unclear
about their future in the land to which they had been carried, they
brought with them a part of their "Africa"—cultures, religions, languages, cuisines, memories.

For the first generation of enslaved, "Africa" was not the concept or place it would become in the imagination of their descendants. They were physically tied to it, having been born on the
continent, and with a real connection to it. They were Igbo,
Yoruba, Kongo, Mende, Ewe. If asked what Africa meant to them,
they would have given concrete answers: named places, told stories, spoke languages of the communities from which they came.
As one historian has noted: "They had lived as members of specific
societies in Africa, so that although their lives were altered by
enslavement, they continued to be informed by both the African
antecedent and by the unique combinations of their distinctive
backgrounds in the various locales of the Americas. Their cultural
and social provenances, therefore, become critical to grasping the
totality of their sojourn and its relation to corresponding experiences elsewhere." In other words, although Africans came to the
United States under traumatic circumstances, and left much behind, they did not completely leave their individual homelands and
cultures. These were part of them. In America they attempted, as
best they could, to reconstruct elements and patterns of life from
these various places, passing them on to their children and grandchildren. Michael Gomez's argument that "Africans in the New
World were very much aware of who they had been in the Old,
and engaged in patterns of collective behavior that sought to recapture and reinforce Old World realities" is accurate.[5] Nonetheless, it was easier for some than others.

In 1773 the poet Phillis Wheatley "answered" a version of Cullen's question by attempting to make sense of why she had been
enslaved:

Once I redemption neither sought nor knew.
Some view our sable race with scornful eye,
Their colour is a diabolic die.
Remember, *Christians*, *Negros*, black as *Cain*,
May be refin'd, and join th' angelic train.

For Wheatley, Africa was in the past; she believed that her life in the United States was superior to the one she had left behind.[6] Wheatley internalized the prevalent negative stereotypes about her birthplace. Like many of her contemporaries, she subscribed to what would become known as providential design, the view that Africans were enslaved for divine purposes. Their time in the United States exposed them to the Christian religion. Wheatley's poem highlights the virtues of that religion and the Africans who adopted it. In Wheatley's understanding of her experiences of enslavement, the possibilities for redemption made her capture justifiable. In an attempt to understand the reasons for the oppressive conditions of slavery and racism, many black Americans sought answers to explain their plight, and found them in the idea that being enslaved opened up a path to Christianity. Given the negative representations of Africa in this era, it is not surprising that blacks in America sought to distance themselves from a place their captors regarded as primitive and heathen.

Throughout the late eighteenth and nineteenth centuries, African Americans continued to pose questions regarding their connection and link to Africa, and the answers changed over time. By the end of the nineteenth century, there were few African-born blacks in the United States, and the experience of the Middle Passage in the slave trade became a story from ages past. Vestiges of Africa and its culture remained in the communities of these American-born Africans, but they had few tangible links to it. Some had elements of African religions and languages passed down to them. Most had only reminiscences of native-born parents or grandparents, songs, and stories of Africa. Many might not even have identified elements of their culture, language, and religion as African.

African American history during the nineteenth century is marked by black American attempts to understand their place in American society and how Africa defined them. Those enslaved on

Southern plantations more readily embraced their African roots by holding onto elements of their cultures, while the newly freed black populations in Northern states strove to discover where they fit into the new nation. The 1790 census recorded an estimated 59,000 free blacks in the United States. Of those, 27,000 resided in the North.[7] By 1830 there were about 319,000 free blacks, with 150,000 in the North. As Northern states slowly eradicated slavery beginning in the 1790s, and as a small free black community emerged in some Southern states, newly freed black populations struggled to integrate. They made claims on those who had once enslaved them, urging them to afford them equal status. Relegated to second-class citizenship, they objected to the status quo, searching for ways to gain acceptance. Thwarted by increasingly oppressive legislation, some turned their gaze to Africa and the possibilities of freedom they imagined it offered by promoting "back to Africa" initiatives. Small movements arose among some whites and blacks calling for repatriation to Africa. Those who sought to "return" would create an image of Africa stretching out its hands to its sons and daughters in the United States. Invoking the idea of a divine calling, they cited the well-known verse of Psalm 68: "Princes shall come out of Egypt. Ethiopia shall soon stretch out her hands unto God."[8]

Others would turn their backs on Africa, embracing their new homeland, rejecting any association with the continent of their forebears. The emigration movement and the subsequent settlement of African Americans in Sierra Leone and Liberia allowed for a more positive vision of Africa as some imagined settling there as an alternative to oppressive conditions in the United States. The rhetoric surrounding the "back to Africa" effort, which would come to fruition in the second decade of the century with the settlement of Liberia, focused on the special relationship black Americans had with Africa, and the role they were destined to play. Divine providence, back to Africa proponents argued, had brought them to the United States, allowing conversion to Christianity and its concomitant civilization and preparing them for a "return" to Africa. There they would uplift their African brothers and sisters through the light of Christianity. This rhetoric of uplift would endure into the twentieth century, with representations of Africa as primitive, savage, backward, and heathen, in need of help from its more progressive sons and daughters in the Americas.

African Americans' own assessment of Africa was heavily influenced by prevailing images of Africa among white Americans and Europeans.[9] In the nineteenth century the German philosopher Georg Wilhelm Friedrich Hegel wrote: "Africa proper, as far as History goes back, has remained—for all purposes of connection with the rest of the world—shut up; it is the Gold-land compressed within itself—the land of childhood, which lying beyond the days of self-conscious history, is enveloped in the dark mantle of Night. . . . At this point we leave Africa never to mention it again. For it is no historical part of the world; it has no movement of development to exhibit."[10] Hegel's was the predominant view of Africa presented in newspaper articles, visual representations, and in public discourse, both in Europe and the United States. A black American picking up an American newspaper in the late nineteenth century might have been faced with headlines such as "Dangers in Africa," whose accompanying article chronicled the exploration of Jules Boreill, who wrote of savagery and treachery in the lands he visited. They would have read a report called "Four Young Savages," the story of four Liberian boys sent by missionaries to be educated in Tennessee, or "Cannibal Race Found in Africa," chronicling Arthur Sharp's foray into Central Africa in 1899.[11]

By the late nineteenth century more factual knowledge about Africa was available. While the continent continued to be constructed as backward, more inroads were made as European and American explorers mapped its terrain, "discovered" its rivers and lakes, and studied its people. Yet lingering ideas of Africa as primitive continued to influence how African Americans engaged with their ancestral homeland. Even so, not all black Americans accepted this negative view, and they tried hard to present an alternative image. There were voices for Africa in the nineteenth century, particularly after the 1850s, that refused to accept the derogatory picture painted of the continent. While scholarship was inadequate (indeed, the research university with a graduate school was just being invented), and access to accurate views of the continent limited, knowledge about Africa increased in the nineteenth and twentieth centuries, at least among some African American intellectuals.

Leading thinkers on Africa and its relationship to African Americans would emerge in this era.

African American Intellectuals and Africa

Perhaps the most significant individual to present Africa and its people historically during the nineteenth century was the black American historian and journalist George Washington Williams. Throughout his life Williams made it his mission to combat negative ideas about Africa. Born in Bedford Springs, Pennsylvania, Williams joined the Union army in 1864 while still a teenager. After the war he graduated from Newton Theological Institution in Massachusetts in 1874 and went on to become a pastor, politician, and historian. Williams developed an interest and pride in Africa from an early age. While otherwise no different from many of his white contemporaries, he accepted that because of his ancestry his history was intricately bound up with that of the continent. His religious and theological training led him into an exploration of Christianity in Africa. In 1874 he wrote of Africa: "My heart loves that land, and my soul is proud of it. It has been the dream of my youth that that country would be saved by the colored people of this country."[12]

It seems that Williams too subscribed to the theory of providential design. As one of twelve graduating students to speak at his commencement, he delivered as his address "Early Christianity in Africa." This speech marked the beginning of his abiding love for the continent, which he would write about for the rest of his life. The speech traced the development of Christianity in parts of Africa. He argued that the slave trade had stunted the religion's growth, but with the trade now over, other parts of the continent could become Christianized. African Americans, he believed, had a role to play in that endeavor because "for nearly three centuries Africa has been robbed of her sable sons. For nearly three centuries they have toiled in bondage, unrequited in this youthful republic of the west. They have grown from a small company to be an exceedingly great people—five millions in number. No longer chattels, they are human beings; no longer bondmen, they are freemen, with almost every civil disability removed. ... With his Saxon brother, the African slakes his insatiable thirstings for knowledge at the same fountain. . . . The Negro of this country can turn to his Saxon brothers and say, as Joseph said to his brethren who wickedly sold him, 'As for you, ye meant it unto evil, but God meant it unto good; that we, after learning your arts and sciences, might return to Egypt and deliver the rest of our brethren who are yet in the house of bondage.' That day will come!"[13] Like Phillis Wheatley, he believed that Africa needed Christianity. The lessons blacks had learned in America and the strength gained from the country's Anglo-Saxons would benefit Africans.

George Washington Williams answered the question Cullen would later ask by writing his 1882 *History of the Negro Race in America from 1619 to 1880; as Negroes, as Slaves, as Soldiers, and as Citizens.* Among the many reasons the author cited for writing such a comprehensive history was "a growing desire among the enlightened Negroes in America to learn all that is possible from research concerning the antiquity of the race." He noted the enslaved's connection to Africa, wondering, "If the Negro slave desired his native land before the Rebellion, will not the free, intelligent, and reflective American Negro turn to Africa with its problems of geography and missions, now that he can contribute something towards the improvement of the condition of humanity?"[14]

Williams's work presented an Africa of which black Americans could be proud. The first eleven chapters outlined the histories of various African societies and examined African philology, ethnology, and Egyptology. Williams writes in great detail about Benin, Dahomey, and the Yoruba, ancient kingdoms in Africa, with particular focus on slavery in those regions. Devoting a whole chapter to the powerful Asante kingdom (in contemporary Ghana), he spends a great deal of time on the longevity of African civilizations and cultures. Having set the foundation, Williams begins the second part of his book with the section "Slavery in the Colonies," and the rest of the book concentrates on the experiences of Africans in the Americas. Having presented a picture of the many prosperous societies from which African Americans came, he discusses the settlement of the American colonies, the evolution of slavery and its negative impact on black Americans, African American contributions to American society, and their legal status in the United

States. According to a modern scholar, Williams's book had a "great impact" and was well received by African American readers and the white press.[15]

George Washington Williams traveled to Africa at the end of the nineteenth century, becoming well known for his criticism of the horrors perpetuated by Belgian colonizers in the Congo. In a 1890 letter to the Belgian king Leopold, he made a searing indictment of Belgian rule in the Congo, labeling it a "crime." He had come with high ideals as a descendant of Africa and was disappointed by what he found—a system of brutal oppression of African men and women. As he stated in his letter: "When I arrived in the Congo, I naturally sought for the results of the brilliant programme: *'fostering care,' 'benevolent enterprise,' an 'honest and practical effort'* to increase the knowledge of the natives *'and secure their welfare.'*"[16] During his time in the Congo he strived for this vision, and would later be instrumental in exposing Belgian atrocities.[17]

Williams's biographer, the historian John Hope Franklin, who contributed much to our knowledge of African American history, describes how he came to his subject. While browsing in a college library in 1945, he discovered *History of the Negro Race in America*. Surprised by the title and the contents of the book, Franklin wondered at his own ignorance. Although he had not studied any black American history, Franklin reproached himself for not knowing who George Washington Williams was. He understood that the great man's obscurity "was the result, at least in part, of social forces at work in this country in the late nineteenth century. Those forces dictated that Afro Americans were not to be remembered for their constructive contributions to society, for their involvement in the literary history of the country, or for their revelations of the rape of Africa by Europeans and Americans."[18] John Hope Franklin would go on to become a leading historian of the African American experience in the United States. His seminal textbook, *From Slavery to Freedom*, first published in 1947, is now in its ninth edition.

Other activists, intellectuals, and scholars championed the cause of Africa in the late nineteenth and early twentieth centuries. Men like Carter G. Woodson, Leo Hansberry, and W. E. B. Du Bois would write about Africa. Like Williams, they sought to examine Africa's history, and by extension that of African Americans,

George Washington Williams.
(From George W. Williams, A History of Negro Troops in the War
of Rebellion, 1861–1865 *[New York: Harper & Brothers, 1888], p. ii.*
From Wikimedia Commons/Public Domain.)

from their own point of view.[19] While they sought to rectify negative stereotypes of the continent, they sometimes unintentionally
created some of their own, so steeped were they in Western understandings of Africa.

Perhaps more than any other African American in the late nineteenth and twentieth centuries, W. E. B. Du Bois understood the
connections between African Americans and Africa, making it his
lifelong goal to educate Americans—black and white—about the
plight of Africans and their counterparts in the diaspora, but also
about their contributions and achievements. Du Bois's long life,
spanning from 1868 to his 1963 death in Africa, perhaps best

illustrates the relationship between a small number of African Americans and the continent of Africa and its people. His 1896 Harvard dissertation, "The Suppression of the African Slave Trade to the United States of America, 1638–1870," explored the transatlantic slave trade and its consequences for Africans. In 1939 he expressively described the incident that led him to take up the study of Africa and its history. In 1906, he writes, the anthropologist Frank Boas in his commencement speech to Atlanta University graduates urged them to take pride in their African heritage. Du Bois later remembered Boas's words and their impact on him. "Franz Boas came to Atlanta University where I was teaching history in 1906 and said to a graduating class: You need not be ashamed of your African past; and then he recounted the history of the black kingdoms south of the Sahara for a thousand years. I was too astonished to speak. All of this I had never heard and I came then and afterwards to realize how the silence and neglect of science can let truth utterly disappear or even be unconsciously distorted."[20]

W. E. B. Du Bois went on to publish many works emphasizing the importance of Africa and its history to African Americans, writing of Africa and its place in the world in *The Souls of Black Folk* (1903), *The Negro* (1915), *Africa: Its Geography, People, and Products* (1930), *Africa—Its Place in Modern History* (1930), and *Black Folk Then and Now* (1939), among many other books. The first eight chapters of *The Negro* are devoted to Africa, looking at the history of Ethiopia and Egypt, examining the role of Islam in West Africa, and discussing African cultures.

He opens the book with a map of the continent's geography. The first paragraph reads: "Africa is at once the most romantic and the most tragic of continents. Its very names reveal its mystery and wide-reaching influence. It is the 'Ethiopia' of the Greek, the 'Kush' and 'Punt' of the Egyptian, and the Arabian 'Land of the Blacks.' To modern Europe it is the 'Dark Continent' and 'Land of Contrasts'; in literature it is the seat of the Sphinx and the lotus eaters, the home of the dwarfs, gnomes, and pixies, and the refuge of the gods; in commerce it is the slave mart and the source of ivory, ebony, rubber, gold, and diamonds. What other continent can rival in interest this Ancient of Days?" In this paragraph we see the ambivalence many black Americans felt toward Africa. It was at one and the same time a romantic home with a glorious past and the tragic site of the enslavement of millions. Yet Du Bois recognized that "there are those, nevertheless, who would write universal history and leave out Africa."[21] Throughout his life he ensured that Africa would never be left out.

In subsequent work Du Bois, like Cullen, continued to query the nature of the relationship between African Americans and Africa. In 1940 Du Bois attempted to answer a version of Cullen's question. Although acknowledging that he did not know what constituted a tie between himself and Africa, he knew that "on this vast continent [Africa] were born and lived a large portion of my direct ancestors," and "since the fifteenth century these ancestors of mine and their other descendants have had a common history; have suffered a common disaster and have one long memory." Du Bois identified a common experience of oppression in Africa and in America, asserting, "It is this unity that draws me to Africa."[22] He understood that there is no universal African culture, that Africa is made up of different ethnic, religious, and language groupings. He was nonetheless drawn to Africa by what he called "one long memory." By this, he meant that African Americans were sustained by their "memory" of Africa, real or imagined, through the centuries. Whether on the voyage to enslavement or in the stories told by family members born in Africa, these memories became history in the hands of men like Du Bois and his contemporary Carter G. Woodson.

Carter G. Woodson's writing in the 1920s and 1930s stressed the links between African Americans and Africa. Books like *The African Background Outlined; or, Handbook for the Study of the Negro*, published in 1936, emphasize African cultural influences on African American culture and on his own writings. Woodson examined how African folktales, religious beliefs, languages, and other elements of African cultural practices impacted African American communities.[23] He challenged the negative representations of Africa and criticized the omission of Africa and its history from the curriculums of black schools. In *The Miseducation of the Negro*, he writes: "In history, of course, the Negro had no place in this curriculum. He was pictured as a human being of the lower order, unable to subject passion to reason, and therefore useful only when made the hewer of wood and the drawer of water for others. No thought was given to the history of Africa except so far as it had been a field of exploitation for the Caucasian. You might study the history as it was offered in our system from the elementary school throughout the university, and you would never hear Africa mentioned except in the negative."[24] Carter Woodson went on to lead the Association for the Study of Negro Life and History (ASNLH) and found the *Journal of Negro History*. Woodson instituted Negro History Week in 1926. It would become Black History Month in 1976.[25]

A number of early twentieth-century African American intellectuals like Woodson progressively came to underline their connection to Africa. Leo Hansberry, who taught the first African history courses at Howard University in the 1920s, was another. In 1916, having read Du Bois's *The Negro*, he pursued the study of Africa and its history. One scholar has reflected that "in his teaching Hansberry made no secret of his desire to combat notions of black cultural inferiority by demonstrating the dynamism and complexity of African societies. He saw his classes in ancient African history as part of a movement to help African Americans improve their self-concept by developing pride in their African past."[26] Hansberry published several works drawing attention to the importance of African history.

Although these scholars endeavored to rebut claims of African inferiority, they encountered deep-seated ideas perpetuated by European colonizers in their bid to justify colonization and bolstered by white Americans to justify racism. Cullen's generation was far removed from Africa. Accordingly, many African Americans in this era and later shared an imagined portrait of their ancestral homeland because they knew so little about Africa. In the twentieth century, more concrete knowledge, largely produced by European imperialists, allowed black Americans to form more complex and varied opinions about Africa and its people. Still under colonialism, Africa and Africans continued to be represented by their colonizers as backward, needing European tutelage, and incapable of governing themselves. Nevertheless, more information, and more positive representations in the writings of black scholars, however limited, allowed African Americans to articulate their feelings on what they saw as their role and responsibility to the continent.

In the early twentieth century African Americans often encountered "Africans" for the first time as men and women from the continent continued a practice, begun in the late nineteenth century, of coming to the United States as students and visitors. Arriving from colonial spaces, these individuals often subscribed to the view that Christianity was a path to civilization for African-descended peoples. They were mostly Christian, missionary educated, and not very different from black Americans in their ideas about how to uplift Africa. As we shall see, Africans coming to the United States were often from elite and privileged classes, educated in colonial schools, with Christian training. Often studying in historically black colleges, these young men, and sometimes women, presented a different and perhaps unexpected view of Africa. These were not the heathen and primitive natives so frequently featured in popular representations of Africa, but individuals offering a view of Africa that black Americans could be proud of—one that did not tally with the stereotypes they had previously encountered.

It is no surprise, then, that the black press especially found these Africans interesting subjects for coverage. Articles on Africans abounded in the pages of late nineteenth- and early twentieth-century black newspapers. Papers such as the *Chicago Defender, Baltimore Afro American, Pittsburgh Courier, Amsterdam News, Atlanta World*, and *Washington Bee*, to name a few, brought light to the movement and activities of students, visitors, and dignitaries from the continent. Mundane stories like "Native African Student Likes American Food" described Asuquo Udo Idiong, a Nigerian visiting Chicago, as being "sold" on America because it is "friendly, peaceful and prosperous." More sensational ones, like "Says Minister Took His Wife; Given Divorce: African Student Steals Love of Friend's Wife while Roomer in Home," reported on the relationship that developed between a South African student and the wife of an African American minister with whom he lodged.[27]

Humorous articles on African encounters with American society were also popular. A 1931 article with the headline "African Student Visitor to City" profiled Everett Davis, a Sierra Leonean graduate student at Yale who, while visiting his friend in Chicago, asked, "Where are all the gangsters you read about?" Davis went on to observe: "I've read so much about Chicago gangsters that I rather expected to see everybody wearing armored suits when I stepped from the train."[28] Given the derogatory picture Americans had about Africa, seeing the tables turned with an African articulating his stereotyped ideas about America changed people's point of view. These real-life portraits of Africans in the United States allowed black Americans to envisage an Africa that was not filled with primitive natives, dressed in grass skirts and carrying spears. Yet ignorance persisted.

Inadequate knowledge of Africa and its history gave rise to these erroneous perspectives. Most African Americans in the early twentieth century still lacked access to an education. A largely poor population, still concentrated in the South, may have preserved elements of Africa in their cultures but often did not recognize them as such. In a 1985 article in the popular magazine *Essence*, the historian John Henrik Clarke traces his journey to the study of African history. He was the son of illiterate sharecroppers from Georgia. His father was puzzled by young John's desire to become a teacher, urging him instead to follow his path of becoming a farmer. Supportive teachers led Clarke to an interest in what became "black studies." The historian recollects that a Bible study class in a Baptist church was where his "search for the identity and place of African people began and where a conflict started within me that took me 20 years to resolve." While the African setting of many biblical stories was recognizable, he recalls, "I saw no African people in the printed and illustrated Sunday school lessons. I began to suspect at this early age that someone had distorted the image of my people. My long search for the true history of African people the world over began."[29]

Clarke was following in the footsteps of predecessors like George Washington Williams in the nineteenth century and the better known twentieth-century scholar W. E. B. Du Bois in seeking to rectify the distorted image of Africa to which most African Americans were exposed. Like these nineteenth- and early twentieth-century giants, John Henrik Clarke devoted his life to sharing his knowledge of Africa and its history. In 1979 he chronicled the long relationship African Americans had had with the continent, arguing that an "Africa consciousness" had always been present in the African American psyche. Clarke chronicled the work of early black

writers who championed Africa and their African heritage.[30] Many,
like Joel Augustus Rogers, brought to the fore the achievements of
"great" men and women in Africa and America. Writing in the
1920s and 1930s, he sought to instill pride in black Americans by
showing them the greatness of their African past.[31]

While not as well known as Woodson or Du Bois, Joel Rogers
did much to showcase black accomplishment and instill pride in African Americans. A Jamaican by birth, Rogers immigrated to the
United States early in the twentieth century, becoming an American citizen. He studied art in Chicago and anthropology in France,
and worked as a Pullman porter as well as a newspaper reporter.
More than anyone else in the 1920s through the 1950s, Rogers pop-
ularized black history for African Americans. With a vast array of
writing, he introduced elements of their history to African American lay readers. His weekly column "Your History" in the *Pittsburgh
Courier* showcased black history and achievement. He frequently
published his own books, making sure they were accessible. In
books such as *World's Great Men and Women of African Descent*
(1935), *Real Facts about Ethiopia* (1935), *Your History: From the Beginning of Time to the Present* (1940), *Real Facts about the Negro* (1957),
and *Africa's Gift to America: The Afro-American in the Making and
Saving of the United States* (1959), Rogers contested claims of black
inferiority, instilling pride in African Americans. When he died in
March 1966 his obituary in *The Crisis* lamented that his death "removed from the American scene one of the great popularizers of
Negro history. Rogers always said that he wrote his books for the
man-in-the-street."[32]

"African American" in the Twentieth and Twenty-First Centuries

Countee Cullen's century would see continuity and change in the
relationship between black Americans and Africa. Some would continue to embrace the continent, arguing that African Americans had
a special role to play in regard to Africa and linking their predicament with its people. Others would see the struggle for civil rights
and equality in the United States as different and separate from the
conditions of Africans. Yet the twentieth century was also a period

when African Americans began to encounter and interact more significantly with Africans. Africa became more real than imagined for
most African Americans, as they met men and women from the
continent and acknowledged their similarities and differences.

Since the dawn of the twenty-first century, with the large-scale
migration of Africans from the continent to the United States, the
question "What is Africa to me?" has taken on a significantly different meaning for those labeled African American. To the 2.1 million
African-born people now living in the United States, the answer is,
once again, self-evident. They are Nigerian, Ethiopian, Sierra Leonean, Liberian, or Ghanaian, with direct experiences of Africa. This
"new" African American population is generating a different image
of Africa, as it attempts to understand what it means to be a black
American. African immigrants have strong ties to their countries.
Many lead transnational lives, moving back and forth between Africa
and the United States. They retain a connection to Africa not possible for the first Africans brought to the United States in the seventeenth century, and their influence in the United States is gradually
being recognized. As African fashion, food, and culture become
more readily available in the United States, African Americans are
increasingly exposed to a variety of African cultural practices.

Beginning in the seventeenth century, Africans brought their
cultural practices to the United States and struggled, often with
great dignity and difficulty, to maintain them. They held onto the
things that made them who they were, their memories, and as
many elements of their African past as they could, allowing them
to sustain a link to the continent from which they had been forcibly removed.

CHAPTER TWO

"I tried to keep their voices in my head"

In his novel *Someone Knows My Name*, Lawrence Hill provides a fictional account of an enslaved girl's life.[1] His protagonist, eleven-year-old Aminata Diallo, tells of her childhood in the fictional town of Bayo in the eighteenth century, her capture and enslavement, and her subsequent freedom and return to Africa. Although a work of fiction, the book gives readers a feel for how the millions of anonymous men, women, and children taken into slavery might have lived before being forcibly taken to the Americas. It is particularly poignant because it is written from the point of view of a child. The young Aminata paints a rather mundane picture of childhood in her village as she comes of age, assisting her mother, a midwife, in her duties, learning how to read Arabic from her father, and preparing to become a woman. Everything is snatched away when she is kidnapped by African slavers, taken to the coast, and loaded on a ship bound for the Americas. Throughout her life, as she is sold several times, given a new name, and endures hardship and sorrow, she clings to her name, Aminata Diallo, and to her identity as an African and "freeborn Muslim." She retains memories of her homeland throughout her life.

Aminata's story could be that of the real-life ten-year old Priscilla, enslaved on the coast of Sierra Leone in 1756. Taken to the United States, she was sold to Elias Ball, a prominent South

Carolina planter. Priscilla undoubtedly endured great hardship. Like the novel's protagonist, she lived long enough to have children, ensuring the continuation of her lineage in the United States. Hill's heartbreaking account of Aminata's life personalizes the slave trade and slavery in ways historical accounts often cannot. It allows us to get at the emotions that being forcibly wrenched from one's homeland must produce. His fiction wonderfully captures how a child understood and came to grips with enslavement.

The millions of Africans like Aminata Diallo enslaved in the Americas came from diverse societies with complex political, religious, and social organizations and institutions. Scholars now know the regions in Africa from which those who ended up in the Americas came—Senegambia, Sierra Leone, Windward Coast, Gold Coast, Bight of Benin, Bight of Biafra, West Central Africa, and Southeast Africa. Africans forcibly taken from their homelands came from many different backgrounds, from small segmented societies to more centralized polities, villages, towns, cities, chiefdoms, and kingdoms. They came from nomadic and sedentary societies and were farmers, fisherman, pastoralists, and hunter-gatherers. Most came from kin-based societies, where ties to family by blood and through marriage were central. These societies practiced a variety of religions and produced art, music, and architecture. They were diverse in their attitudes toward those who belonged to their societies and those who did not. Some of the communities that produced enslaved Americans already had their own—African-based—slavery. Others had little experience of slavery. A woman in fifteenth-century Mali under the reign of Mansa Musa would have lived out her life in an entirely different setting and manner than her counterpart in the Kingdom of Kongo, depending on her marital status, religion, kinship ties, and class. The experiences of women of slave origin in both societies, however, would have been comparable.

Kinship in African Societies

Although there are periods in African history we cannot easily or accurately reconstruct, scholars now know a great deal about African civilizations before their encounter with Europe, and about ways of life in communities stretching down the West African coast. Most African societies were kin-based, consisting of clans and extended families, descendants of a common ancestor. Kinship was a major principle of social organization in African societies, and kinship practices operated in all types of societies from small village communities to more centrally organized state polities. They connected people through blood and marriage. In these societies, "a person was a person only insofar as he or she belonged to a broader community." Kinship ideology enabled the survival of the group, and Africans understood the importance of cultivating and maintaining family ties, as this was crucial to defining one's place in a group. A Yoruba proverb reinforces this idea: "Your extended family members act as your closest apparel." In other words, kin members, like clothes, are the closest thing to a person's body.[2]

A world defined by kinship relationships, not unlike European feudal society, was not always ideal, for along with the rights it guaranteed came burdens and a set of obligations. Because these societies had beneficiaries and providers (takers and givers) and dominants and dependents, there were often tensions and strains. Social and family obligations could be irritating. As a contemporary Nigerian proverb explains, "We cannot choose who our relatives should be, even though we may come to like some better than others." Although these obligations could be onerous, membership in a kin group accorded an individual ties of affection, a sense of belonging, and unquestioned affiliation to a group that brought love, respect, protection, and identity. In the many communities in West and Central Africa, biology was important, but kinship was not always defined through blood ties. Family ties were often socially constructed, and fictive kinship relations, based neither on ties of blood nor of marriage, were common in Africa, as they would later be in the Americas. In other words, individuals not related by blood could be considered family with the same rights, duties, and obligations as those with blood ties.

Age was revered in African societies. Elders, both men and women, played important roles in kinship systems, often making decisions concerning family issues, keeping members in check, overseeing the community's customs, laws, and traditions, and controlling access to land and the means of production. Deemed wise because of their length of time on earth, older members of a group commanded respect from the young in all social relations. Though they did not hold unqualified superiority, they wielded tremendous power because, as a common adage maintains, "Old age does not come in just one day."[3] For that reason, despite the complexity of a community's social organization, kinship ideology often prevailed. In other words, family ties were sometimes more important than political alliances or ties based on a common religion.

The African Background: Political and Social Organization

Although kinship structures were at the heart of many societies, African communities had diverse social and political structures. Along the West and West Central African coasts and further inland, small fishing and farming villages existed alongside more centrally organized states and kingdoms. New social and political organizations developed over the centuries as migration, environmental changes, and other influences affected how and where people lived.

Given that most enslaved Africans eventually settled on plantations, it is important to understand the role of agriculture in African societies. Settled communities began to emerge in Africa about 20,000 BCE along the Nile River. In West Africa farming communities emerged around 3000 BCE. With greater settlement and stability came increased social and cultural change, resulting in the emergence of a multiplicity of cultures. As food-producing economies developed, populations were more firmly tied to territories. In Western Africa, large and dense populations resulted in the growth of primarily agricultural societies and the development of iron-working technology. Agriculture also provided increased interaction between settled communities for mutual benefit through trade, intermarriage, and a search for security and protection. As larger, long-term settlements developed, methods were devised to cope with issues of conflict and cooperation. Farming communities usually had abundant land, but labor was scarce. Wealthy individuals could often control labor and gain greater access to land, intensifying class and, to some extent, gender differences. It was in these more settled societies that social inequalities such as slavery could be found.

As people became more sedentary, they continued to organize themselves in a variety of ways, forming different types of government and administrative structures. By the fifteenth century, some populations chose to organize themselves into states; others remained in stateless organizations with little concentration of authority. Stateless societies such as the Igbo had no political or professional class as such, but did have structured authority such as a council of elders. The Igbo in Nigeria had no kings, but although a ruler was absent, authority was not. Age, knowledge, and personal achievement often provided standards by which authority was established, with communities choosing to solve their problems as a unified body. Disputes were typically settled without resort to force, and the units in which they were settled were small, such as a "palaver" presided over by community elders. This meant that a wide population had a relatively equitable amount of political influence. Furthermore, in these societies social mobility was often based on merit rather than inherited status. The fame of Chinua Achebe's fictional character Okonkwo, for example, "rested on solid personal achievements." His father had not been well regarded in the village of Umuofia, but Okonkwo "was clearly cut out for great things" and, though a young man, "was already one of the greatest men of his time. Age was respected among his people, but achievement was revered."[4]

Some communities formed into centrally organized states or kingdoms with a concentration of authority in the form of a ruler (a chief or king) who wielded authority as a full-time occupation. States and kingdoms were highly structured, administered and organized by a small elite, able to mobilize their people and resources effectively, and capable of offering increased protection. The region known as the Western Sudan made an early transition from hunting and gathering to sedentary culture through animal domestication, the development of agriculture, and the formation of states. The Western Sudan stretches from the Sahara Desert to the north and the tropical rain forests of the Guinea coast to the south. The name derives from the Arabic term *bilad-al-sudan*, meaning Land of Blacks, a consequence of the area's significant relationship with the Arab world. Beginning in the fifth century a number of powerful states and kingdoms arose in this locality, largely as a result of trade.

With more settled and organized ways of life made possible in a centralized state, Africans opened themselves up to new experiences and interactions. For example, the impulse to express themselves artistically is evidenced by the many rock art and paintings uncovered by archaeologists. Depicting the everyday life of these communities, they allow us to see how people lived. In the Western Sudan the introduction and spread of Islam, predominantly through the artery of trade, was a major development. The new religion and the trade that often accompanied it became important aspects of life in African societies south of the Sahara after the fourth century. The rise of the great empires, such as Ghana, Mali, Songhai, and Kanem Bornu, among others, contributed to this trend. While populations from these regions did not end up in the Americas in significant numbers, the influences of trade and religion from the three major empires figured in the history of regions further south, from which Africans were taken. Furthermore, these kingdoms played a significant role in African American consciousness and connection with Africa.

Trans-Saharan Trade and African Kingdoms

Long-distance trade across the Sahara went on for many centuries before Europeans encountered African societies. Berber pastoralists in the northern Sahara were traders long before they made contact with populations further south of the desert. The introduction of the camel in the first century CE changed the nature of trade. In contrast to the horses and pack oxen previously used in trade, the camel facilitated larger-scale and longer-distance trade. During the third and fourth centuries, the use of camels spread among Berber nomads of the northern Sahara, becoming the major form of transport by the fifth century. This ungainly animal, with its ability to withstand desert conditions, revolutionized the scale and scope of the trans-Saharan trade, allowing traders to travel longer distances, and explore and establish new trade routes. Berbers and the Sudanese populations in the Sahel region (Serer, Soninke, Songhai, and Wolof, among others) were major participants in the trade. Trading settlements quickly developed on both sides of the Sahara Desert as Africans from various places engaged in economic and cultural exchanges. The Sahel, or "shores" of the desert, with settled towns where caravans were offloaded and reloaded for transport across the desert, was a point of contact. As commerce increased, the products of sub-Saharan Africa—and the area's black population—became more accessible to the Mediterranean world and later to Europe via North Africa. Trade in West African gold expanded and demand for other goods, such as ostrich feathers, ivory, and furs, increased. The trade routes featured people as well as goods, establishing an African slave trade.[5]

The trans-Saharan trade brought many changes to West African societies. It increased their awareness of a larger world, brought new goods to their people, and led to social and political changes. As trade items such as gold, salt, and ostrich feathers were exported from the region, horses, cloth, beads, and metal goods made their way into the Western Sudan. Perhaps the most important development was the exposure of West Africa to Islam. Between the seventh and eleventh centuries, Islam spread from Egypt to the Maghreb region and south of the Sahara into West Africa.[6] The religion's first converts were nomadic desert-dwelling Berbers, who then became key to its spread in West Africa. Berbers introduced Islam further south through the trans-Saharan trade, first to the Saharan nomads, later to populations in the Western Sudan. Islam won converts among traders and rulers, for a long time remaining the religion of these two elite groups, while making little impression on commoners. In later centuries it would spread more widely, either peacefully or through force. By the sixteenth century, Islam, well established in the Sudanic regions, became a familiar part of the cultural landscape, if not a widely practiced religion.

The spread of Islam in West Africa would later contribute to its spread in the Americas through captured and enslaved Muslim men and women. The fictional Aminata Diallo, who guessed her birth date to be 1745, was born a Muslim. The ruling classes of the great empires often converted to Islam, at least in name, and the new religion played an important part in the fortunes of the Western Sudanese states of Ghana, Mali, and Songhai.

Ghana, the earliest of these states, reached the height of its power between the fifth and thirteenth centuries. Its major ethnic group, the Soninke, were largely settled farmers and fishermen.

Ghana grew on the strength of the trans-Saharan trade as its rulers became rich and powerful with the expansion of the gold trade. During the height of its power, the gold trade flourished, bringing visitors to the kingdom from North Africa and the Arab world. All remarked on its great wealth. Ghana's decline began at the end of the eleventh and early twelfth centuries. As it fell, other states, such as the Susu kingdom, broke away, rising to power. Known for its iron working and military power, by the end of twelfth century the powerful Kante clan had emerged as leader, with Sumanguru Kante at its head. Under Kante, the Susu seceded from Ghana, and he ruled until his defeat by the Malinke.

Oral tradition credits Sundiata Keita with founding the Mali Empire in 1235. Overcoming adversity, this legendary ruler consolidated several Malinke chiefdoms to build a great empire. The most famous of Mali's kings, Sundiata, is remembered for his military power.[7] Subsequent rulers Mansa Musa (1312–37) and Mansa Suleyman (1341–60) strengthened the administrative machinery of the kingdom, building on the work of Sundiata. Under Mansa Musa, in particular, Mali enjoyed stability and good government as well as unprecedented wealth and economic prosperity, attracting traders from north and south. Mali took advantage of trade with populations north of the Sahara, profiting from participation in the trans-Saharan trade. Commerce increased, with merchants coming from as far away as Egypt and Morocco. Both Musa and Suleyman were Muslim converts and used their network and connections with the Islamic world to bring trade and knowledge to the empire. Mali's decline began around the second half of the fourteenth century as the kingdom of Songhai came into its own.

Songhai too rose predominantly through trade brought by Muslims from the north and the Arab world. Strong rulers built up the kingdom until its decline in the sixteenth century. Likewise, Kanem Bornu, situated in the region around Lake Chad, rose to prominence in the eleventh century. Largely pastoralist, the kingdom grew through trade, reaching its height in the thirteenth century. Other kingdoms rose and fell, propelling change, dislocating populations, and generating migrations of all sorts.

Although documents tell us mostly about elites in these three successful kingdoms, occasionally we gain a glimpse of the lives of ordinary men and women. When the Arab traveler Ibn Battuta made his way south into Mali in 1352 during the reign of Suleyman, he described the hospitality Africans extended to him, their cultural and religious practices, and their customs. Battuta also described the lives of women, a picture Aminata Diallo would likely have recognized. In Walata, he marveled at the beauty of women, their relative freedom, and the matrilineal customs of the society, which traced descent through the mother line: "Their women are of surpassing beauty, and are shown more respect than the men. The state of affairs amongst these people is indeed extraordinary. Their men show no signs of jealousy whatever; no one claims descent from his father, but on the contrary from his mother's brother. A person's heirs are his sister's sons, not his own sons. This is a thing which I have seen nowhere in the world except among the Indians of Malabar. But those are heathens; these people are Muslims, punctilious in observing the hours of prayer, studying books of law, and memorizing the Koran. Yet their women show no bashfulness before men and do not veil themselves, though they are assiduous in attending the prayers. Any man who wishes to marry one of them may do so, but they do not travel with their husbands, and even if one desired to do so her family would not allow her to go."[8] Indeed, the fictional Aminata's picture of her family life shows her very independent mother traveling long distances alone and her father according her great respect. But Battuta also observed inequalities in the communities he visited, making it clear there were subservient groups.

West and West Central African Communities

Further down the coast similar societies emerged. Agriculture and iron working were just as important to these communities, and many of the same patterns in political development emerged. African people in the Senegambia, the Rice and Slave Coasts, and the Gold Coast lived in kin-based societies, developing their own ways of life and adapting to their environment. For our purposes, the emergence of states such as Benin, Oyo, and Asante in West Africa and Kongo, Lunda, and Lundu in West Central Africa are important. Benin, located in what is today southern Nigeria, emerged with village communities as the basic political unit. Kinship was the basis of social interaction, and agriculture and fishing were the mainstays of the economy. Over time kingship developed, with a more complex and centralized political mode of organization.

By the fifteenth century, Benin was the most powerful empire in the forest region of West Africa. One of its first rulers, (Oba) Ewuare, built up the empire, strengthening its capital and seat of power. Subsequent leaders expanded the empire toward the coast of the Atlantic Ocean. Benin began to decline in the late seventeenth century, as many of its vassal states broke away. Ife and Oyo, two important Yoruba states, were strategically located between the forest regions and the Western Sudan to the north, giving them a trade advantage.

Oyo, in particular, built up its power as result of trade with these regions and later with Europeans. The Alaafin, believed to be a sacred ruler personifying reincarnated ancestors, served as the link between the living and the dead and governed based on the idea of divine right. As in Benin, trade with Europeans was important to this community. Oyo began to decline gradually in the late eighteenth century. The Akan-speaking people located in what is today the country of Ghana built up their power beginning in the late seventeenth century when Osei Tutu consolidated the Asante Empire. Gold was central to its growth and success through the eighteenth and nineteenth centuries. All these West African kingdoms, located on the edge of the forest region, took agriculture and fishing as their mainstays because of their location near rivers such as the Volta and the Niger. They also made use of mineral resources native to their environment. Trade with neighboring communities and later with Europeans became central to the development of these states and empires.

Kongo originated with small communities that sprang up along the banks of the Congo River. Largely fishing and agricultural societies, they had, by the fifteenth century, organized themselves into more centralized political systems. Early accounts of Kongo described it as a highly bureaucratic state with close to four hundred thousand people and many vassal states. Kinship relationships still remained significant, in particular the role of fictive kinship as a way of mobilizing people. As in Mali, women played important roles. In his examination of elite women in the kingdom of Kongo in the sixteenth and seventeenth centuries, the historian John Thornton argues that women accessed power by influencing their male relatives, noting that "women with the right genealogical position, of acceptable age and connections to males, could exercise influence and—at a later period—real power in their own right."[9] As in the Western Sudan, commerce was important as Africans traded with each other and later with Europeans. In the seventeenth and eighteenth centuries, several states along the West African coast built up their power due to trade with Europeans, particularly the slave trade. Oyo, Dahomey, Asante, and Benin, all centralized states, reached their power at the height of the slave trade. Many men and women from these societies found themselves enslaved on plantations in the Americas, often as a result of internecine wars.

The stateless societies along the West African coast also saw their women and men forcibly removed to the Americas. While it has been more difficult for scholars to reconstruct the histories of communities that were not centralized, and those leaving none or few written records, we know something of some of the populations inhabiting a stretch of the West African coast line known as the Upper Guinea Coast, stretching from the Gambia to Sierra Leone. The Rice Coast region in particular, in the countries that are now Sierra Leone, Guinea, and Liberia, proved to be significant to the United States. The region was inhabited by ethnic groups such the Baga, Nalu, Balanta, Fula, Jolonke, Mandinka, Temne, and Mende, whose communities were largely agricultural. Known for their rice growing and other agricultural techniques, these communities were multilingual, multiethnic, and mobile, with overlapping and multiple identities. It would not have been unusual for women and men to marry outside their ethnic group, or to practice Islam while also adhering to their traditional religions. The historian Donald Wright, for example, describes the village communities making up the precolonial kingdom of Niumi in the Gambia River region. Men and women in Niumi had "several levels of identity," including family or kinship, class, village, and an identity with the kingdom itself. Further down the coast in the region of Guinea, Liberia, and Sierra Leone, village communities were the principal form of social organization.[10]

Indigenous Religious Practices in African Communities

Regardless of their form of government or social organization, Africans placed a high value on their religious beliefs. West and Central Africans had a wide variety of belief systems. Religion permeated people's lives and their everyday activities. Africans developed religious systems that conformed to their lifestyles and were reflected in their prayers of gratitude in bounteous times and entreaties in times of need. Like kinship, religion conferred identity on the individual and the group. While there was no universal religion, some similarities can be identified. Africans approached their religious beliefs holistically, with little or no lines or divisions between the spiritual, natural, social, or political worlds, and practices were often intimately related to their concepts of culture, language, and ethnic identity. These governed marriage and death, farming and hunting, and community living.[11]

The function of religion in these societies, as in others around the world, was to unearth the meaning of life, to understand the proper relationship among humans, between humans and spiritual powers, and between humans and the natural world. African religions also sought to understand and explain the persistence of evil and suffering. Important to religious practice was upholding proper behavior and enforcing rules. Belief in the afterlife ensured adherence to the prescribed codes. These ideas could be found in sacred oral traditions, passed down through the generations, as well as through education gained during rites of passage ceremonies and through the performance of rituals.

Oral traditions and stories were important to African religious beliefs. Origin stories in particular were significant for explaining how communities came to be. The various traditions of origin found in African societies illustrate how people understood their world, performed rituals, and explained why and how things happened to them. Art and dance were vital to religious practices, whether in the form of masking traditions, the wearing of particular cloths and colors, the specific design of an object or material, or the direction and steps a dance might take.

Central to many African religions was a belief in a supreme being responsible for the creation of the universe. Although variations on how important the supreme being was and the role he/she played could be found among cultures of West and Central Africa, most conceived of the supreme being as a remote figure with minimal involvement in the daily lives of individuals. Although distant, the supreme being was responsible for giving life and judging the conduct of individuals after death. For example, the Yoruba believe that their supreme being, Olorun (Olodumare), gives life to a newly born child and controls his or her destiny. Likewise, when a person dies, Olorun decides his or her fate and determines whether the person will become an ancestor or go for eternity to the place of broken pots, reserved for those who led destructive lives. The place of broken pots, like hell, was believed to be hot, heated with peppers rather than fire.

Ngewo or Leve, the supreme god of the Mende of Sierra Leone, is said to have created the universe before withdrawing to the heavens. Some accounts of Leve cast the god as female. Although remote, the supreme being continued to oversee the destinies of Mende people. The creator and supreme being Nzambi a Mpungu, central to Kongo/Bakongo cosmology, spoke of two worlds: the land of the living (*nza yayi*) and the land of the dead (*nsi a bafwa*), divided by a body of water. Though separate physical spaces, life in both places went on simultaneously, affecting one another. Sun and moon traveled around both lands, making it day for the living when it was night for the dead and visa versa. The dead lived similar lives to the living but in a separate physical realm. This idea, that dead individuals had the capacity to interact with those they left behind, can be found in many African religious traditions.

Ancestor reverence and a belief in spirits were also central to African religious belief systems. People attained ancestor status in different ways. Among the Jola of Gambia and the Yoruba of Nigeria, only those who led good lives could become ancestors. In some belief systems ancestors were more present in the lives of the living than the supreme being. Some communities believed ancestors had mystical powers. While benevolent for the most part, they could also be capricious if they thought they had been neglected by the living. For that reason those left behind made sure the ancestors were not forgotten.[12]

Lesser nature spirits played a substantial role in African belief systems. These were spirits designated as helpers by the supreme being, deriving their powers from him/her. The Yoruba Orishas, perhaps best known in the Americas, had special power and distinct characteristics with specific duties. Spirits such as Oshun, a female deity associated with water and femininity, Ifa, a spirit of divination (the practice of finding the cause and significance of events), or Shango, god of thunder, were greatly revered by the living. They influenced the daily lives and activities of people more meaningfully and were often feared more than the supreme being figure in the cosmology.

Lesser spirits sometimes identified themselves to humans through spirit possession. Believed to have more control and power over people's everyday lives than the supreme being, they had specific functions in the life of the community. In Kongo people believed in lesser spirits (*simbi/bisimbi*), each of which had its own function.[13] The Jola of Gambia associated lesser spirits with fishing, governance in the community, blacksmithing, women's fertility, male initiation, and rain. In an agricultural society with patrilineal forms of kinship, spirits deemed important often reflected the needs of a farming community: rain, an abundance of crops, and so on. In other African societies lesser spirits were linked to oceans, rivers, springs, and other places in the natural world. The Dogon of Mali believe lesser spirits are connected with specific forces of nature. Nommo, an ancestral spirit, is linked with the life-giving properties of water. Displeasing the spirits could be the difference between a bountiful harvest and famine, and people did all they could to follow the rules.

A central aspect of many African belief systems was the attempt to understand and explain suffering and evil. Because people needed to explain what brought harm to their communities, spirits or other humans were often blamed for things that could not otherwise be explained. Eshu among the Yoruba spirits was believed to be a purveyor of negative events and occurrences. Other societies attributed suffering and bad luck to spirits. Humans were also targeted as the source of evil in some contexts, accused of being responsible for death, illness, and other misfortunes. Accusations of witchcraft and wrongdoing were common, particularly in troubled times. In the centuries during which the slave trade flourished, and as Africans encountered Europeans coming to the continent with their own religions, societies ravaged by loss doubtlessly called on elements of their religions for succor.

Africa, Europe, and the Transatlantic Slave Trade

The encounter with Europe would immeasurably alter those civilizations. When the first Portuguese ships sailed down the coast of West Africa, the lives of men and women in Africa would change forever. The Portuguese first reached West African shores in 1443 at the mouth of the river Senegal. This began a centuries-long link between the two continents that had considerable ramifications for people of African descent globally. By 1462 the Portuguese had sailed down the coast to Sierra Leone. Twenty years later Portuguese traders built a trading fort they called Sao Jorge da Mina (later Elmina) in what is today the nation of Ghana. A relationship initially beneficial to Africans and Europeans alike soon disintegrated into great suffering as a transition from trading in goods to trading in human beings ensued.

Europeans had little knowledge of sub-Saharan Africa before the fifteenth century, although European mapmakers had produced rudimentary maps of Africa as early as the thirteenth century. Drawn largely from rumors and hearsay, what they knew was scanty and rife with misinformation. Although some contact had occurred between Europeans and Africans from East and North Africa, not until the Portuguese made their first maritime voyage south did Europeans gain more information about these societies. The trans-Saharan trade had allowed African goods to flow into Europe long before direct encounters. By the time the Portuguese sailed for the coast of Africa, for example, West African gold was already being used to mint European coins. As news of African wealth abounded, more Europeans came, attracted by gold and possibilities for more trade.[14]

In 1482, when Diogo Cão sailed down the West African coast to the river Congo and encountered the Kingdom of Kongo, he was the first European to travel that far south, opening the way for significant events in the relationship between Europe and Africa. This was one of the first meaningful and well-documented relationships between an African ruler and his European counterpart.

As illustrated in subsequent correspondence between Manikongo/
King Affonso of Kongo and King Henry of Portugal, the early relationship between Portugal and Kongo was founded on mutual
exchange and respect, as Europeans pursued knowledge of the African societies they encountered and Africans brokered trade with
the newcomers from across the seas.[15]

The Portuguese were the first to trade with Africans, but other
European nations soon entered the trade, including Spain, France,
Britain, the Netherlands, and Denmark. The initial relationship between Africans and Europeans was that of host and guest. Africans
extended courtesies under prevalent customs of hospitality as gifts
and information were exchanged, but in African territories Europeans followed African rules. But in the ensuing years, as African rulers and traders became more dependent on European goods, they
lost much of the power they had wielded. The relationship was not
one-dimensional, as African men and women engaged with Europeans in particular ways. Women, for example, often married or
had sexual relationships with European men. While we know that
some of these relationships were coercive, it was sometimes in the
interest of women to enter into them. Likewise, men chose to trade
with Europeans for a variety of reasons, including aggrandizement,
protections, and political ascendancy.[16]

The exchange of goods other than humans continued until the
settlement of the Americas. This development prompted a shift in
terms of trade and changed the fate of some Africans forever. Millions of men and women were drawn into a network of trade that
resulted in their enslavement. In the Americas they encountered
bondage as they had never understood it before, for while slavery
was common in many parts of the world, racial slavery would
emerge in the New World.

Slavery and slave trading were not unfamiliar to some African
societies. Scholars have recognized slavery as a universal phenomenon practiced in societies all over the world long before the Atlantic slave trade era. While Atlantic slavery has largely come to be
associated with the institution, its nature in other societies has long
been understood. Recent studies have examined these institutions
in greater deal, making a distinction between "societies with slaves,"
where slavery was one of many systems of labor, and "slave societ-

ies," in which slave labor and slavery served as the foundation of a social and economic order. Both forms of slavery could be found in Africans societies in the coastal regions of West and West Central Africa, although most scholars agree that societies with slaves predominated in these regions. But slavery was not one-dimensional.[17]

It is important to understand that African societies were not static. The nature of slavery changed over the course of the many centuries this book examines. Furthermore, as demand for labor intensified in the Americas, the nature of slavery in Africa also changed. In some societies the enslaved were a minor part of the labor force and were not crucial producers; in others they were central to production.

Slavery developed in different ways in the places where it existed. Enslaved men and women were treated as outsiders, as people without a history. Held against their will by the threat of force or through coercion, they could sometimes nevertheless have a great deal of autonomy, and their status or position could change over time. With no ties or links with those considered members of the society (even the lowest classes), enslaved men and women were completely dependent on the will of their owners, making them vulnerable. Although they were not unique in the work they did or in the fact that they had no control over their lives, there were marked differences in the rights of the enslaved. Members of a clan or kin group could be put in temporary conditions of servitude. What often distinguished those considered slaves was their perceived rootlessness and the absence of kinship ties.[18]

In societies where slavery came to be recognized as an important institution, lack of ties to a community, absence of family connections, and inability to access land often distinguished slaves from other workers. This was particularly true in the case of women, who performed similar tasks regardless of their status as slave or free. Given that in some African societies enslaved women were often preferred as wives because they lacked kinship ties, they frequently performed the same tasks as the free women who were members of the lineage. Some scholars have argued that because of their value in African societies as child bearers and farmers, they were not initially sold in large numbers to Europeans. However, women would not be spared in the centuries to come.[19]

By the eighteenth century, the transatlantic slave trade came to define the connection between Europe and Africa, changing the nature of slavery in societies where it existed and introducing it in others. Yet African men and women did not always accept the notion of trading in human beings. While many participated actively in the trade, scholars have noted that there was also active resistance to the slave trade. Africans found various strategies to counter the devastation wrought by the slave trade.[20]

Enslavement

The forced enslavement of Africans across the Atlantic began with the initial transportation of Africans to European cities and to islands off the African coast. Some of the earliest African captives were taken directly to Portugal between 1441 and 1443 to be used for local labor purposes. As Europeans settled the Caribbean Islands and the Americas, the need for labor intensified, and in 1502 the first Africans were transported directly from Africa to the Americas. This enforced movement of Africans to the Americas intensified in the middle of the sixteenth century as Europeans found a need for more labor. Millions of men and women were enslaved before the transatlantic slave trade came to a halt by the end of the nineteenth century.

American labor demands transformed Africans into human commodities. The historian Stephanie Smallwood describes the process: "The method by which traders turned people into property that could move easily, smoothly through the channels of saltwater slavery took the form of both physical and social violence. Along the coast, captives felt the enclosure of prison walls and the weight of iron shackles holding them incarcerated in shore-based trade forts or aboard ships that functioned as floating warehouses as captives were accumulated."[21] Women, men, children, and sometimes the elderly were transported on slave ships across the Atlantic Ocean, leaving loved ones behind. Aminata Diallo, the young protagonist in Hill's novel, expresses surprise at her capture, asserting her humanity as she cries out to her captors: "This is a mistake. I am a freeborn Muslim." Her pleas are to no avail, and all she can do is ask, "How could this be? I prayed that this was a dream."[22]

Scholars estimate that between 12 million and 15 million Africans left Africa during the course of the trade as Africans were transported from regions in the Upper Guinea Coast, Gold Coast, Bight of Benin, Bight of Biafra, and West Central Africa. They came from diverse ethnic groups—Ewe, Yoruba, Mende, Temne, Malinke, Kongo, and others—and many of them, like Aminata, were practicing Muslims. Enslaved Africans contributed greatly to the development of American colonies and, as we shall see, had a lasting demographic impact on those regions. Recent scholarship shows the various regional, religious, and cultural origins of Africans brought to American shores, allowing for greater understanding of their influences on the societies in which they settled.[23]

The United States, which did not grow labor-intensive sugar as did the Caribbean colonies, received less than 5–7 percent of the total number of Africans who settled in the Americas. These Africans came from a wide variety of places, including the Senegambia region, Sierra Leone, the Bights of Benin and Biafra, the Windward Coast, and a small number from Southeast Africa. The United States received Bambara, Igbo, Mandingo, and Mende people, among others. Recently scholars have also highlighted the important role of West Central Africans, who made up about one-third of the Africans brought to the United States. An estimated sixty thousand West Central Africans could be found dispersed in the Carolinas, Georgia, Virginia, Maryland and, in smaller numbers, elsewhere in the country.[24]

The departure of large numbers of men and women left a void in the societies from which they were taken. This wrenching of millions from their homeland, loss of lives, and separation from family brought many changes. While slave merchants and rulers prospered, production capacity and manpower were lost, hindering African development and creating insecurity in the population left behind. Scholars have examined patterns of social organization that emerged during the slave trade era and the changes wrought to African communities. Work by archaeologists illuminates the trade's impact on social organization, cultural practices, and economic relations. While scholars have long recognized its effect on labor needs, retardation of market industries, and economies, these examinations are now revealing other consequences—depopulation in some areas, evidence of large-scale movements as Africans fled their communities to settle new ones further inland or took refuge in European settlements. People fleeing enslavement constructed defensive villages, towns, and cities away from places they could be captured. As one scholar writes, "The period can be considered one of major demographic upheaval characterized by new manifestations of power and cultural memory that had profound effects on the way people lived in and thought about the world around them."[25] For those unfortunate men and women who could not escape enslavers, the route to their final destination in the Americas was terrifying.

Middle Passages

While the ship's voyage across the Atlantic Ocean has traditionally defined and shaped our understanding of the Middle Passage, enslaved Africans often endured several middle passages. The path to enslavement began at the moment of capture and continued with the long journey to the coast, confinement in a slave fort, boarding the ship, and the journey across the ocean. Mahommah Baquaqua in 1854 describes his capture: "In the morning when I arose, I found that I was a prisoner, and my companions were all gone. Oh, horror! I then discovered that I had been betrayed into the hands of my enemies, and sold for a slave. Never shall I forget my feelings on that occasion; the thoughts of my poor mother harassed me very much, and the loss of my liberty and honorable position with the king, grieved me very sorely."[26] Belinda, "the African," a seventy-year-old woman petitioning the Massachusetts legislature in 1783, remembers her captivity and transportation to America. During the ship's voyage, "Scenes which her imagination had never conceived of, a floating world, the sporting monsters of the deep, and the familiar meeting of billows and clouds, strove, but in vain, to divert her attention from three hundred Africans in chains, suffering the most excruciating torment; and some of them rejoicing that the pangs of death came like a balm to their wounds."[27]

The moment of capture has also been described in fiction by the Afro-Canadian writer Lawrence Hill and the African American novelist Alex Haley, who depicted the capture and subsequent enslavement of his protagonist Kunta Kinte in similar terms. These fictional accounts echo the real experiences of the enslaved on the ship's journey to the Americas. Aminata Diallo narrates her long journey from where she was captured to the coast, as the coffle picked up more captives along the way. She tells of attempted escapes and recapture and of death and separation as enslaved Africans are taken farther and farther from their homes.

The voyage to the coast could last several weeks to months before an enslaved individual embarked on a ship. On the coast the enslaved could languish for weeks in slave forts or barracoons. In his famous autobiography, first published in 1789, Olaudah Equiano describes his enslavement in Africa in great detail, outlining his initial capture and sale to several African owners before even leaving the continent. Having been for several months imprisoned in factories on the continent, Equiano wrote of his arrival at a coastal port in West Africa: "The first object which saluted my eyes when I arrived on the coast was the sea, and a slave ship, which was then riding at anchor, and waiting for its cargo. These filled me with astonishment, which was soon converted into terror when I was carried on board."[28] On the coast the enslaved were "processed," branded with hot irons to indicate to whom they "belonged," perhaps baptized (to guarantee their salvation if they were to die en route), and either housed at a slave fort until loaded on ships or, as in Equiano's case, loaded directly on a ship.

The ordeal of the Middle Passage frequently continued with the "coasting" of the ship along the West African coast, as it picked up more human cargo until it finally sailed for the Americas. This process could last weeks, sometimes months. All the while men, women, and children were tortured by their memories of those dear to them. In Hill's fictional account, Aminata struggles to hold onto memories of her parents: "I tried to keep their voices in my head," she remembers, "but I could not feed those thoughts. Each and every time they were starved, flattened, and sucked out of my mind."[29] Eventually, those loved ones and homes would be physically left behind as the ship sailed to the Americas.

The journey across the Atlantic could take several months, depending on time of year, port of sail, and type of ship, among other factors. We know much about these voyages, and the experience for those enslaved aboard those vessels was horrifying. Baquaqua proclaimed about the slave ship, "Its horrors, ah! who can describe?

None can so truly depict its horrors as the poor unfortunate, miserable wretch that has been confined within its portals. ... We were thrust into the hold of the vessel in a state of nudity, the males being crammed on one side and the females on the other; the hold was so low that we could not stand up, but were obliged to crouch upon the floor or sit down; day and night were the same to us, sleep being denied."[30]

Enslaved Africans resisted their capture whenever they could, whether by running away from barracoons on the coast, jumping overboard in coastal waters, or outright revolt on the seas. Slave revolts were frequent on voyages across the Atlantic. Scholars estimate that there were around four hundred shipboard revolts during the era of the transatlantic slave trade, the most memorable perhaps being the rebellion of enslaved men and women aboard the *Amistad* in 1839. Led by Sengbe Pieh (also known as Joseph Cinque), the captives succeeded in taking over the ship. They hoped to sail back to Africa, but unfortunately, the surviving ship's crew navigated the ship to the United States, where the ship was seized. A famous court case regarding the question of the enslaved's status ensued. The Amistad case made headlines in its day as the courts tried to decide whether the African captives were illegally enslaved or whether they were, in fact, property. Sengbe Pieh and his compatriots were represented by former president John Quincy Adams, who defended their right to freedom on both moral and legal grounds. The court ruled in their favor and they were released. [31]

The experience on board created a bond among those who survived the journey, forming ties of friendship and kinship as they endured the long journey to an unknown world. In his examination of African captives on board the *Emilia*, a slave ship bound for Brazil in 1821, Walter Hawthorne has explored the slave ship "as a place where individuals died but communities were born." Long-lasting relationships were created by those lucky enough to end up in the same place on the other side of the Atlantic. This "community of shipmates" and the bonds they established were "the foundation upon which new communities were constructed and reinforced preexisting identities."[32] Though fictional, Alex Haley's central character, Kunta Kinte, movingly illustrates how these ties were created over the course of the voyage:

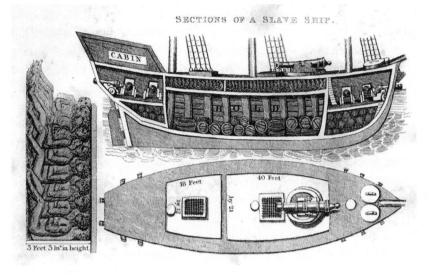

SECTIONS OF A SLAVE SHIP.

Cross-section of a Brazilian slave ship.
(From Robert Walsh, Notices of Brazil in 1828 and 1829 *[London, 1830].*
From Wikimedia Commons/Public Domain.)

The steady murmuring that went on in the hold whenever the toubob [white men] were gone kept growing in volume and intensity as the men began to communicate better and better with one another. Words not understood were whispered from mouth to ear along the shelves until someone who knew more than one tongue would send back their meanings. In the process, all of the men along each shelf learned new words in tongues they had not spoken before. Sometimes men jerked upward, bumping their heads, in the double excitement of communicating with each other and the fact that it was being done without the toubob's knowledge. Muttering among themselves for hours, the men developed a deepening sense of intrigue and of brotherhood. Though they were of different villages and tribes, the feeling grew that they were not from different peoples or places.[33]

Thus even before landing on American shores some men and women from the continent had become "Africans," as they would later be designated.

As men, women, and children made their involuntary journey to the Americas, they did not leave Africa completely behind. Although they left loved ones and life histories in their various homelands, they took much with them. As Smallwood writes: "Each person pulled onto the slave ship embodied a social history: one or more distinctive places that were called 'home' and an indelible web of relationships comprising ties with immediate family and the extended network of kin."[34] The enslaved took memories and cultural patterns, including kinship structures and ideas about how families should interact and function, from the particular communities from which they hailed. They took memories of kin and community: mothers, fathers, spouses, and children they would never see again. Years after being enslaved, Venture Smith would remember his father as "a man of remarkable stature. I should judge as much as six feet and six or seven inches high, two feet across his shoulders, and every way well proportioned. He was a man of remarkable strength and resolution, affable, kind and gentle, ruling with equity and moderation."[35] Likewise, throughout Hill's narrative his fictional heroine recollected her parents and her homeland, and the values they had given her.

Africa and the idea of Africa would, in the ensuing centuries, comfort and strengthen enslaved Africans and their American-born descendants in the United States. Africans retained words, idioms, and other elements of their languages. They clung to religious and sacred beliefs, which sustained them through their ordeal, and kept alive oral traditions and origin myths that would help them explain their plight and understand the new world they were encountering. They maintained ideas about good and evil they would use to recognize friends and enemies in the Americas, and memories to remember those they had left behind. Africans held onto ideas about how to organize themselves politically and an understanding of the social and cultural formations that had sustained them throughout their lives. They kept memories of enslavement within their communities, which they doubtlessly compared to their new lives in bondage. Most important, the many women and men taken from the continent held onto their resilience and strength, which nourished them in their new lives as enslaved people. They would pass on all of these things to successive generations of African-descended people in America.

CHAPTER THREE

"We, the African Members, form ourselves into a Society"

I n his autobiography, printed in 1798, Venture Smith, now free and living in New York, writes that before he finally attained his freedom he was sold three times, encountered many misfortunes and tribulations, and suffered great personal loss. Yet at the age of sixty-nine, when he wrote his life story, he was able to reflect positively on his life and express gratitude for his independence: "My freedom is a privilege which nothing else can equal. Notwithstanding all the losses I have suffered by fire, by the injustice of knaves, by the cruelty and oppression of false hearted friends, and the perfidy of my own countrymen whom I have assisted and redeemed from bondage, I am now possessed of more than one hundred acres of land, and three habitable dwelling houses."[1]

Smith surely did not take his life of freedom or his ability, however limited, to make his own decisions for granted. Captured in Africa at the age of eight, Venture was enslaved in New York until 1765 when he purchased his freedom. He went on to buy his family's freedom and lived until 1805. His experience of enslavement and freedom was certainly not typical. Most enslaved Africans lived out their lives in slavery.

By 1776, when the American Revolution broke out, over half a million men and women of African descent lived in North America. Africans brought involuntarily to the United States in the seventeenth and eighteenth centuries found a world vastly different from what they were accustomed to in their native lands. The early experiences of enslaved men and women in the United States were fraught with struggles and difficulties they could not have imagined, as they faced uncertain futures in their new homeland. Over the course of three centuries, slavery would emerge as the predominant status of African-descended populations in the United States. Africans and their descendants would strive for freedom and dignity, achieving those ends in some cases, failing in others.[2] For the most part, they were constrained by the institution of slavery whether enslaved or not, for it circumscribed the lives of all African-descended people.

Slavery evolved differently across the United States, impacting African religions, languages, and cultures, splitting families, and radically changing lives. Race would emerge as the principal ideology in the country, shaping the lens through which men and women of African descent were viewed and would, eventually, view themselves. As some blacks escaped slavery and moved into freedom, notions about race influenced how they could, and would, live. A unique slave culture developed among enslaved Africans in Southern states as they relied on elements of their African background, while Northern blacks, small in number and often isolated in the communities in which they lived, grew increasingly distant from their ancestral culture, though many fought to hold onto it. While slavery became entrenched in the South, it slowly eroded in the North, and the two regions took different economic and political paths. Depending on which region of the country they dwelled in, the lives of African Americans emerged differently. Laws addressing their role and place affected their lives, North or South, free or slave. Yet they strove to maintain real and psychological connections to their African past by reconstructing and reconstituting elements of their customs and traditions. In the process distinct African American culture(s), informed by Africa, developed in the United States.

Although Africans had come to the New World with Spanish conquistadors as early as the sixteenth century, they did not become permanent residents until the seventeenth century. As Europeans settled the American colonies in the seventeenth century, labor demands prompted the importation of millions of Africans into the United States. Each colony had to decide where and how blacks would fit into an established hierarchy, which included land-owning and landless whites, white indentured servants and, in some regions, Native Americans. Slavery evolved differently in the regions where it took root, impacting not only how Africans adapted to their new environment but also how much of their African past they could retain.

Slavery Emerges

The best-documented "first arrival" of Africans was that of the men and women sold to British settlers in the Jamestown colony of Virginia by a Dutch ship in 1619.[3] Other colonists in North America followed suit, importing Africans to work in homes, plantations, and public works. Settled in 1609, Jamestown, Virginia, in many ways served as the template for how slavery would develop in the rest of the colonies, particularly in the South. When the first Africans arrived in Virginia ten years after its settlement, their status was initially unclear. Their primary purpose was to perform labor. An English colony, Virginia had no established laws on slavery—an age-old institution worldwide, but one the British had declared unlawful on English soil. In many ways, except for their color, the enslaved were like the white indentured servants, serving in the same capacity and doing similar work. But European servants contracted out their labor for a number of years with the understanding they would be granted their freedom after fulfilling their terms of labor. Africans never had that option, making their status different from indentured servants. The men, women, and children from Africa were clearly identified as captives, property, and perpetual servants.

Early records of the first Africans in Jamestown categorized them as servants rather than slaves, and a number of them were listed as free persons who owned their own property. Antonio "the negro," who arrived in Jamestown in 1621, was listed in the census as a servant. Later anglicizing his name to become Anthony Johnson, he married Mary, also a servant. Antonio was probably

LANDING NEGROES AT JAMESTOWN
FROM DUTCH MAN-OF-WAR, 1619

Howard Pyle, Landing Negroes at Jamestown from Dutch Man-of-War, 1619.
(From Harper's Monthly Magazine, *January 1901, p. 172. Library of Congress,
Prints and Photographs Division. From Wikimedia Commons/Public Domain.)*

Christian, converted in Angola, or his Portuguese captors may well have given him the name. His claims to Christianity likely allowed him to petition for his freedom. Some Africans were already Christians, having been converted in Africa after long contact with Europeans or in the Caribbean. Historian James Sweet has referred to an "African-Christian identity" of the twenty West Central Africans in Jamestown that allowed the early Africans to integrate more easily into the colony.[4]

The population of Virginia was small. Consequently, blacks worked and lived side by side with whites, allowing them to integrate "into the day-to-day affairs of English colonial life, including the practice of Christianity." Because they were Christians, they "used their prior knowledge of Christianity as a tool to integrate the communality of servants in Virginia. By becoming like servants instead of like slaves, Central Africans challenged notions that they were chattel, opening the way for manumission and roles as freedmen."[5]

During most of the seventeenth century there was some fluidity in the lives of Africans, as colony laws had not yet defined a specific place for those of African descent. African men and women gave testimony in court against whites, sued them, and petitioned for freedom from servitude, often on the basis of being Christian. They served in colony militias and lived alongside whites. However, slavery gradually became codified in law as Virginia planters, requiring more reliable labor for their tobacco plantations, imported Africans into the colony in greater numbers. By 1650 there were four hundred Africans in Virginia. Some, like the Johnsons, free by then, owned property they passed on to their children. Others were bound to those for whom they worked. Labor demands augmented the number of Africans brought to the colony, and as their numbers rose so did the erosion of their rights.

By the end of the seventeenth century, a clear correlation existed between the growing number of Africans and the diminution of their freedoms and rights. This pattern of settlement and importation would be repeated, with some variation, in all the thirteen colonies as different labor demands determined the status and treatment of Africans. By the 1640s it was clear that a distinction between indentured servants and those who would be called slaves would now be made on the basis of African heritage.

The first laws systemizing slavery emerged in the seventeenth century, and involuntary servitude for life came to mark Africans as slaves. In 1641 Massachusetts became the first colony to legally recognize slavery. Other states followed suit, adopting laws that determined that those of African ancestry would remain enslaved. In the 1660s, Virginia law made its first reference to slavery, and by 1705, when the Virginia General Assembly declared, "All Negro, mulatto and Indian slaves within this dominion ... shall be held to be real estate," it was evident that Africans would be enslaved in American society. The 1705 code "An Act concerning Servants and Slaves" outlined the many restrictions to be put on the enslaved, enumerating punishments that would be meted out to those, black enslaved and white indentured servants, who disobeyed the law. The law established the property rights of slave owners, allowing them to sell their enslaved, set up separate courts for trying Africans, and prevented blacks from hiring whites, among other things. This pattern was repeated in other colonies—Maryland, Dutch New York, Pennsylvania, and later in colonies further south like the Carolinas and Georgia.[6]

Maryland, settled in 1634, increasingly came to rely on African labor. Following neighboring Virginia's suit, in 1664 the colony legalized slavery, resulting in the enslavement of children with white mothers. In 1681 the law was amended to recognize the black children of white mothers and the children born to free black women as free. It did not change a 1671 law ruling that conversion to Christianity did not affect the status of Africans. Thus the path to freedom through Christianity closed by the end of the seventeenth century, as "race" became the criterion distinguishing free from slave. African ancestry and perpetual servitude became linked. The noted historian Peter Wood observes: "Perhaps in the middle of the seventeenth century, if you were one of several thousand Africans living in Virginia you certainly knew that your children would be free—you might have that expectation. To suddenly find themselves involved in lifelong servitude, and then to realize that in fact their children might inherit the same status, that was a terrible blow, that was a terrible transformation."[7]

Africans were different, and for early American settlers the most obvious difference was their physical appearance. Long held ideas and stereotypes about the continent led to ethnocentric, if not yet racist, attitudes toward people of African descent. For many, their strange customs marked them as inferior to Europeans, who commented on their "harsh jargons" and "gross bestiality and rudeness of manners."[8]

As African heritage was increasingly associated with labor and servile status, the belief that Europeans were superior emerged. By the mid-seventeenth century there were clear differences between black and white laborers on Southern plantations and in Northern states, where blacks could often be found performing domestic tasks within white homes. Laws separating the races slowly made their way into colonies as first subtle, then more obvious distinctions were made in how Europeans and Africans were treated. Gradually, perpetual servitude came to be seen as suitable only for Africans. The small freedoms many blacks had enjoyed were curtailed, and the rights and privileges some had been afforded were stripped from them.

Hence, those of African ancestry saw their rights slowly disintegrate. Although all blacks were not automatically deemed slaves, the association of their color with servitude became an accepted part of American society, resulting in the diminution of status even of free blacks. Blacks were now restricted from carrying arms, voting, testifying in court, mingling with whites, and even holding office—all things they had been able to do with some fluidity in earlier years. Conversion to Christianity was no longer a path to freedom, and the differences between those classified as free and those labeled slaves were strengthened.[9]

Northern slavery, not as extensive, emerged differently, with its own peculiarities. States in the North did not require large-scale use of African labor, and a plantation economy did not shape the lives of blacks in this region. Large numbers of enslaved were brought from the Caribbean rather than directly from Africa, though some men and women came directly from the continent. Africans were used in a variety of ways, performing diverse tasks. Northern colonies often had smaller ratios of blacks to whites. For example, in 1790 Massachusetts, there were about 5,250 blacks in a population of over 370,000. The enslaved often lived and worked alongside their owners and other whites on small farms or in households. They were also craftspeople, artisans, and domestic servants.

From region to region, the status and condition of blacks differed. Although Northern colonies did not have the large-scale plantations typical of the South, harsh laws affected black life nonetheless. In fact, court documents, which provide the best glimpse into African American life in these regions, illustrate that blacks faced some of the harshest treatment in New England. They encountered laws restricting their rights and daily activities, and their movement was circumscribed. In 1703 Massachusetts legislation barred blacks from going out after 9 p.m. unless on an errand for an owner. Other laws governed marriage, ownership of property, trade, and travel. In 1672 Sylvanus Warro's owner prosecuted him for going out at night, fornication, and disobedience. Warro ran away, no doubt to escape punishment. In the seventeenth century blacks could not bear arms, fight in the militia, legally board ships without permits, or be on the streets at night. The harshest laws prohibited interracial unions. Over the course of the seventeenth and early eighteenth centuries, stringent laws prevented and punished those who dared enter into these types of relationships.[10]

Similar laws governing blacks' lives and actions were passed in Pennsylvania. Enslaved men and women were used as skilled laborers in iron manufacturing and as bakers, goldsmiths, sail makers, masons, and carpenters. In 1700 the colony established different legal statuses for Africans and whites. Blacks were not tried in regular courts, could not go more than ten miles from their masters' residence, could not be out after 9 at night, and could not meet in groups larger than four. As in New England, intermarriage was forbidden.

Further north in New York, as the legal enslavement of Africans was upheld in 1710 and as fear of uprisings grew, harsher slave codes governed black lives. At the end of the eighteenth century, as Northerners moved to end slavery in their colonies, free blacks could now, within limits, choose their destinies in a way forbidden to their Southern brothers and sisters. Venture Smith, despite a life of hardship, was grateful, ending his autobiography with these words: "It gives me joy to think that I *have* and that I *deserve* so good a character, especially for *truth* and *integrity*."[11] Smith's narrative is a glimpse into the life of an African in the North as he transitioned from slavery to freedom. His life mirrored that of many African Americans in the colonies, North and South. It was an existence filled with grief, loss, and pain.

But Smith finally achieved his freedom, however constrained. Despite harsh laws, enslaved Africans in the North had more mobility than their Southern counterparts. For example, Richard Allen, who would later become the founder of the African Methodist Episcopal church, was born a slave in Pennsylvania. He later wrote of moving between Pennsylvania, Delaware, and New Jersey, hiring out his labor.[12]

By the eighteenth century racial slavery was an accepted part of life in America. New colonies being settled further south took their cue from earlier settlements in crafting legislation and in their attitudes toward Africans. First settled in the 1660s, South Carolina sanctioned slavery from its inception. In 1663 settlers were offered twenty acres for every black male slave and ten acres for every female slave brought into the colony. The state's 1669 constitution sanctioned slavery as a way of life, stating that "every Freeman of Carolina shall have absolute power and authority over Negro slaves of what opinion or religion soever."[13] In the early years, between one-fourth and one-third of the population arrived in the colony as slaves, mostly men brought to work on rice plantations.

After 1700 rice production increased and so did the demand for labor. White planters recognized how useful Africans could be because of their knowledge about cultivating rice. Africans who engaged in rice production in their homelands in West Africa were targeted for enslavement in South Carolina. That colony imported more slaves than any other through the end of the eighteenth century, many of them directly from Africa. In later years, South Carolina would become one of the colonies in North America where Africans could be found in the largest numbers. As slavery became profitable for European plantation owners in the American South, they continued to import Africans in greater numbers. Increasingly they were brought directly from Africa to the United States, rather than from Caribbean slave islands (where, among other things, the mortality rate was high).[14]

By the end of the eighteenth century the large community of enslaved, influenced by African antecedents, had devised ways to sustain itself through the traumatic ordeal of slavery. Here it might be important to reiterate, as Michael Gomez has noted, the importance of examining the enslaved as "Africans with distinct heritages,"

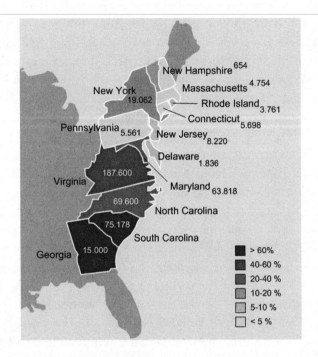

Population of African Americans in the thirteen colonies, 1770.
("Slavery in the 13 colonies" © Stilfehler 2008. From Wikimedia Commons.
Copyleft: This is a free work, you can copy, distribute, and modify it under
the terms of the Free Art License, http://artlibre.org/licence/lal/en/.)

forced to create new lives for themselves.[15] Scholars have long de-
bated how much of their African past enslaved Africans brought to
the United States and how much they retained. Early scholarship
argued that the brutality of the Middle Passage and slavery in the
Americas stripped Africans of their culture. More recent scholarship
has shed light on the many ways Africans held onto elements of
their cultures, religions, and ways of life.

Components of African life and cultures, real and imagined, remained in African American consciousness. Africans made many
cultural accommodations in their quest to survive. Much of that required drawing from their African past. They mixed and matched
elements of their African ways with European ones, adapting and
combining them in order to survive in the New World. As one historian has reminded us, just as Africans were influenced by Europe-

ans and their ways, "African ideas and political cultures 'colonized' Europeans and Native Americans just as readily as the other way around."[16] In other words, Europeans and Native Americans also adopted African practices.

In assessing how much of their cultural practices enslaved Africans retained, we must understand that some arrived in the Americas having already encountered Europeans and their customs. African societies, as we have seen, were not monolithic or static. Over the many centuries with which this book is concerned, they changed as a result of numerous factors. While many had their first extended experience with Europeans in the Americas, there were others who had been aware of a European presence since the fifteenth century. Along coastal regions trading relationships developed, resulting in African communities conversant with European ways. Some have called them "Atlantic Creoles," men and women whose origins lay in the encounter between Europe and Africa. This "charter generation" had gained some understanding of Europeans customs by the seventeenth century. They often spoke European languages, so were sometimes able to understand their captors once enslaved. Ira Berlin argues that they were "very much at home in the new environment."[17] How "at home" they were is debatable. Nonetheless, we can imagine that the acculturation of some to their new environment was eased by their previous encounters with Europeans.

For the most part, however, Africans enslaved in the United States arrived with little knowledge of European ways, having been taken from inland regions. The shock and trauma of their encounter with Europeans under conditions of enslavement must have been horrifying. Olaudah Equiano, enslaved as a young boy in West Africa, was worried that the first Europeans he encountered would eat him: "Their complexions too differing so much from ours, their long hair, and the language they spoke (which was very different from any I had ever heard), united to confirm me in this belief. Indeed such were the horrors of my views and fears at the moment, that, if ten thousand worlds had been my own I would have freely parted with them all to have exchanged my condition with that of the meanest slave in my own country. When I looked round the ship too and saw a large furnace or copper boiling, and a multitude of black people of every description chained together, everyone of their countenances expressing dejection and sorrow, I no longer doubted of my fate."[18] Despite the brutality of capture and subsequent enslavement, Africans held on tightly to their memories and their past, clinging to their humanity.[19]

How did Africans succeed in holding onto their humanity? As we have seen, the men and women captured in Africa came from societies organized in a variety of ways where every individual had a role to play. In the Americas the cultures that emerged reflected what Africans had left behind and showed up in socialization and family patterns, religion, and recreation. Although maintaining stable families in North America was difficult, kinship structures prevailing in most African societies allowed the enslaved to cope and develop new relationships in captivity. Given how broadly kin could be defined in their societies, Africans saw no obstacles to creating new family ties.

Scholars have examined how African forms of kinship were re-created in the Americas, observing how slaves formed "fictive kinship" bonds. In slavery, the "principal kinship organization was a malleable extended family that, when possible, provided its members with nurture, education, socialization, material support, and recreation in the face of the potential social chaos that the slaveholder imposed," one scholar writes. Africans brought with them flexible understandings of family that served them in slavery as they bound themselves to new communities. Forming these family ties allowed those enslaved to cope with their bondage, permitting them to pass on cultural norms, values, and other elements of their African past to subsequent generations. Furthermore, familial practices brought to the United States were adapted to suit American needs. Central to family life in Africa was the extended family group, and Africans in the United States re-created these patterns on plantations and households in the Americas. While exact forms of family could not be re-created, enslaved men and women attempted to build kinship relationships. As scholars of enslaved families have observed, Africans re-created familial patterns in the Americas in various ways. Adopting this fictional form of kinship allowed them to "strategize the survival of the entire slave community."[20]

Often less supervised than labor, recreational activities brought the enslaved together, allowing them to use this time to create ties with one another and to hold onto their cultural practices. Utilizing the limited free time they had, usually on Sundays, blacks created community through music and other cultural forms. African rhythms and harmonies drew Africans from different ethnicities together as they recognized familiar strains and tones in the music of their enslaved counterparts. Music served as solace to many in their new lives in bondage and uplifted others as they sought to adjust to their new circumstances. A variety of instruments, like drums, banjos, rattles, kora, balafon, and other string and percussion instruments used in Africa were replicated in the United States.

Storytelling was also a significant part of socialization, and during free moments enslaved Africans shared stories and tales of their various homelands. Telling stories allowed them to remember home and gave them opportunities to share elements of their languages and cultures with others. Thus many African words survived, making their way into the American vocabulary. As Joseph Holloway has shown, words from African languages were assimilated into the English language, including *zombie, honky, bebop,* and *tote.* As Africans lost elements of their native languages and became more acculturated, they slowly created communities with other enslaved people.[21]

Africans had to adjust not only to their European captors and the Native American populations they encountered, but also to other Africans with whom they had little in common besides their enslaved status. Acculturation often began in the Middle Passage, with further cultural changes occurring as Africans settled on plantations in various colonies. Remembrance of Africa persisted as enslaved Africans retained elements of their "Africanity" while assimilating to European cultures. Holding onto aspects of their cultures and belief systems was a way Africans resisted and coped with their enslavement. As cultures mingled, men and women applied old ways to face new challenges, retaining and adapting their customs, religions, and cultural patterns. The process of adjusting and acculturating themselves to the new society, and to each other, depended on where they lived, their will to maintain their cultural practices, and sometimes on the relative size of the African population.[22]

There was a surge in the slave trade to the United States in the second half of the eighteenth century, and Africans continued to be

brought to America until the early nineteenth century. Direct importation brought new infusions of African culture to America. By
the eighteenth century, the Chesapeake Bay colonies had distinct
African and Creole populations that increasingly became acculturated, while the Carolinas and Georgia often had black majorities in
some regions. In rural areas and on rice plantations in South Carolina, relative isolation of the black population afforded a certain
amount of independence and meant that into the nineteenth century Africans were able to retain many of their cultural practices,
speech patterns, religious practices, and social customs.[23]

"Free" Blacks in Early America

Although African ancestry progressively came to be associated with
servitude and slavery, not all blacks were enslaved. Frequently, alongside those in bondage lived a small free black population. From the
very beginning, a small number of individuals of African ancestry, for
whatever reason, managed to escape enslavement. Others found a
way out of slavery through manumission and self-purchase. In the
early colonies, before slavery was entrenched, free blacks were able to
build self-sustaining and independent lives. Anthony Johnson gained
his freedom not long after he arrived in Virginia, becoming a land-
owner able to hire his own indentured servants. He bought property
in Virginia in 1640 and because free blacks had some mobility, in
1665 moved to Maryland, where he leased a three-hundred-acre
plantation. Before 1770 free blacks, most of whom lived in the North,
made up a small percentage of the colonies' population. This small
group had little influence in white society and few rights. But some,
like the Johnsons, owned property, which they passed on to their
children.[24]

As slavery became entrenched, the lives of men and women not
enslaved were constrained in numerous ways. By the eighteenth
century, as racial attitudes hardened and slavery became ingrained,
laws targeted both free and enslaved blacks. In 1723 the governor
of Virginia decreed that whites should put "a perpetual brand upon
Free-Negroes & Mulattos by excluding them from the great Privi-
ledge of a Freeman." He argued that doing so would "make the
free-Negroes sensible that a distinction ought to be made between

their offspring and the Descendants of an Englishman, with whom they never were to be Accounted Equal.[25] For a time in Virginia, free blacks interacted socially with whites, owned joint property with them, and even sued them in courts. By the eighteenth century, most Southern states had a small free black population whose status was often indistinguishable from its counterparts in slavery.

The American Revolution, with its rhetoric of equality and liberty, brought an increase in the number of free blacks as benevolent slaveholders freed some of their enslaved. The growing number of free blacks in the postrevolutionary period posed the problem of what to do with them. Increasingly stringent legislation targeted them, curtailing their rights and privileges. In South Carolina and other colonies few were able to acquire property. In 1791 free blacks in Charleston protested against a law forbidding them to testify under oath in court, and preventing them from suing in court. They petitioned the legislature, claiming citizenship rights and condemning the act that deprived them of the "Rights and Privileges of Citizens." They asked for these rights on the basis of their contributions to the government in the form of taxes. While not putting themselves on an equal footing with whites in Charleston, they believed that "as your Memorialists have been and are considered as Free-Citizens of this State they hope to be treated as such."[26] The legislature rejected the petition. Despite the restrictions placed on them, free blacks had opportunities not possible for their counterparts in slavery. This was true of blacks in the Northern colonies also.

With the War of Independence won, Northern states moved to end slavery. The 1790 census enumerated fifty-nine thousand free blacks in the United States. A little over twenty-seven thousand were in the North. Even before widespread emancipation there was a community of free blacks in most Northern colonies. Massachusetts, Vermont, and New Hampshire never had large slave populations and hosted a small number of free black residents. In the 1770s all three colonies had language in their constitutions opposing slavery. The black population in these regions grasped its freedom with both hands, immediately creating independent communities, taking advantage of opportunities, accessing wealth and education, and establishing autonomous institutions. In these

communities and organizations, we are able to see the continuing
engagement with Africa, whether in how blacks chose to label their
institutions or in their cultural expressions of music, dance, and
worship practices.

Recent excavations of an eighteenth-century settlement of free
blacks in New England have shown that Northern blacks, like their
Southern counterparts, strove to hold onto elements of their African past. Free African Americans settled Parting Ways, a town near
Plymouth, after the Revolutionary War. Archaeologists found that
its residents had designed their homes very differently from their
white neighbors and "drew on their African past to build a settlement that, in important ways, was at variance with those of their
Yankee neighbors." Prince Goodwin, Cato Howe, Plato Turner,
and Quamany, all residents of Parting Ways, were free men. Likewise, excavation of African burial sites in New York shows African
cultural continuities. In the newly discovered gravesites, there is
evidence of African rituals being used in burial practices.[27]

In Northern colonies, largely characterized by urban living and
fewer numbers of Africans, it could have been harder to maintain
cultural practices, but we now have evidence that black communities retained African social customs like dance, folklore, and song.
Some scholars have argued that continued African religious practices characterized Northern slave resistance. Having autonomy
over their lives allowed Africans to continue the ways of their
homeland. Because their numbers were smaller, it was often difficult for Africans in the North to interact with one another. Even
though blacks made up only a small percentage of New England's
population in the eighteenth century, some managed to hold onto
elements of their African past. Marriage practices, building styles,
medicinal practices, and forms of music and dance were retained
among Northern blacks during the colonial period. In Boston African funeral rites were observed, while in Massachusetts whites, not
understanding blacks' religious practices, often levied accusations
of sorcery and witchcraft at African-descended populations.[28]

By the end of the eighteenth century the Northern black population was significant enough to create its own distinctive communities and organize social events. Two such festivals, Negro
Election Day in New England and Pinkster in New York, allowed

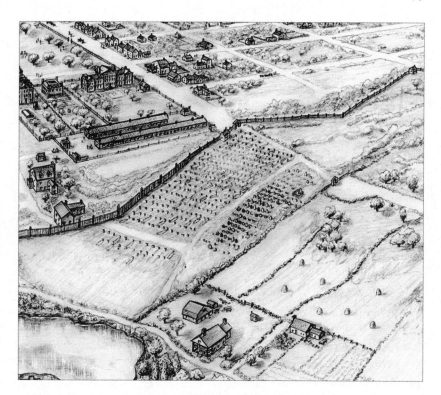

African burial ground in Manhattan, late 1700s.
(From Wikimedia Commons/Public Domain.)

blacks to create communities that helped them sustain elements of
their African past. These festivals allowed blacks to socialize with
one other and perform rituals that drew on their African antecedents. During Negro Election Day, an African-born slave was often
chosen as "king" or "governor" to preside over the ceremonies, as
African Americans came out in full force, in their best clothes, to
"elect" a leader. These events were "infused with memories of
Africa, evidenced in the music and dance that were at the crux of
these festivals, as well as in the frequency with which African-born
slaves assumed the positions of governor or king."[29]

African-descended men and women connected with their ancestral home in varying degrees. They exhibited their bond with
the continent by highlighting different elements of their "Africanness." The scholar Leslie Alexander has persuasively illustrated the

many ways blacks in Northern cities took pride in their African heritage. Whether in the work of those like Phillis Wheatley, who sought Africa's redemption through Christianity, or those who highlighted their African ancestry as they petitioned for rights, Africa loomed in the imagination of Northern blacks. In the attachment of some free blacks to the designation "African," black Americans indicated pride in their heritage by labeling their institutions to reflect their continuing connection to Africa. As they set up churches, schools, and benevolent societies they proudly labeled them African. It was common in this era for black Americans to refer to themselves as Africans. In 1776 Prince Hall led a group of free blacks to establish the African Lodge No. 1, a Masonic lodge in Boston.[30] Hall went on to establish the African Grand Lodge in Philadelphia in 1797. In New York, the African Free School was founded in 1787 largely through the work of white benefactors, but free black children received instruction from black teachers.

In 1787, when Richard Allen and Absalom Jones founded the Free African Society in Philadelphia, they proudly proclaimed themselves "two men of the African race" in the society's preamble, and referred to members of the group as "Free Africans and their descendants of the City of Philadelphia." In 1792 Allen and Jones established the African Church. Two years later the first services were held. The two later split and Absalom Jones founded St. Thomas Episcopal Church. Richard Allen and Daniel Coker would go on to establish the African Methodist Episcopal Church in 1816. Likewise, when the Boston African Society was founded in 1796, its rules for members read, "We, the African Members, form ourselves into a Society . . . for the mutual benefit of each other."[31] In 1802 the Female African Benevolent Association (FABA) was established with two hundred members; in August 1805 Thomas Paul, a preacher from New Hampshire, formed the First African Baptist Church.[32] Samuel Cornish established the African Presbyterian Church in Philadelphia in 1811. Throughout Northern cities blacks created institutions that identified them with their heritage.

David Walker, perhaps the loudest voice decrying white racism in the United States in the early nineteenth century and, as we shall see, a strong critic of colonization, embraced his African heritage even as he claimed his rights as an American. Walker, born free in Wilmington, North Carolina, to a free mother and enslaved father, later settled in Boston, where he recognized that blacks were discriminated against no matter where they lived. In 1829 he published *Walker's Appeal, in Four Articles; Together with a Preamble, to the Coloured Citizens of the World, but in Particular, and Very Expressly, to Those of the United States of America, Written in Boston, State of Massachusetts, September 28, 1829*. In this indictment of white Americans, directed at blacks, David Walker frequently referred to the population he appealed to as "Africans." At the end of the *Appeal* he wrote: "If any are anxious to ascertain who I am, know the world, that I am one of the oppressed, degraded and wretched sons of Africa, rendered so by the avaricious and unmerciful, among the whites."[33]

Walker recognized black American ties to Africa. Unlike Wheatley, he highlighted the historical greatness of his ancestral continent, urging black Americans not to be ashamed of their ties to Africa. He even challenged Thomas Jefferson, who in his *Notes on the State of Virginia* had called for the colonization of African Americans, maintaining that blacks "are inferior to the whites in the endowments both of body and mind."[34] Walker took issue with Jefferson's characterization of blacks as inferior and his calls for colonization. Walker asserted: "They think because they hold us in their infernal chains of slavery, that we wish to be white, or of their color—but they are dreadfully deceived—we wish to be just as it pleased our Creator to have made us, and no avaricious and unmerciful wretches, have any business to make slaves of, or hold us in slavery." African-descended people, he emphasized, were proud of their heritage and long history. He pointed to "wise legislators—the Pyramids, and other magnificent buildings—the turning of the channel of the river Nile, by the sons of Africa or of Ham, among whom learning originated," stressing the achievements of great Africans such as Hannibal, "one of the greatest generals of antiquity, who defeated and cut off so many thousands of the white Romans or murderers, and who carried his victorious arms, to the very gate of Rome."

By invoking the greatness of Africa's past and highlighting famous African leaders, Walker hoped to show that black Americans were worthy of inclusion in American society. Citing Africa's importance, he blamed slavery for black degradation in the United

States, remarking sarcastically that while other "races" were considered men, "we, (coloured people) and our children are *brutes!*! and of course are, and *ought to be* SLAVES to the American people and their children forever!! to dig their mines and work their farms; and thus go on enriching them, from one generation to another with our *blood* and our *tears!*!!!" Ultimately, Walker believed that black Americans had a responsibility to Africa, but did not have to meet that obligation by leaving the United States.

Maria Stewart, a fervent admirer of David Walker, also used strong language to embrace her African identity and challenge African Americans to action. A political activist, abolitionist, and feminist, Stewart was born in 1803, orphaned at five, and was employed as a domestic servant until she was fifteen. She received her education through religious instruction. In 1831 Maria Stewart became a public figure and activist, an act that required courage, when she got involved in the movements to abolish slavery and for women's rights. The millions of blacks in slavery were a stain on a nation that claimed to be Christian. Stewart challenged white Americans, appealing to their Christian sensibilities and calling for an end to racism and slavery. Demanding justice for black Americans, she declared: "African rights and liberty is a subject that ought to fire the breast of every free man of color in these United States."[35]

As an early feminist, Stewart demanded equal rights for black women. In 1831 she asked, "Shall it any longer be said of the daughters of Africa, they have no ambition, they have no force? By no means. . . . How long shall the fair daughters of Africa be compelled to bury their minds and talents beneath a load of iron pots and kettles? . . . Possess the spirit of independence. Possess the spirit of men, bold and enterprising, fearless and undaunted. Sue for your rights and privileges. Know the reason that you cannot attain them." She urged black women to take action: "Oh ye daughters of Africa awake! Awake! Arise! No longer sleep nor slumber but distinguish yourselves. Show forth to the world that ye are endowed with noble and exalted faculties." With these words Stewart called for African Americans to take action within the possibilities afforded them at the time. In her limited capacity as a black woman at that time, she nevertheless raised her voice boldly to improve her community, urging blacks to take pride in their African ancestry.

Yet not all black Americans readily embraced their African heritage or connection to the continent. In the aftermath of the War of Independence, blacks attempted to integrate as free men and women in Northern communities. Frequently rebuffed, some wondered whether their African heritage explained whites' reluctance to accept them. Alexander argues that "displays of African culture fell into disrepute" as black Americans tried to move toward respectability and acceptance.[36] Some eschewed, for example, the public demonstrations and parades celebrating African culture. Eventually the parades were abandoned completely. Different ideas about the relationship to Africa emerged, as we will see in chapter 4.

Like Walker, many Northern blacks embraced their African heritage, took pride in their ancestry, and continued to demonstrate their pride in naming their institutions. However, this pride did not always translate into a more significant attachment to Africa. Rather, advocating for change in the United States was paramount for most. At the end of the eighteenth century members of the thriving free black population in Northern cities were instrumental in challenging continuing discrimination. African American leaders like Richard Allen, Absalom Jones, and Samuel Cornish called attention to the plight of those still enslaved on Southern plantations. David Walker, in tribute, highlighted the achievements of Richard Allen. He expressed hope that future black historians, writing about the ordeals of those who preceded them, would "do justice to the name of Bishop Allen, of Philadelphia" and recognize him as a champion of black American causes.[37]

Free blacks were involved in the antislavery and abolition movements of the late eighteenth and early nineteenth centuries. In 1797 Absalom Jones petitioned Congress demanding abolition, arguing that slavery was a violation of the nation's constitution. In the wake of the American Revolution free blacks frequently drew attention to the inconsistency and contradiction of a white population calling for freedom, liberty, and equality from the British Crown while maintaining slavery on its own soil.

With Northern slavery ended by 1790, free blacks continued the call for emancipation of their brothers and sisters in the South. In 1800 Absalom Jones once again petitioned Congress, condemning the Fugitive Slave Act of 1793 and pressing lawmakers to end

Raphaelle Peale, Portrait of Absalom Jones, *1810.*
(Delaware Art Museum. From Wikimedia Commons/Public Domain.)

the African slave trade. An act of Congress, the fugitive slave law guaranteed the right of slave owners to recover runaway slaves, and made it legal for Northern states to return them to their owners in the South. Southern free blacks also challenged laws restricting their mobility. When North Carolina passed a law forbidding the manumission of slaves in 1775, strengthening it in 1788, giving whites the authority to apprehend blacks believed to have been freed illegally, African Americans responded. In 1797 Jacob Nicholson, Jupiter Nicholson, Joe Albert, and Thomas Pritchet, North Carolinians who had escaped to Philadelphia, petitioned Congress on the matter. In this petition, believed to be the first such document presented to Congress, the men called attention to their heritage, underscoring, "That being of African descent, late inhabitants and natives of North Carolina, to you only, under God, can we apply with any hope of effect, for redress of our grievances, having been compelled to leave the State wherein we had a right of residence, as freemen liberated under the hand and seal of humane and conscientious masters."[38] The petitioners explained their particular circumstance and situation but also took the opportunity to condemn slavery in general. Congress rejected the petition after some debate, deciding it could not accept a petition from fugitive slaves. Laws like the one passed in North Carolina increasingly targeted the Southern free black population, prompting flight to the North and thoughts of "return" to the ancestral homeland.

At the end of the eighteenth century and into the nineteenth, African Americans would express different views on the subject of their place in American society and their relationship to Africa. For some their African heritage was a cause for pride while for others, it was a cause for moral uplift. These different ideas with respect to their relationship with Africa would lead African Americans to seek different solutions to their plight. Some chose to seek justice and fight for a place in the United States; others, seeing no possibility for an equitable place, elected to leave.[39]

CHAPTER FOUR

"It is the will of GOD for you to come into the possessions of your ancestors"

I n January 1830, a year after David Walker published his *Appeal*, fifty-one-year-old George M. Erskine of Tennessee set sail for the newly settled colony of Liberia. With him aboard the brig *Liberia* were his wife Hagar, fifty; seven of their eight children—Jane, thirty; Wallace, twenty-one; Mary, seventeen; Weir, fifteen; Martha, thirteen; Hopkins, ten; and Sarah, seven—and his seventy-one-year-old mother-in-law, Martha Gains, said to be African-born.[1] George Erskine was literate, and all his children could read as well. Records show the family arrived in Africa a month later. Sadly, the documents also note that within a year of their arrival, George, Hagar, and four of their children had died. Cause of death for George and his daughter Mary was listed as unknown, although we know from later correspondence that Mr. Erskine died of a fever. Weir died by drowning. The rest were reported to have died of fever. Only two of the Erskine children would survive to adulthood.

What, we might ask, prompted a free black man to take his family from a life he knew and understood, even with all its hardships, to a place he had never seen? We do not know exactly what motivated the Erskines to leave Tennessee, but George's response to a query about why he was leaving tells us much: "I am going to a new country to settle myself and family as agriculturalists; to a country where we shall at least be on a level with any of our fellow citizens; where the complexion will be no barrier to our filling the most exalted station. I shall cultivate the land assigned me ... and if it pleases God to spare my life, shall always be ready to do good as opportunity offers."[2] The Erskines sought a better life. Although George Erskine would not live to see it, his son would in adulthood fill an "exalted station," while his daughter Martha was offered many opportunities, as her father had hoped.

From the moment Africans were enslaved in their native lands, they sought ways to (re)connect with Africa and expressed the desire to return. Those captured in coastal areas often tried to escape before being loaded on ships. Once on board, some attempted to return by jumping overboard, which often resulted in death. On the high seas, en route to their lifetime of bondage, suicide was frequently a way for the enslaved to gain their freedom and "return" home. In the early days of slavery, African-born men and women continued the practices and customs brought from their native lands, articulating their continued link to Africa. In South Carolina and Virginia, enslaved men and women frequently expressed their hope of going "across grandywater," the Atlantic Ocean. As we have seen, even in Northern states African-descended men and women preserved elements of their past, whether in the parade traditions, Negro election days, the music and dance they continued to practice, or in their burial rites.[3]

As the number of those who were American-born grew, blacks in the United States found other ways to maintain their connection to Africa. Often, as we have seen, it was in the naming of their institutions. At other times, it was in how they articulated their longing to "return" to lands from which their mothers and fathers had been taken. For many, this was more an aspiration than a reality, an attempt to highlight their ties to Africa. By the end of the eighteenth century most African Americans were reconciled to their position in the new American nation. Those enslaved in Southern states for the most part had their lives determined for them by slave owners. The newly freed and free black population, particularly in Northern states, had to decide what their identity and place in the new nation would be. Many questioned their place in the United States, high-lighting "their connection to Africa, and their doubts about whether Blacks, as a race, could achieve equality in the United States." Others strove to prove they were worthy of inclusion.[4]

In the eighteenth and nineteenth centuries, some African Americans sought to establish permanent relationships with Africa by physical migration and settlement. Others came together to oppose any form of out-migration. The Negro Conventions that began in the early nineteenth century were a vocal rejection of colonization and emigration. As blacks negotiated their status and place in American society, Africa featured prominently in the many debates. We can see the many ways African Americans engaged with Africa. Some identified with the continent, highlighting their heritage and ties to it, while others showed interest in being involved with African issues, recognizing that their fate was inextricably linked with dominant, largely derogatory, perceptions of the continent. The ambivalence we see in many reflections on Africa had to do with the negative way Africa was represented. How African Americans perceived those representations frequently affected their status in the United States and influenced their choice to stay or leave. It also shaped their relationship to the continent.

"Therefore, we had rather be gone": Emigration and Colonization

The idea that black Americans, because of discrimination and racism, could never achieve full equality prompted some to consider whether the solution to the problem was to leave the United States. Some white Americans, believing that removing blacks from America would gradually end slavery and the slave trade, proposed the idea of colonizing blacks in Africa. In 1773 Reverend Samuel Hopkins, a Newport, Rhode Island, pastor, educated two African congregants in his church, training John Quamminei and Bristol Yamma in the hope they would return to Africa as missionaries. Hopkins later educated Newport Gardner and Salmar Nubia with the same purpose. Other white Americans proposed emigration as a solution to the growing number of free blacks in various colonies.[5]

Blacks also embraced the idea that they would be better off in the land of their ancestors. In the late eighteenth century free blacks in Boston sent several petitions to the legislature asking for equal treatment and parity with their white counterparts. If that was not possible, they asked to leave. Likewise, in 1773 free blacks in Boston petitioned the Massachusetts legislature for a variety of rights, including abolition of slavery and permission to leave the United States for Africa. Peter Bestes, Sambo Freeman, Felix Holbrook, and Chester Joie, encouraged by the rhetoric of freedom and equality espoused by their white masters in their bid for freedom from Britain, asked for their own emancipation. They promised that if freed they would obey the laws of the state "until we leave the province, which we determine to do as soon as we can, from our joint labours procure money to transport ourselves to some part of the Coast of *Africa*, where we propose a settlement." The petitioners sought to leave the United States voluntarily, hoping they would find a better life in Africa. They were unsuccessful and, more than likely, continued to champion their cause in America, fighting for equality.[6]

Again, in 1787, with the war won and liberty for whites achieved, blacks in Boston petitioned the legislature to allow them to emigrate to Africa. Predominantly members of the African Lodge, the seventy-three signatories asked that in the absence of equal rights in the United States, they be allowed to leave. The supplicants pointed out that their ancestors had been forcibly "brought from Africa and put into a state of slavery in this country." Their condition was downtrodden and unlikely to change "so long as we and our children live in America." They asked, therefore, to "return to Africa, our native country, which warm climate is much more natural and agreeable to us; and, for which the god of nature has formed us; and, where we shall live among our equals, and be more comfortable and happy, [than] we can be in our present situation." Drawing attention to their African ancestry, the men pointed to the many inequalities and indignities to which they were subjected. In their view settling in Africa was the ideal solution to the problem. Not only was its climate conducive, but they would also bring what they had learned in America to Africa: "The execution of this plan will, we hope, be the means of enlightening and civilizing those nations, who are now sunk in ignorance and barbarity; and may give opportunity to those who shall be disposed, and engaged to promote the salvation of their heathen brethren, to spread the knowledge of Christianity among them, and persuade them to embrace it." They would establish schools and churches to promote these values. Furthermore, they argued that a settlement of black Americans in Africa "may also lay a happy foundation for a friendly and lasting connection between that country and the United States of America, by a mutual intercourse and profitable commerce." These petitions and pleas did not result in emigration to Africa. Rather, their significance lies in the strong pull Africa had on these men, and their desire to contribute to its uplift.[7]

In these early petitions, blacks brought up arguments that would be made by African Americans seeking to emigrate to Africa over the next two centuries. They could escape the indignities placed upon them as second-class citizens, settle in the more hospitable land from which their ancestors had come, and bring the skills they had acquired in the United States to Africans. The petitioners also highlighted numerous reasons subsequent migrants would cite for returning to Africa: a desire to civilize Africans, to bring Christianity to the continent, to promote trade between Africa and the United States, and to attain freedom. African Americans who would emigrate in later years would find that these goals, while admirable, were not always possible.

Facing marginalization and discrimination in communities all across the United States, African Americans increasingly looked to Africa. In the late eighteenth century it finally became possible for African Americans to fulfill their wish to leave the United States. When war broke out between Britain and its American colonists in 1775, African Americans, like many white colonists, made a choice regarding their loyalties. In hopes of gaining their freedom many cast their lot with their British overlords. When in November 1775 the Earl of Dunmore, governor of Virginia, issued his proclamation offering freedom to blacks who fought on the British side, many African Americans ran to British lines. Dunmore declared free "all indentured Servants, Negroes, or others, (appertaining to Rebels,) . . . that are able and willing to bear Arms, they joining His Majesty's Troops as soon as may be, for the more speedily reducing this Colony to a proper Sense of their Duty, to His Majesty's Liege Subjects, to retain their [Quitrents], or any other Taxes due or that may become due, in their own Custody, till such Time as Peace may be again restored to this at present most unhappy Country, or demanded of them for their former salutary Purposes, by Officers properly authorised to receive the same."[8] These Black Loyalists seized the chance to emancipate themselves. At the end of the war Britain fulfilled its promise, evacuating hundreds of Black Loyalists to Britain or Canada.

Along with whites loyal to the Crown, many African Americans settled in Nova Scotia, Canada, at the conclusion of hostilities in 1783, hoping to create new lives for themselves. Hill's fictional character Aminata Diallo made this journey to Nova Scotia and later to Africa. Dissatisfied with the treatment they received from their white counterparts and disenchanted by the broken promises regarding land, some Black Loyalists petitioned for removal from Nova Scotia. In 1792, after years of negotiation and with the support of British humanitarians, over a thousand Nova Scotian blacks settled in the small colony of Sierra Leone, established by Britain in 1787. Formerly enslaved men and women from the United States believed they had finally found the freedom they sought, exhibiting a "feisty attachment to their rights as free men and women."[9]

Thomas Peters, David George, Mary Perth, Boston King, and John Kizell, all former slaves on Southern plantations, were among those who ultimately made it to Africa. David George had been born on a Virginia plantation around 1742 to parents enslaved in Africa. He ran away to South Carolina, where he lived among Native Americans of the Creek and Natchez Nations. Sold by a Natchez chief to a plantation in Silver Bluff, South Carolina, George later converted to Christianity, becoming a preacher. In 1775 he founded one of the earliest black churches in the United States, the Silver Bluff Baptist Church. Three years later George fled to British lines, gaining his freedom, and in 1782 was among the Black Loyalists evacuated to Halifax, Nova Scotia. Runaway Henry Washington, formerly the slave of George Washington, also escaped behind British lines; he was evacuated to Canada and settled in Sierra Leone.

In an account of his life published in 1793, George remembers his feelings upon seeing the shores of Africa for the first time:

"There was a great joy to see the land the high mountain, at some distance from Freetown, where we now live, appeared like a cloud to us." George brought the religious fervor he had imbibed in South Carolina to his new home, influencing not only his fellow Americans but the Africans he encountered as well. In Sierra Leone he ministered to a Baptist congregation in his own chapel until his death in 1810. David George fulfilled a dream that eluded many African Americans. He saw his parents' homeland.[10]

While we know more about Black Loyalist men than their female counterparts, we do know the story of Mary Perth. Born around 1749, Mary was enslaved to one John Willoughby in Norfolk, Virginia. She took the opportunity given by Dunmore to leave the United States for Nova Scotia, later leaving for Sierra Leone, where she became a businesswoman. Zachary Macaulay, a governor in Sierra Leone, regarded her highly, and we know that she was a staunch Methodist. John Clarke, a Scottish Presbyterian, was so impressed by Perth that he wrote, "I am as happy in her company as I ever was in that of any Christian of my own colour."[11]

These men and women, some African-born and others born in the United States, expressed a desire to return to their original homeland. Many articulated the providential design argument, underscoring that they had been brought to the United States to adopt Christianity in order to take its tenets back to Africa. There were many preachers among the Nova Scotians. David George and Moses Wilkinson, a blind preacher, both had congregations. Boston King, a teacher, wrote of his desire to go to Africa to spread Christianity and "commiserate my poor brethren in Africa." In fact, King used this argument to gain passage to Sierra Leone and to explain his decision to emigrate: "I was under no necessity of leaving Nova Scotia, because I was comfortably provided for," he remembered. However, he told the Sierra Leone Company agents "that it was not for the sake of the advantages I hope to reap in Africa, which induced me to undertake the voyage, but from a desire that had long possessed my mind, of contributing to the best of my poor ability, in spreading the knowledge of Christianity in that country. Upon which they approved of my intention, and encouraged me to persevere in it."[12] This calling prompted many African Americans in the eighteenth and nineteenth centuries to consider settlement in

Africa. Like Phillis Wheatley, they accepted that Christianity made them superior to Africans and believed it their duty to take what they had learned to Africa. African-born Americans in the North also argued that their experience in America had equipped them to serve as missionaries to Africa.

While the Boston petitioners were largely ignored and Newport blacks were ineffective in their bid for settlement in Sierra Leone, other moves to promote African American migration to Africa were more successful. In 1794, encouraged by the Nova Scotian settlement in Sierra Leone, the African Society in Providence, Rhode Island, sent one James Mackenzie to Sierra Leone to negotiate the settlement of black Americans. Mackenzie met with British officials who subsequently rejected the idea of a black American settlement. The Nova Scotian settlers had turned out to be too American for the British administrators of the colony, who complained about their ingratitude. Many of these men had fought in the American War of Independence for the very freedom they believed they had achieved in Sierra Leone, but British officials found these sentiments objectionable. In 1799 the Nova Scotians rebelled against the colonial administration of Sierra Leone for alleged injustices in the colony. The rebellion was crushed, but the Black Loyalists continued to press for their rights.[13]

In 1808 a British governor in Sierra Leone, frustrated with this streak of independence, blamed their American experience for giving the former slaves ideas about liberty and equality. The Nova Scotians, he maintained, were "a race of traitors ready to imitate the example of their former lords and masters."[14] Another governor, Zachary Macaulay, labeled Mary Perth "vain, worldly, and arrogant, harsh and violent in her tempers."[15] Unlike their counterparts in the United States, the Nova Scotians seized an opportunity for self-determination and to craft their own destinies. For them, Africa became a reality, as it did for others in later centuries.

Early in the nineteenth century New England–born merchant Paul Cuffe became interested in the prospect of trade with Africa. In 1809 Cuffe wrote of his desire to make a trip to Sierra Leone to assess its potential for trade and for the spread of Christianity. He pointed out that "as I am of the African race I feel myself interested for them and if I am favored with a talent I think I am willing that they should be benefited for them."[16] The following year he traveled

PAUL

CAPTAIN

CUFFEE

1812.

ENGRAVED FOR ABRM. L., PENNOCK, BY MASON & MAAS.
From a Drawing by JOHN POLE, M. D. of Bristol, Eng.

Paul Cuffee died in 1817 aged 66.
He was a worthy negro Captain of his own ship.

Captain Paul Cuffee, 1812. Engraved for Abrm. L. Pennock
by Mason & Maas, from a drawing by John Pole.
(Library of Congress. From Wikimedia Commons/Public Domain.)

to Sierra Leone to assess the feasibility of trade and African American settlement. Returning two years later with glowing reports, he began a campaign to persuade free African Americans to emigrate. Cuffe succeeded in drumming up interest for his enterprise among black leaders in New York, Boston, and Philadelphia. Although the War of 1812 stalled his activities, Cuffe sailed to Sierra Leone with thirty-eight African American settlers in 1816. The black Americans were welcomed in Sierra Leone; the local press announced their arrival, and the colony's administrators provided them with land. Perry Lockes, a blacksmith, encouraged relatives and friends in the United States to emigrate. "It is the will of GOD for you to come into the possessions of your ancestors," he said, drawing a connection between African Americans and their ancestral homeland.[17] White Americans, for a variety of reasons, sought to help black Americans achieve this.

The American Colonization Society (ACS), spearheaded in 1816 by the Reverend Robert Finley, a New Jersey minister, proposed a solution to the plight of black Americans. Witnessing the discrimination against free blacks in his community, Finley concluded that their salvation lay in removal from the United States. "We would be cleared of them; we would send to Africa a population partially civilized and Christianized . . . [and] blacks would be put in a better condition," he argued to his black and white supporters.[18] Finley believed white prejudice would not allow black Americans to attain equality if they stayed in the United States.

Finley's plan was attractive to many white Americans. Southern slaveholders in particular liked the idea of emigration for free blacks because they believed that the very existence of free blacks posed a threat to slavery. In 1820 the American Colonization Society sent its first group of settlers to West Africa. Daniel Coker, born free in Maryland and co-founder of the African Methodist Episcopal Church with Richard Allen, led the group. In 1821 the settlers established Liberia on the West Coast of Africa next to the British colony of Sierra Leone. From 1820 to 1867, between ten thousand and twelve thousand African Americans settled in Liberia under the auspices of the ACS. Others came independently during the course of the nineteenth century. Emigrants had different reasons for going, but the idea of divine providence predominated.

The long-standing belief that there was a divine purpose to African American enslavement motivated many to emigrate. The American Colonization Society, still in its infancy, actively recruited free blacks, offering them the equality and opportunity for upward mobility they could never achieve in the United States.

George Erskine's heartbreaking story certainly illustrates this theme. Erskine realized he had no hope for equality in the United States and chose to leave. The sketchy details of his life show that on September 26, 1815, Isaac Anderson and Abel Pearson manumitted him in Blount County, Tennessee. Erskine had been enslaved for thirty-six years. Soon after gaining his freedom, George petitioned to be received into the Presbyterian ministry. As a licensed preacher, he traveled to Northeastern cities like Boston and Philadelphia as well as cities in the Midwest, preaching to raise money. Described as a "preacher of impressive ability," Erskine began purchasing freedom for his wife and children sometime after 1818. In June 1828 *Freedom's Journal*, an African American newspaper in Philadelphia, reported that Erskine would be preaching at a Presbyterian church, "at which time there will be a collection taken up to aid him on redeeming his children that are at this time in bondage in East Tennessee."[19] An 1829 article reported that "from the charitable and pious, he has since been enabled to redeem his family at an expense of $2,400, and has resolved to emigrate to Liberia, in the hope that he may there do something to rescue his enlightened brethren from their superstitions, crimes, and miseries, and to conduct them to the knowledge of the true God."[20]

By 1830 Erskine had sailed to Liberia with his family. Erskine's African-born mother-in-law, who also made the long trip to Liberia, was returning to her homeland.[21] On April 3, 1830, Erskine wrote of his arrival in the colony: "I can say I am well pleased with this country; and I believe it is a general feeling among the late emigrants. We have been here one month, in which time we discover something of the customs of the country and productions of the soil; and are fully persuaded that the honest and industrious can, with great ease, secure a comfortable living, accompanied with many of the luxuries of a tropical climate. There is but little sickness in the Colony this season."[22] Upon arrival in Liberia the family took up farming. Unfortunately, Erskine would succumb to death within a year from fever.

John Russwurm, c. 1850.
(National Portrait Gallery, Smithsonian Institution; transfer from the
Library of Congress. From Wikimedia Commons by Cliff [Creative
Commons License; Attribution 2.0 Generic (CC-BY-2.0)].)

Erskine's reasons for leaving the United States were not unusual. John Russwurm, an 1826 graduate of Bowdoin College, edited the very newspaper that reported Erskine's endeavor. Russwurm, a staunch critic of the American Colonization Society, opposed colonization for years before becoming disillusioned with the plight of free blacks in the United States. In 1829, before sailing for Liberia, he explained to readers of *Freedom's Journal* why he had finally decided to abandon the United States. Citing unending prejudice and discrimination, Russwurm lamented that blacks were considered "a degraded people, deprived of all the rights of freemen in the eyes of the community, a race who had no lot or portion with them."[23]

Perhaps Abraham Camp, a free black from Illinois who lacked Russwurm's opportunities, better expressed what a man like Erskine felt when he chose to leave the United States. Like the petitioners in Massachusetts decades before, Camp pointed out the lack of opportunity for black Americans: "We love this country and its liberties, if we could share an equal right in them; but our freedom is partial, and we have no hope that it ever will be otherwise here; therefore, we had rather be gone, though we should suffer hunger and nakedness for years."[24] Camp, like Erskine and Russwurm, recognized the limits of staying in a country that would not fully accept him as a citizen.

Yet George Erskine was not just a migrant escaping oppression. He was also a missionary. Though he chose to leave the repressive conditions of a slave society that restricted and circumscribed the movement of free blacks, he was also deeply committed to bringing Christianity to Africa. He could not be the man he wanted to be in America.

George Erskine was not disappointed in Liberia but, like most settlers, his view of the indigenous African population was negative, shaped by the attitudes of his white counterparts. He complained that education did not seem to be a priority and that the indigenous Africans were not civilized. God had brought him to Liberia, he believed, to "preach the gospel extensively in Africa." Africans were "extremely in favor of their groveling superstition," and he feared that if the African American settlers did not educate themselves they would soon "become like them."[25]

Because of his untimely death George Erskine did not leave a significant legacy of Christian work in the colony. Had he lived, we can speculate that he would have been as tireless a missionary in Liberia as he had been in Tennessee. Nevertheless, George Erskine left a legacy in his surviving children and grandchildren, and their stories tell of the success of some settlers in Liberia. His son Hopkins became active in Liberian politics, holding significant political positions in government. Hopkins Erskine was elected to the Liberian cabinet in 1852. Ordained as a Presbyterian minister in 1860, he served as attorney general of Liberia from 1864 to

*The Reverend Hopkins Erskine, November 1866. Photograph
by Theodore M. Schleier.
(Library of Congress, Prints and Photographs Division.
From Wikimedia Commons/Public Domain.)*

1868, and as superintendent of Montserrado County from 1870
to 1871.[26]

George Erskine's daughter Martha gained fame as the old lady
who presented Queen Victoria with a handmade quilt. Martha, an
avid quilter, described by a contemporary account as a "philanthro-
pist and race agitator," fulfilled a lifelong dream of meeting Queen
Victoria when in 1892 at the age of seventy-five she traveled to
England. Ricks presented the queen with a quilt depicting a coffee
tree. Queen Victoria would later make a note of meeting Martha
in her diary: "Afterwards [after lunch] saw, in the Corridor a very
loyal old Negress, 76 years of age, who had for 50 years longed to
see me, & had saved money to do so, walking a long distance, to

Martha Ann Ricks, 1892.
(Library of Congress, Prints and Photographs Division.
From Wikimedia Commons/Public Domain.)

arrange for her departure. At last she came with friends, & Mrs. Blyden, (also coloured) the wife of the very black Liberian minister brought her. The old [woman] was short & very black, with a kind face. I shook hands with her & she kept holding & shaking mine."[27]

In July 1842 the *African Repository* reported on Zion Harris's trip to Tennessee. Harris, Erskine's son-in-law, visited the state to fulfill one of George Erskine's last requests: to "bring to Africa the surviving relatives left behind." Harris succeeded in returning to Liberia with thirteen family members.[28]

There were others like Erskine and Russwurm who chose an uncertain life in Africa over a life of racism and discrimination in the United States. These formerly enslaved men and women took up the challenge to civilize their African brothers and sisters. Even a newly freed settler like Diana Skipwith James was derisive of what she considered to be heathen practices. In a letter to Sally Cocke, her former owner's daughter, James wrote of her surprise that the Africans she encountered could not "read & write like white man (they call us all white man) & had not as much Sence as the white man & he said that it was thire own fault; that God give them the Choice either to learn book proper as they says or make Rice & they told god they had rather make rice." She was, however, hopeful that "we will be able to get them out of their Supisticious Idears & at last they will become Siverlise."[29] Despite being enslaved, Diana Skipwith James believed that her experience in the United States had given her advantages over her African counterparts. She was civilized. It is important to observe that these attitudes of superiority toward indigenous Africans created an elite caste that would become problematic in later years in Liberia's history.

Throughout the nineteenth century African Americans from all classes and walks of life, from regions all over the United States, accepted the offer of the American Colonization Society to leave the United States. Daniel Coker was born in the United States but lived most of his life in Sierra Leone. Born Isaac Wright in Maryland to an enslaved African man and white indentured servant, making him free by law, he nonetheless lived as a slave. He later changed his name to Daniel Coker. In an 1810 pamphlet he made his views on slavery evident. *A Dialogue between a Virginian and an African Minister*, a conversation between a slaveholder and a black minister, enumerated the many proslavery and antislavery debates of the day, with the African minister making a plea for emancipation and challenging ideas of white superiority and black inferiority. It was a strong treatise on the equality of African-descended people and a condemnation of slavery. He organized the Bethel Charity School, serving as a teacher. Unlike Richard Allen, he chose to leave the United States, accompanying the first group of settlers bound for what would become Liberia in 1820.

Coker's journal of the trip is a chronicle of an African-descended man expressing his hopes for a better future in Africa and a desire to proselytize among its people. Before embarking he prayed: "Oh God! help me to be true to my trust, and to act for the good of my African brethren in all things. I feel a great responsibility to rest upon me."

Joshua Johnson, Portrait of a Gentleman—Daniel Coker? *c. 1805–c. 1815.*
(American Museum in Britain. From Wikimedia Commons/Public Domain.)

He was grateful at the end of the sea journey, exclaiming, "Thank the Lord I have seen Africa," but despondent to find out that the slave trade, despite its abolition, endured. On arrival he was happy to reunite with Perry Lockes, a Cuffe colonist, "a friend," who "was so happy at seeing us he could not contain himself." Coker remained in Sierra Leone working as an educator until his death. He recorded his safe arrival in Sierra Leone and urged his "dear African brethren in America" to consider missionary work in Africa, "where we find the land to be good, and the natives kind," and where "there is a great work here to do. ... God grant that many such may come over to help with this great work."[30]

Edward Jones, born free in Charleston, a member of an affluent black family, also left the United States, settling in Sierra Leone as a missionary. His father Jehu Jones was a hotelier in Charleston who began his career as a tailor on the city's Broad Street and later ran a boarding house. As a member of the Brown Fellowship, an elite self-help organization established by the "mulatto" population of Charleston, he would have enjoyed high status in the free black community. By the time his son Edward set off for Amherst College in 1822, the senior Jones was proprietor of a hotel patronized exclusively by white clients. Jehu's affluence allowed him to educate his children, and Edward benefited from a higher education, becoming the first black graduate of Amherst in 1826. He went on to study theology and was ordained a priest in the Episcopal Church. By 1831 he was in Sierra Leone in his first job as schoolmaster. Jones was active as an educator, journalist, and missionary, working tirelessly for the benefit of the colony's indigenous population. He became the first black principal of the Christian institution that would become Fourah Bay College in 1841, serving until 1859 and influencing many in the colony to pursue higher education.[31]

"Our claims are on America; it is the land that gave us birth": Anti-Emigration Sentiment

In 1774, objecting to the suggestion that she go to Africa as the wife of a black missionary, Phillis Wheatley wrote: "Upon my arrival, how like a Barbarian Should I look to the Natives; I can promise that my tongue shall be quiet for a strong reason indeed being an utter stranger to the Language of Anamaboe."[32] Reflecting on the dangers of such a trip, Wheatley recognized that she was too long removed from Africa and would be a stranger in the land of her birth. She believed herself unfit to be a missionary, and certainly could not conceive of a permanent move to Africa. Wheatley rejected the notion that her blackness and African ancestry obligated her to Africa.

Although thousands left the United States in search of a better life, millions more cast their lot with the fledgling nation despite all its disadvantages for people of color. Many understood the impulse to flee a place that continually rejected their pleas for equality and citizenship, but many more recognized their significant contribution to building America and resisted those who would see them leave. There was a surge in the slave trade to the United States in the second half of the eighteenth century, bringing more Africans to the United States and allowing for retention of their cultures. Nonetheless, African Americans had adopted and adapted cultural patterns of Europeans and Native Americans, even as they influenced these other groups. Many, therefore, rebuffed the idea of an African "return," distinguishing between emigration, the voluntary migration of a few blacks, and colonization, which they saw as a deportation scheme.[33]

Blacks opposed colonization because they understood it as a coercive attempt by white Americans to get rid of free blacks. Some argued that emigrating meant abandoning the millions of African Americans still enslaved in Southern states. Although the importation of slaves had ceased by 1808, a domestic slave trade continued as African Americans were moved within and between regions in the South. With the increase in the number of those enslaved, and as slavery became more entrenched, the status of blacks, slave or free, declined and progressively more restrictions were placed on them. The status of free blacks was intricately connected with that of slaves, making their freedom precarious.

When American colonists rebelled against Britain in 1774, African Americans anticipated their own liberty. Although some blacks were ambivalent toward the American cause, they supported the colonists' bid for independence, hoping the rhetoric of freedom and equality espoused by their masters would apply to them. In contrast to those like David George, Thomas Peters, and Boston King, who cast their lot with the British, many chose to bear arms for the rebel cause when given the opportunity to do so. These black patriots fought bravely in the war with hopes of gaining full citizenship. The American Revolution was, therefore, a watershed moment in race relations. In its wake many blacks did receive their freedom. At the same time blacks saw an increasing diminution of their rights, opportunities, and privileges as divisions between the races were strengthened and Americans confronted their ideas about democracy. Revolutionary rhetoric espoused freedom and equality, with God-given inalienable rights for everyone, yet the nation that emerged after the War of Independence had slavery woven into its economic and social fabric.

The new nation did not allow for easy acceptance of African Americans as equal and full citizens. By labeling blacks inferior white Americans could justify their shameful treatment of them. In the new century the expansion of democratic rights for whites accompanied a lessening of black rights. The swelling number of free blacks in the postrevolutionary period posed a major problem, particularly in the South. The United States essentially had a free black problem, as those newly emancipated faced more legal restrictions. The flexibility and mobility they had enjoyed in the seventeenth century was gone by the nineteenth. Although Northern blacks had a little more autonomy than their counterparts in the South, they still confronted restrictive legislation and racism. The federal government itself behaved in discriminatory ways, passing immigration and naturalization laws limiting citizenship to whites, and restricting blacks from enlisting in militias or serving as mail carriers, among other things. Individual states also imposed onerous legislation curbing the rights of free blacks.

In the South free blacks, especially those who thrived, like the Jones family, exposed the myth of black incapacity. The many successes of free blacks belied Southern justifications that slavery was necessary because those of African descent needed the care and protection of whites to survive. The expanding number of successful blacks like Jehu Jones challenged the very idea of black inferiority. Slaveholders feared a thriving free population might incite the enslaved to rebel or run away. Consequently, they assigned them to the inferior category in which slaves had been placed. With the growing number of them in the North at war's end, Southern legislatures passed restrictive laws targeting the free blacks in their states, and curtailing the possibility of freedom for those still in slavery. There were very few free blacks in states like South Carolina and Georgia, although Charleston and Savannah had small populations of affluent blacks.

Although laws in many Southern states recognized free blacks, their status was conditional, relying on recognition and validation from white citizens. Regardless of their class and status, all blacks faced restrictions and prohibitions. In most Southern states free blacks had no voting rights and were forced to prove their status. This required them to register with authorities, sometimes to find a white protector or, as in the case of North Carolina, wear a patch that proved their freedom. Free blacks also faced economic challenges. Maryland prevented them from selling agricultural products, and in Virginia and Georgia blacks could not work as riverboat captains or pilots. Many Southern states levied special taxes on their free black residents. As property, the enslaved often had the protection of their owners. Their free counterparts had no means of defense, and were frequently forced to establish relationships with whites who could vouch for their status.

Northern blacks often fared no better. Low wages and high unemployment marked their condition. Blacks in the North had been sought after as skilled craftsmen and artisans. After 1815, as immigration from Europe increased, they lost jobs to the growing white immigrant population. Northern blacks found work as common laborers and domestic servants, digging, loading, carrying, sweeping, or performing other menial jobs. As more blacks came north, whites feared that if given equal rights and privileges, they would become a menace to society, bring incivility to social gatherings, and compete for economic opportunities. The prevalent attitude of whites was that blacks were different and therefore inferior. They characterized blacks as uneducated and uneducable, unproductive, shiftless, and unpleasant.

Many Northern states passed restrictive legislation that sought to exclude blacks from the state if they couldn't prove their citizenship. In January 1804 the Ohio state legislature required free blacks to give bonds and security of $500 for their good conduct. In 1819 the Illinois legislative assembly passed laws making it almost impossible for blacks to enter the state. A free black wanting to live in Illinois had to post $1,000 bond guaranteeing that he or she would not become a public charge. All free blacks in Illinois had to register and be certified, and anyone who hired an uncertified black could be fined. In addition, an uncertified black was treated as a runaway slave. Although these laws were not often rigidly enforced, they served to keep blacks out of these states and made life inhospitable for those already living there. It was in this context that Abraham Camp petitioned to emigrate, Erskine fled with his family, and Russwurm gave up hope. But others stayed.

Blacks had few rights in the legal system and little room to ma-
neuver. Many states restricted blacks from serving on juries. Massachusetts allowed blacks to serve as jurors in the years before the
Civil War, but later took that right away. Some states did not allow
blacks to testify in court; others did not accept their testimony if it
would be detrimental to whites. By the 1820s residential segregation was common as blacks, faced with hostility from whites, were
restricted to living in certain areas. Many whites believed that
blacks lowered the value of property. In 1834 white residents in
New Haven complained that the value of their property had
decreased as a result of black presence.

When legislation was unsuccessful, public sentiment often prevailed. Mob violence was common in Northern cities during the
nineteenth century as economic competition between free blacks
and poor whites often led to social tension and conflicts. Between
1820 and 1850, major race riots erupted in Northern cities. Interracial unions were outlawed. Many whites saw blacks as a threat to
racial purity, and this fear often led to violence. In 1824 a mob of
whites tore down twenty buildings in the black section of Providence, Rhode Island. Two years later in Boston, a white mob de-
stroyed homes in the Negro Hill section of the city. Between 1829
and 1831 there were riots in Philadelphia; Portsmouth, Ohio;
Hartford, Connecticut; and Providence, Rhode Island. In 1829 a
riot in Cincinnati led the city government to enforce its black laws,
which required blacks to pay $500 bond for good behavior. Threats
and intimidation forced many to leave. Between July and December 1829, more than one thousand blacks left Cincinnati.[34]

A particular danger facing free blacks in the North was the
threat of kidnapping. The Fugitive Slave Act passed by Congress in
1793 heightened their insecurity. In the mid-1820s and 1830s some
Northern states challenged the act by passing personal liberty laws
to protect free blacks, but kidnapping was still a threat. The 1850
Fugitive Slave Act further strengthened the penalties for those who
did not abide by the law, forcibly compelling citizens to assist in
the capture of African Americans identified as runaway slaves.
These restrictive laws showed blacks they were not welcome residents of the United States. In 1857, when the ruling in the Dred
Scott case decreed that blacks were not considered citizens of the

United States, it seemed to many their place was elsewhere. State and federal regulations, social customs, and popular pressure had relegated them to lower social, economic, and political positions. Nevertheless, there were more opportunities for blacks in the North than there were in the South, and free blacks had thriving institutions. As we have seen, blacks established social institutions to support their communities—churches, mutual aid societies, and schools. For many whites this symbolized upward mobility and independence, and many of these institutions were threatened. Nonetheless, African Americans persevered, refusing to be driven from a country they had helped build.

Early in the nineteenth century blacks, particularly in Northern cities, came together to oppose colonization and slavery and to promote moral uplift. Africa featured prominently in these discourses because many African Americans opposed large-scale emigration. The Negro Convention movement, as it has come to be known, was an organized response to inequality and a challenge to colonization. Recognizing, as one prominent African American declared in 1830, that the "rights of men are decided by the colour of their skin," Northern blacks sought redress for their predicament.[35] The first convention, held in 1830, denounced the American Colonization Society. While its members supported voluntary migration to Canada, they opposed Liberian colonization. The participants called instead for improvement in their condition. They asked for manual training colleges for blacks and pushed for educational equality, suffrage, the right to enlist in militias, and fuller participation in American society. Finally, the conventions urged that the station of free blacks be improved through moral reform. In other words, if African Americans could prove by their rectitude and Christian behavior that they were fit for citizenship, whites should accept them.

A quest for respectability and acceptance often required African Americans to distance themselves from Africa, commonly represented as heathen, backward, and morally corrupt. One scholar has argued that as African Americans pushed to gain acceptance and full citizenship in American society through the Negro Convention movement, they "simultaneously renounced their African heritage."[36] At these conventions, held regularly in Northern cities through the 1840s, blacks reinforced their determination to stay in the United States to fight for their freedom and demand full rights of citizenship. In 1828 Thomas Jennings, a free black New Yorker, maintained,

> Our claims are on America; it is the land that gave us birth; it is the land of our nativity, we know no other country, it is a land in which our fathers have suffered and toiled; they have watered it with their tears, and fanned it with sighs. Our relation with Africa is the same as the white man's is with Europe, only with this difference, the one emigrated voluntarily, and the other was forced from home and all its pleasures. We have passed through several generations in this country, and consequently we have become natural-ized, our habits, our manners, our passions, our disposi-tions have become the same. ... I might as well tell the white man about England, France or Spain, the country from whence his forefathers emigrated, and call him a European, as for him to call us Africans; the argument will hold as good in the one case as the other. Africa is as foreign to us as Europe is to them.[37]

Others shared these sentiments. In the 1830s African Ameri-cans increasingly distanced themselves from Africa, abandoning ra-cial designations and dropping the "African" label from their institutions in favor of more closely identifying themselves with the United States. Africa took on negative connotations for many who understood it as the cause of their rejection and exclusion by whites. As the nineteenth century progressed, more black Ameri-cans opposed colonization, perceiving it as a ploy to remove free blacks from the United States. In particular, this movement criti-cized the American Colonization Society, condemning its activities as a deportation scheme. While individual blacks wishing to emi-grate were welcome to do so, the view of the anti-emigrationists was that they should not be forced to leave the United States.

The strongest voices against colonization and emigration dur-ing the nineteenth century were those of David Walker and Fred-erick Douglass. Walker, as we have seen, was very proud of his African heritage. Nonetheless, in his *Appeal* he argued that African

Americans had the right to live as equals in America. Africa was not their home. In Walker's rhetoric we see that African Americans were able to assert their African heritage while also making a claim on an American identity. Unlike those who saw a conflict in embracing their African heritage while asserting rights in America, Walker freely used the term *African* to describe himself. Nevertheless, he argued that colonization and emigration were tantamount to abandoning those still enslaved. He insisted that those whites encouraging Liberian emigration understood the threat a free black population posed: "Can we not discern the project of sending the free people of colour away from their country?" he asked. "Is it not for the interest of the slave-holders to select the free people of colour out of the different states, and send them to Liberia? Will it not make their slaves uneasy to see free men of colour enjoying liberty? It is."[38]

Although Walker criticized the American Colonization Society and its white founders and members, he was also derisive of blacks that supported the organization, wondering why they would choose to leave given that "this country is as much ours as it is the whites, whether they will admit it now or not." As far as Walker was concerned, America, not Africa, was the African American's home. He urged blacks to stay in the United States and fight against slavery, encouraging them, if necessary, to take up arms. For free blacks to leave was to abandon those in slavery: "Do they think to drive us from our country and homes, after having enriched it with our blood and tears, and keep back millions of our dear brethren, sunk in the most barbarous wretchedness, to dig up gold and silver for them and their children?" He continued: "Surely, the Americans must think that we are brutes, as some of them have represented us to be. They think that we do not feel for our brethren, whom they are murdering by the inches, but they are dreadfully deceived."[39]

Frederick Douglass agreed. Like David Walker, Douglass did not see the solution to the plight of African Americans in Africa. A former slave, Douglass frequently argued that emigration was an abandonment of those still enslaved, describing colonization as "an evasion." In 1849, echoing Walker, he wrote in the columns of his *North Star* newspaper: "We are of the opinion that the *free* colored people generally mean to live in America, and not in Africa. . . . We do not mean to go to Liberia. Our minds are made up to live here if we can, or die here if we must; so every attempt to remove us will be, as it ought to be, labor lost. Here we are, and here we shall remain. While our brethren are in bondage on these shores, it is idle to think of inducing any considerable number of the free colored people to quit this for a foreign land."[40]

Critical of those who would encourage emigration, Douglass forcefully asserted that for centuries blacks had "toiled over the soil of America, under a burning sun and a driver's lash—plowing, planting, reaping, that white men might roll in ease, their hands unhardened by labor, and their brows unmoistened by the waters of genial toil." Now that voices were being raised against slavery, "the mean and cowardly oppressor is meditating plans to expel the colored man entirely from the country." Douglass rebuked those who proposed colonization: "We live here—have lived here—have a right to live here, and mean to live here." Douglass opposed African emigration throughout his life, although even he, faced with discrimination and racism, briefly entertained the possibility of black settlement in Haiti.

To Africa We Must Go: Emigration Discourse, 1840–1900

Despite strong anticolonization voices, and regardless of the Negro Convention movement's pleas for inclusion, acceptance, and equality, African Americans were rebuffed again and again in their claims for citizenship. For that reason, some black Americans held onto the idea of African emigration. In the 1840s and 1850s the strongest pro-emigration voices, laced with a strong dose of African pride, were those of Henry Highland Garnet and Martin Delany.

Born into slavery in Maryland, Garnet escaped to New York at the age of nine with his father and became an active abolitionist. He came to support emigration, believing the largely white-led antislavery movement was not strident enough in its demands on the white ruling class. In the 1840s Garnet, becoming more radical, called for blacks to take up arms to end slavery. In 1843, during a Negro National Convention, he delivered a strong indictment of slavery in which he challenged African Americans to "act for yourselves." He proclaimed, "Let your motto be resistance! *resistance! resistance!* For no oppressed people have ever secured their liberty without resistance."[41] Garnet proudly embraced his African ancestry, urging others to take pride in that part of their past. In 1858 Garnet formed the African Civilization Society with the motto, "No man should deprive me of my love for Africa, the land of my ancestors." In 1881 Garnet emigrated to Liberia, where he died a year later.

Like Garnet, Martin Delany was a vocal proponent of emigration and black pride. Delany was born free in Charles Town, Virginia (now West Virginia), in 1812. He learned to read at home since it was illegal for blacks to receive formal education in Virginia. In 1822 the family moved to Pennsylvania, where he and his siblings attended school. Training as a doctor's assistant, he also worked briefly as a dentist. From 1843 to 1847 Delany edited a weekly newspaper, *Mystery*, in Pittsburgh. From 1847 to 1849 he was the assistant editor of the *North Star*, Frederick Douglass's paper. In 1850 he was admitted to Harvard Medical School, but after a year he was dismissed along with other black students when white students objected to their presence. Delany argued that whites in the antislavery society presuming to speak for blacks were hypocritical and paternalistic. He urged blacks to "act for themselves" and to form all-black antislavery societies. Though initially not interested in emigration, he came to support the movement as he lost hope that blacks could integrate. First he urged blacks to create separate institutions within the United States, but he later promoted emigration, first to Central and South America, then Canada, and finally Africa.

Always a critic of Liberian colonization, Delany traveled to Africa in 1859 and negotiated a site for black American settlement with local African chiefs in what is today Nigeria. While in Africa he wrote to Garnet: "Lagos is a fine, and will be a very great commercial city. It is destined to be the great metropolis of this part of the world. Entirely under a black Government, it only wants a few of the right stamp of black men and women to make it one of the most desirable cities in the world. They bid us come, and to that end the authorities have presented me with two acres of land in the heart of the city plot, on which to build my residence." He spoke with great pride and almost surprise about the black population he encountered: "There will be for you, and also Mr. J. T. HOLLY, after our return to Africa, a fine prospect in this rich city of Lagos, where thousands are civilized Christians, and speak the English language, and like black people generally, desire to have black instead of white preachers."[42] Nothing came of the expedition, and Delany abandoned emigration efforts when the Civil War erupted in 1861. He turned to recruitment efforts for the Union army with the optimistic belief that if blacks participated in the war it would demonstrate they were worthy of becoming citizens. Later in the century others took up the call for emigration.

While not American-born, Edward Wilmot Blyden was a strong voice for the pro-emigration argument. Born in St. Thomas, Danish Virgin Islands, Blyden was raised by free black parents from the Caribbean island of St. Eustatius. A precocious boy with an interest and facility for languages, he was taken under the wings of Henry Knox. A Presbyterian minister, Knox sponsored the young Blyden for admission to the seminary at Rutgers University in New Jersey. Denied admission, Blyden took the offer of passage to the young colony of Liberia under the auspices of the American Colonization Society. He would live out his days in Africa.

During the nineteenth century Blyden made several trips to the United States on lecture tours, urging African Americans to leave the United States for Africa. Preaching black pride, he argued that African Americans would never be accepted as full and equal citizens of the United States. He became well known as an advocate of African emigration, appealing not just to elite and educated black Americans but to rural and working-class men and women. In 1891 he was so well known he was impersonated by a man calling himself "Dr. Blyden" who defrauded blacks in Arkansas with an offer of passage to Liberia. The impostor was arrested. In the late nineteenth and early twentieth centuries Blyden turned his attention away from active recruitment, focusing more on issues on the continent.[43]

By the end of the nineteenth century Bishop Henry McNeal Turner was the most outspoken African American advocate of emigration. Born free in South Carolina, by the 1850s Turner had become a preacher and in 1858 was admitted to preach in the African Methodist Episcopal (AME) Church. Like Delany, he lobbied

*Henry Highland Garnet, Alexander Crummel, Henry Osawa Tanner, and
Edward Wilmot Blyden.*
(From John W. Cromwell and John Wesley, The Negro in American
History: Men and Women Eminent in the Evolution of the American
of African Descent *[Washington, DC: American Negro Academy, 1914.]*
From Wikimedia Commons.)

for black soldiers to be allowed to fight in the Civil War, and he became a chaplain in the Union army. However, he too grew disillusioned by the refusal of white Americans to accept blacks as equal. After the Civil War Turner was elected to serve in Georgia's legislature. White Democratic legislators expelled the black members on grounds of race. In September 1868 Turner denounced them in the assembly, declaring, "I am here to demand my rights and to hurl thunderbolts at the men who would dare to cross the threshold of my manhood." Censuring those assembled for thinking him less than they were, he asked, "Am I a man? If I am such, I claim the rights of a man. Am I not a man because I happen to be of a darker hue than honorable gentlemen around me? Let me see whether I am or not."[44]

Turner increasingly explored emigration as a solution. His "back to Africa" message was well received by many poor Southern farmers who in the post-Civil War era faced conditions akin to slavery as they entered tenant farming and sharecropping arrangements with white plantation owners. Turner came under heavy criticism from African Americans when he became vice president of the American Colonization Society in 1876. He traveled to Africa four times during the 1890s, visiting Sierra Leone, Liberia, and South Africa. Like Walker, Garnet, and Delany before him, he expressed great pride in his African heritage, even preaching that God was black. He supported the "African Fever" movement, organized by the International Migration Society in 1894, to send emigrants to Liberia.[45] Although he never emigrated, Turner maintained a lifelong interest in Africa, publishing the *Voices of Mission,* a journal of the AME church, and the *Voice of the People* (1901–4), which informed readers of developments on the continent. He promoted missionary activity and sponsored African students in the United States with the hope they would return as missionaries to uplift their homeland. Neither Delany nor Turner succeeded in generating large-scale interest in emigration, but their criticism of the country's treatment of its black population resonated with many black Americans.[46] Bishop Henry McNeal Turner never settled in Africa but left the United States for Canada, where he died in 1915. W. E. B. Du Bois eulogized him in a tribute that would surely have made him happy: "Turner was the last of his clan: mighty men,

BISHOP HENRY McNEIL TURNER, D.D., LL.D., D.C.L.
Senior Bishop of the A. M. E Church.

A.M.E. Bishop Henry McNeal Turner.
(From H. B. Parks, Africa: The Problem of the New Century: The Part
the African Methodist Episcopal Church Is to Have in Its Solution
[New York: Board of Home and Foreign Missionary Dept. of the A.M.E.
Church, 1899]. From Wikimedia Commons/Public Domain.)

physically and mentally, men who started at the bottom and hammered their way to the top by sheer brute strength; they were the
spiritual progeny of ancient African chieftains and they built the
African church in America."[47]

For every Garnet, Delany, Blyden, or Turner promoting African
American ties to Africa, there were those who sought integration
within the United States, believing they had as much claim on the
country as white citizens did. Those not interested in migrating were
involved with African issues, promoting Christianity and development on the continent and seeking its uplift and elevation. In their

Masthead of The Voice of the People, *September 1, 1901.*

bid to show they were fully American, some African Americans deni-
grated Africa, accepting prevailing stereotypes about the continent's
backwardness. Even those who promoted emigration often inadver-
tently perpetuated negative stereotypes about Africa. Both Garnet
and Turner, though proud of their African heritage, imagined emigration as an opportunity for African Americans to provide the benefits of Christianity and economic progress to "savage and backward"
Africans, to demonstrate African American accomplishment free of
racial discrimination and prejudice, and to establish a homeland to
which all African Americans could return. Their language had a
redemptionist tone to it, stressing the duty of African Americans
to save Africa from its retrograde ways. Although they romanticized
Africa as pristine and underscored African ingenuity, civilization,
and cultural advancement, they still believed Africa was uncivilized,
a heathen land that could be advanced by its sons and daughters
abroad. The language of divine providence was prevalent in nineteenth-century emigration discourse.

   As the century came to a close, African Americans were further
removed from Africa, but many still held onto elements of their
African cultural heritage, embracing nomenclature and labels that
highlighted their African identity. They continued to show an interest in the welfare of Africa and its people and to believe they

had an obligation to the home of their ancestors. While many opposed migration, they embraced their African heritage. Hoping to gain equality and citizenship in the United States, African Americans had to decide if they could be both African and American. Some found ways to influence and contribute to the continent while staking their claim to American citizenship and all the rights it afforded.

CHAPTER FIVE

"Africa is their country.
They should claim it."

I n 1861, describing his first impressions of Africa, Alexander Crummell recalled: "When I went to Liberia my view and purposes were almost entirely missionary in their character, and very much alien from anything civil and national; but I had not been in the country three days when such was the manliness I saw exhibited, so great was the capacity I saw developed, and so many were the signs of thrift, energy, and national life which showed themselves, that all my indifference at once vanished; aspirations after citizenship and nationality rose in my bosom, and I was impelled to go to a magistrate, take the oath of allegiance, and thus become a citizen of Liberia."[1] Crummell spoke of an independent nation, governed by African-descended men and women, many of whom had once been enslaved in the United States.

In July 1847 the colony of Liberia had declared its independence. The twelve signatories to the new nation's Declaration of Independence announced to the world their reasons for taking such a step. In words very similar to the document signed by the American founding fathers, they pointed out the need for a nation that would provide "life, liberty, and the right to acquire, possess, enjoy, and defend property." As they could not do in the United States, they sought the opportunity to govern themselves in Liberia. The men described how and why the nation developed, its early history and subsequent growth, and the dissolution of the nation's ties to the American Colonization Society. Liberia, they stressed, had proven to be all they had expected. Explaining why they had left the United States, they wrote that "amongst the strongest motives to leave our native land—to abandon forever the scenes of our childhood and to sever the most endeared connections—was the desire for a retreat where, free from the agitation of fear and molestation, we could approach in worship the God of our fathers."[2] This declaration showed that the Liberians recognized Christianity's influence on African-descended people in the United States. The Anglo Protestant tradition African Americans had adopted during their sojourn in America influenced their engagement with Africa during the nineteenth and twentieth centuries. In the young nation of Liberia, providential design came to fruition.

Some African Americans found a path to maintaining a connection with Africa through missionary, humanitarian, and philanthropic work on behalf of the continent. The theory of providential design loomed large in the consciousness of late nineteenth- and early twentieth-century African Americans who lobbied on behalf of Africa. At the end of the nineteenth century, African American interaction with Africa centered on what African Americans could do to uplift the continent. For black Americans to earn respect, Africa had to be portrayed in a positive light, but most were determined to assert their American identity. Their ancestral ties to Africa motivated their interest in what happened to Africa, but they were Americans. All African Americans had the shadow of Africa thrust upon them, as this part of their history was constantly resurrected by their detractors and supporters alike.

As the twentieth century dawned, African Americans struggled to find a place in American society. The rights brought by emancipation in the form of the Thirteenth, Fourteenth, and Fifteenth Amendments were gradually eroded as segregation and Jim Crow became the law of the land. Across the ocean the lives of many Africans were no better.

By the end of the nineteenth century, with the exception of Liberia and Ethiopia, Africa was under imperial rule. During the colonial era the continent suffered its worst vilification as Europeans, in order to justify their occupation, continued to represent it as heathen, backward, and savage. It was in this context that Hegel would make his assertions about Africa's place in the world. African Americans often accepted these stereotypes of Africa, adhering to the values and norms of the larger Anglo-American society. The rhetoric of providential design would, once again, be important as African Americans took on the mantle of Africa's redemption. Nonetheless, at various junctures, events within the United States forced black Americans to turn their interest away from Africa to focus on creating a nationality within the United States.

African Americans entered the twentieth century with hopes of gaining equality and full citizenship. But growing prejudice and violence, coupled with difficult economic conditions, prompted some to look to Africa once more. Yet as the century progressed, it was evident that most African Americans had cast their lot with the United States, the only homeland they knew. Long removed from their African antecedents, they would strive to make a better life for themselves there. At the same time, they would keep an eye on the continent of their foremothers and forefathers. The rhetoric of nationalism, salvation, and moral uplift was pervasive in the calls for African Americans to help elevate the continent.

Black Nationalism

When David Walker called for blacks to resist slavery by whatever means they could and when Henry Highland Garnet called for African Americans to take up arms, both men expressed a form of black nationalism. Walker, as we have seen, saw no contradiction in embracing his African ancestry and identity and seeking a place in America. The voices of men like Walker, Garnet, and later Martin Delany became louder and more strident as they embraced a black nationalist ideology. A form of black nationalism had permeated African American thought from the moment the first Africans arrived in the United States. Scholars use the term to describe a variety of actions and thoughts among black Americans, ranging from racial solidarity and belief in a common black culture to more organized activity seeking to unite black Americans. In its simplest form, it is the desire of people of African descent in the United States to unify politically. Adherents of cultural nationalism have argued that African-descended people in the United States and throughout the world have a shared culture and way of life. Expressions of religious nationalism also prevailed among a segment of the black population who called for African Americans to create separate religious institutions and political movements.[3]

In the nineteenth century black nationalist activity was a direct result of slavery, the reason for blacks' presence in the United States and the cause of their inferior treatment. African Americans subscribed in varying degrees to some form of nationalism. In their attempt to improve their lives, some called for direct action. No longer content to accept the marginal position to which they had been relegated, they took hold of their own destiny: organizing on the basis of color and oppressed condition, creating separate institutions and communities, and in some cases abandoning the United States completely. Those who called for racial solidarity often spoke loudly against racism, and several were strong proponents of black nationalism.

Despite Walker's opposition to colonization and his argument that blacks should remain in America, he embraced his African identity. Because of these calls for solidarity in response to white oppression, Walker has often been regarded as one of the earliest black nationalists. Later in the century, Martin Delany was possibly the greatest advocate of black nationalist thinking. Delany had come to support emigration after recognizing that African Americans would not be given full equality. In 1854 Delany strongly voiced his support of emigration, contending, "No people can be free who themselves do not constitute an essential part of the ruling element of the country in which they live. . . . The liberty of no man is secure, who controls not his own political destiny. . . . A people, to be free, must necessarily be their own rulers." He disparaged those who argued that black Americans were the same as white Americans and should behave like them, maintaining that "we are not identical with the Anglo-Saxon or any other race of the Caucasian or pure white type of the human family."[4] Delany insisted that African Americans take pride in their ancestry and history. Some contemporaries, including Frederick Douglass, accused him of cultural chauvinism, criticizing his brand of racial pride. But Martin Delany had his share of supporters. Many years after his death the activist Anna Julia Cooper remembered Delany as "an unadulterated black man, [who] used to say when honors of state fell upon him, that when he entered the council of kings the black race entered with him; meaning, I suppose, that there was no discounting his race identity and attributing his achievements to some admixture of Saxon blood."[5]

Although he was tremendously proud of his African ancestry and supported the emigration impulse, Delany did not completely reject his birthplace. Highly critical of the United States' treatment of its black citizens, Delany was not unpatriotic. He promoted an African American exodus more vociferously during historical moments when it seemed black Americans were destined for perpetual subservience and inequality in American society, but he did not give up on the notion that they might find justice in the United States. Thus, when the Civil War broke out, he turned away from emigration rhetoric to focus on changes he believed would benefit African Americans. He even held a commission in the Union army, serving as an officer in the 104th Regiment, and during Reconstruction (1865–76) he sought solutions to the problems facing black Americans within the United States. When Reconstruction-era changes failed to empower his people, Delany once again lost hope for full integration in the country. Although he had previously rejected Liberia as a site of immigration because of its ties to the American Colonization Society, Delany supported the Liberian Exodus Joint Stock Steam Ship Company in the 1870s. It sought to take African American emigrants from Southern cities to Liberia. Denied a diplomatic post in Liberia, he never emigrated, but his interest in Africa never waned.[6]

Throughout the century and into the next, black nationalist voices called for African Americans to separate themselves, either within the United States or by emigrating. Africa figured prominently in these calls, but the discourse often constructed Africa and Africans as secondary players. African Americans from all walks of life believed they were the drivers of any positive change for Africa and its descendants abroad.

Martin Delany, c. 1865.
(National Portrait Gallery, Washington, DC.
From Wikimedia Commons/Public Domain.)

Black Missionaries

Missionaries played a central role in this discourse. In the nineteenth century, black Americans joined a larger movement in England and the United States to serve as missionaries in Africa. Having largely internalized the belief that they were more privileged than their counterparts in Africa, black Americans believed they were culturally distinct because of their exposure to Christianity. Consequently, they "considered themselves peculiarly suited to the task of uplifting and civilizing those Africans who had never left their native shores."[7]

Black American colonists who went to Liberia often subscribed to these ideas. Some were already free; others were freed specifically for the purpose of colonization. All returned to Africa, hoping for a better life away from the discrimination and pain endured in America. Above all, they saw themselves as missionaries, regardless of their training. Like George Erskine and Diana Skipwith, they hoped to civilize and Christianize their heathen African brothers and sisters. Thus the crafters of Liberia's Declaration of Independence felt compelled to take credit for Christianizing indigenous Africans, asserting that "the native African bowing down with us before the altar of the living God, declares that from us, feeble as we are, the light of Christianity has gone forth, while upon that curse of curses, the slave trade, a deadly blight has fallen, as far as our influence extends."[8] Ending the slave trade and converting Africans were the primary motives of those black Americans who chose to go to Africa as missionaries.

African American travelers and settlers in Africa since the eighteenth century had always thought of themselves as missionaries of sorts. Thus Lott Cary, an early settler in Liberia, expressed his desire to leave America, claiming, "'I am an African, and in this country, however meritorious my conduct and respectable my character, I cannot receive the credit due to either. I wish to go to a country where I shall be estimated by my merits, not by my complexion, and I feel bound to labor for my race."[9] Between 1820 and 1980, according to one scholar, of the 30,000 American missionaries who served in Africa 600 were African Americans. By the end of the nineteenth century the African American mission movement to

Africa increased, so that by 1900 there were about 115 black missionaries in sub-Saharan Africa.[10]

Distinct from earlier colonists, black missionaries came to Africa in endeavors similar to their white counterparts, usually under the aegis of white churches. The nineteenth-century missionary movement among Europeans was characterized by a strong belief in the superiority of their way of life and the need to spread Christian civilization. Because of their exposure to Western ideas and conversion to Christianity, blacks espoused the same values. They made the case for providential design, believing they carried a greater responsibility to Africa because of their ancestral ties to it. Walter Williams chronicles the black missionary movement in the late nineteenth century, showing that missionaries in this period had two goals—to teach Christian religion and to Westernize Africans: "Everything Western was sanctioned as the will of God, while everything belonging to the indigenous culture was evil."[11]

African American missionaries took their task seriously. Accustomed to being at the bottom rungs of society in the United States, they were often bolstered by their role as the chosen few designated by God to save a continent. Most held onto the belief that Africa was degraded and needed redemption. Many believed personality and culture were not integrally related, as the case of Alexander Crummell illustrates.

Born in 1819 in New York to free parents, Alexander Crummell grew up among New York's free black community, committed to ending slavery and to the advancement of blacks.[12] He attended the African Free School in Manhattan, went on to Canal Street High School and the Noyes Academy in Canaan, New Hampshire, and graduated from Oneida Institute in 1839. Denied admittance to the General Theological Seminary in New York, Crummell studied privately with Episcopalian clergymen. Ordained in 1844, he pastored a black congregation in New York. Four years later he traveled to England to raise money to build a church. There Crummell became involved in the abolition movement and was offered a place at Queen's College, Cambridge, from which he graduated in 1853.[13]

Rather than return to America, Crummell took up an offer by the Domestic and Foreign Missionary Society to go to Liberia where, upon arrival, he expressed admiration for the colonists. He became a staunch proponent of emigration, urging African Americans to consider leaving the United States. In 1860 he told his black American audience: "There seems to me to be a natural call upon the children of Africa in foreign lands, to come and participate in the opening treasures of the land of their fathers."[14] He took his own advice and served tirelessly as a teacher and missionary in Liberia for almost twenty years.

Yet despite his long years in Africa, Crummell believed the salvation of Africa lay in Christianity. For him, converting Africans to Christianity was simple: "The missionary enters a pagan village. He addresses himself to the salvation of the pagan people around him, and ere long he rejoices in the gain of a convert. The man is a naked pagan. He lives in a rude hut. His clothing is a quarter of a yard of coarse cotton. He eats out of a rude bowl. He clutches his food with his naked hand. He sleeps on a floor, the floor of beaten earth. By the dint of painstaking effort and assiduity, by careful teaching and solicitude, the missionary has succeeded in lodging the clear idea of God, the principles of repentance and faith in the Redeemer; and the heathen man receiving the great salvation is prepared for heaven."[15] This view did not, of course, account for African beliefs, or for the fact that these populations had their own religions. Crummell believed in the rightness of Christianity. Others who believed that Africa's destiny lay in the hands of black Americans took up the call to serve as missionaries. During the nineteenth century many black Americans went to Africa in response to what they believed to be the continent's need of and potential for uplift.

Black American women also answered the call. In the nineteenth century the missionary activity of African American women intensified as black women from all religious denominations went as missionaries to Africa. African American women made up half the number of the missionaries in Africa in the nineteenth century. Like their male counterparts, they believed they had a responsibility to indigenous Africans, particularly to women and children. Although their undertakings were sometimes marginalized compared to the activity of men, women did make an impact on the indigenous African populations. Amanda Berry Smith, born a slave in Maryland, served as an African Methodist Episcopal Church evangelist and missionary in Liberia. She also spent time in Sierra

MISS EMMA B. DELANEY.

Miss Emma B. Delaney, 1902.
(Jean Blackwell Hutson Research and Reference Division. Schomburg
Center for Research in Black Culture, The New York Public Library,
Astor, Lenox and Tilden Foundations. New York Public Library
Digital Collections.)

Leone, where she advocated temperance among African converts.
Maria Fearing, formerly enslaved in Alabama, went to the Congo,
where she worked for more than twenty years as a Presbyterian
missionary. Nancy Jones, an unmarried missionary in Mozambique
and Rhodesia, worked to educate African women and girls, attempted to open up a boarding school, and took in abandoned
children and orphans. The Spelman College Seminary trained
many women for African missions. Nora Antonia Gordon was its
first graduate to serve as a missionary in Congo. Female missionaries continued to serve in Africa into the twentieth century. Emma

Delaney, a missionary in Southern Africa and Liberia, was one of many women to go to Africa in the early twentieth century.[16]

Before 1880 most black missionaries went to Africa under the auspices of white churches and were compelled to follow the philosophies of these churches. Some attempted to understand African cultural practices, trying not to judge them as harshly as their white colleagues did. Others challenged and undermined the prevailing view of African inferiority by demonstrating their own civilized nature. Often their rhetoric was imperial in tone as they extolled the virtues of Christianity and Westernization. Yet, as Brandi Hughes argues in her examination of black Baptists, the work of black missionaries "was integral to the ways black American communities learned how to identify and relate their community with African communities in colonization."[17] Prolonged contact with Africans made them familiar enough with the continent to change their views, condemning European activity in Africa. African Americans often served as a voice for Africans during the colonial period, as exemplified in the life of William Sheppard.

William Henry Sheppard (1865–1927) was an early missionary for the Presbyterian Church. Often referred to as the "Black Livingstone," Sheppard appears in photographs dressed in a white suit and bowler hat, the style of a colonial gentleman. He spent twenty years in Africa, primarily in and around the Congo Free State. He is best known for his efforts to publicize Belgian atrocities against the Kuba and other Congolese peoples. Sheppard's reports made the world aware of the many crimes being committed against Congolese men, women, and children forced to work on rubber plantations. He learned the language of the Kuba people among whom he worked and brought back a rich collection of African art that no doubt gave African Americans another way to think about the continent. Sheppard's collection, now housed at Hampton University, proved to be a valuable resource.[18]

Other black men and women who worked in the Congo Free State during the colonial era called attention to the plight of Africans. Yet even these champions of Africa frequently couched their defense in derogatory language, portraying Africans as children needing the help and protection of their more sophisticated and civilized siblings from across the Atlantic.

Black missionaries frequently continued their efforts on behalf of Africa after returning home. Some adopted African children, bringing them to the United States for education. Missionaries and their church bodies often supported African students. The Colored Baptist Foreign Missionary Convention brought five students to Nashville's Central Tennessee College in 1892. Later the National Baptist Convention missionaries brought South African students to the United States. Bishop Henry McNeal Turner and the African Methodist Episcopal Church sponsored several African students in the late nineteenth century. Delaney informally adopted Daniel Malekebu while a missionary in Central Africa. The young African later received a medical degree at Meharry College of Medicine and returned to Africa as a missionary.[19]

Black missionaries were also influential in the rise of pan-African sentiment. Missionaries played a significant role in linking the plight of Africans to that of African Americans, producing strong ties between the two groups. During the era of high imperialism, Henry McNeal Turner was a strong voice for unity between the two groups. Members of the clergy, journalists, and educators spoke out against European colonialism in Africa, calling for greater black involvement in Africa.[20] Joseph Charles Price, once president of Livingstone College and the National Afro-American League, proposed that African Americans take the lead in colonization. Highlighting their ties to Africa, he pronounced, "The whites found gold, diamonds, and other riches in Africa. Why should not the Negro? Africa is their country. They should claim it; they should go to Africa, civilize those Negroes, raise them morally, and by education show them how to better obtain the wealth which is in their own country, and take that grand continent as their own."[21] Those who promoted emigration and colonization sometimes subscribed to similar values.

Pro-colonizationists argued that American blacks were necessary to uplift and civilize Africa. Even those leaders who rejected Africa as a site of immigration recognized their connection to the continent. In 1896 a conference brought together leading black and white scholars, journalists, and activists in Atlanta, Georgia. Participants spoke on diverse topics pertaining to Africa: the missionary movement, religious beliefs in Africa, the plight of African-descended people in Africa and the diaspora, the American Colonization Society, health and hygiene, and slavery in Africa. Although some of the participants criticized colonialism, many accepted Europe's presence in Africa as largely positive. T. Thomas Fortune, a leading journalist, activist, and adviser to Booker T. Washington, praised the technological advancements Europeans introduced into Africa, pointing to the religious benefits Africans gained. He believed that blacks were "here [the United States] and must make the very best of the situation as we find it," which did not prevent his agitating for better rights for Africans. Fortune looked for a united Africa and during his life was involved with many organizations connected with the continent. This did not preclude him from agitating for change in America. Founder of the National Afro American League in 1890, Fortune called for equality in America—the restoration of black voting rights, redress for violence against blacks, equal funding of black schools, equality in the justice system, and an end to discrimination in public accommodation and transportation.[22] Other speakers at the Georgia gathering stressed the role African Americans could play in Africa. Henry McNeal Turner, true to his principles, delivered a speech entitled "The American Negro and the Fatherland," reiterating his calls for emigration. He insisted it was not possible for black Americans to fulfill their potential in the United States since the divisions between the black and white races were too great. Black Americans, he maintained, lived in the United States on white sufferance. Enumerating the many injustices they faced, Turner argued that "the talk about two races remaining in the same country with mutual interest and responsibility in its institutions and progress, with no social contact, is the jargon of folly." He urged his black compatriots to consider Africa as an alternative. In 1894 he inserted words into the American anthem exhibiting his pride in Africa:

My country, 'tis of thee,
Dear land of Africa,
Of thee we sing:
Land where our fathers died,
Land of the Negro's pride,
From every mountain side God's truth will ring.

My native country, thee,
Land of the black and free,
Thy name I love
To see thy rocks and rills
Thy woods and matchless hills
My heart with rapture thrills
Like that above.[23]

Among the few women who participated in the 1896 conference, Etna Holderness spoke of her life in Africa and her path to
Christian conversion. Born in Liberia, a member of the Bassa
ethnic group, Holderness spoke of the direction she had taken
from her childhood to mission schools and a college education
in Liberia. She served as an example of what conference participants sought for Africa—the potential of Africans to become
Christian and civilized. Holderness was no doubt held up as an
"authentic" African voice, as Americans would have understood
it at the time. Because she had been born on the continent, her
experiences and opinions were valuable to those wanting to help
Africa.

The men and women at this conference were self-appointed
spokespersons for Africa, responsible for showing the continent
positively. On the other hand, we might wonder what Africans on
the continent might have thought of a conference held in the
United States with an agenda purporting to be in aid of their redemption. We can surmise that they did not see themselves as can-
didates for African American beneficence. Nevertheless, throughout
the nineteenth century diasporan blacks lay claim to their duty as
children of Africa to uplift their motherland.

Events affecting blacks in the United States made carrying
out that duty difficult. Black life and race relations in the United
States reached their nadir in the late nineteenth and early twentieth centuries. This era witnessed the rise of Jim Crow and segregation, increased violence, and legal setbacks to the gains African
Americans had made during and after the Civil War. *Plessy vs. Fer-
guson*, the 1896 ruling sanctioning segregation on railroad trains,
affirmed the separate but equal doctrine, requiring that black and
whites could no longer share facilities and accommodations. Afri-

can Americans were separate but, despite the language of *Plessy*, they were certainly not equal. Increasingly, African Americans faced growing violence and terror, particularly in Southern states.

In the last year of the nineteenth century Sam Hose was lynched in Georgia. His body was dismembered and pieces handed out to the more than two thousand white spectators who witnessed his death. This hanging exemplified white disregard for black lives (and the due process of law) at the dawn of a new century and prompted many blacks to assess their place in American society.

Twentieth-Century Challenges and Responses

The twentieth century ushered in new challenges for African Americans. At the beginning of the century lynching was commonplace.[24] Between 1900 and 1915 more than a thousand African Americans were lynched in the South, and hundreds in the North were executed in this way. It was in this context that Henry McNeal Turner called for emigration. In those troubled times African Americans no doubt questioned their place in American society. White Americans, north and south, believed in their superiority. As one historian has written, "The Southern ways had become the American way."[25] Black Americans in the South were disenfranchised, with segregation and racial violence a way of life. This tide of racism, discrimination, and segregation characterized the plight of African Americans through the 1930s.

In the wake of such violence, many looked, once more, for a way out. Early in the century thousands of Southern blacks migrated to Northern states for the opportunities new industries in those regions afforded. Though black Southerners believed life in the North was better, their Northern counterparts faced similar problems of discrimination and economic marginalization. Although blacks could vote in these states, they frequently faced residential and employment discrimination and segregation in education and public accommodations. When the (white) journalist Ray Stannard Baker interviewed black Northerners in 1908, their major complaint was about working conditions—unfair opportunities for jobs, racism, and discrimination. Blacks in the North, he noted, were "compelled to loiter around the edges of industry."[26]

Regardless of legislation that ostensibly protected their rights and afforded black Americans freedom, white Americans perpetuated segregation. Thus in 1934 W. E. B. Du Bois wrote that black Americans "have not made the slightest impress on the determination of the overwhelming mass of white Americans not to treat Negroes as men."[27] Nevertheless, African Americans pushed for political participation and inclusion in the wake of emancipation. They strove for equality and acceptance, celebrated their achievements, took pride in their race, and affirmed their connection to Africa.

Although on the decline, emigration sentiment persisted as some African Americans recognized that they would not achieve full equality in the United States. Early in the twentieth century, Chief Alfred Sam of the Gold Coast (now Ghana) formed the Akim Trading Company to engage in trade, develop industry, and "encourage the emigration of the best Negro farmers and mechanics from the United States to different sections in West Africa."[28] Sam sold stock at $25 to blacks, mainly in Oklahoma, who, the *New York Times* reported, looked upon him as "a leader who will deliver them all from all 'Jim Crow' regulations." Mainly targeting Southern blacks, the movement and its supporters succeeded in transporting Oklahoman emigrants to Africa in 1914. One of its major supporters, Orishatukeh Faduma, a Sierra Leonean living in the United States, saw the importance of this movement for African Americans. Even those across the Atlantic recognized the benefits African Americans could bring to Africa. An editorial in the *Sierra Leone Weekly News* observed that black Americans "had stretched their hands across the Atlantic from America to us in Africa, from one side of the Atlantic to the other. If we give them a grip . . . and let the Blacks in America unite with those in West Africa as one people, this would evoke a force which nothing can resist."[29]

Sadly, Sam's venture was unsuccessful. After reaching the Gold Coast in January 1915, black settlers faced difficulties with colonial officials, prompting many of them to return. African Americans, for the most part, heeded Booker T. Washington's 1895 call to "cast down your bucket where you are."[30] Most African Americans, despite the bigotry they faced, still considered themselves Americans. So it was that a New Orleans cook faced with the prospect of leaving the United States observed, "I don't see why I got to go back to Africa. I'm doin' all right here. I don't need nothin' in Africa."[31] Rejecting Africa, this woman, presumably uneducated, nonetheless acknowledged her ties to Africa by refusing to "go back." Identification with Africa persisted even as black Americans pushed for assimilation in America.

Those with a platform spoke out publicly in defense of the continent. Individuals like W. E. B. Du Bois and Carter Woodson responded to negative images of Africa, "determined to reclaim for Africa its proper heritage as a continent of great peoples with noble pasts and mighty contributions to human progress."[32] Both men, because of their long association with African issues, were often called upon as experts and consultants. In 1927 when Emory Ross, a Disciples of Christ missionary who had served in Central Africa, sought to write a history of the missionary movement in Africa, he wrote to both men asking for their advice and expertise. Although his focus would largely be on white missionaries, Ross hoped to acknowledge the part "played by colored missionaries from America and the West Indies and by Congo's own people."[33]

As "advocates for Africa," black Americans often highlighted their role in the uplift of the continent. Furthermore, in making their case, some adopted the idea that Africa had little of value to offer. Like earlier activists, they believed that American blacks would uplift the continent and "pilot Africans towards a new day in the sun."[34] Although these assertions were meant to vindicate and defend Africa, today these views seem like cultural arrogance. Nonetheless, this belief sometimes propelled African Americans to take unified action.

Du Bois, who wrote extensively on Africa throughout his life, saw the plight of African-descended people worldwide as connected to Africa's. As editor of *The Crisis* magazine, he championed the causes of African Americans and Africans alike. In many of his speeches and writings, he called for organized group action along political and economic lines, with the "express object of making it possible for Negroes to earn a better living and ... more effectively to support agencies for social uplift."[35] In the early twentieth century he pressed for unity between Africans and their sons and daughters in the Americas. The Pan-African Congresses Du Bois organized in 1919, 1921, 1923, and 1927 called for unity among people of African descent, political rights, and a liberated Africa. The delegates stopped short of calling for African independence and self-determination, believing that Africans were not yet ready for self-government.

When Germany was forced to give up its colonies after World War I, African American leaders, led by Du Bois, asked for the internationalization of the colonies. Rather than pushing for Africans to assume the reins of their own government, the black Americans proposed that the colonies be placed under "general control of the civilized nations of the world." The resulting administration would introduce culture, science, trade, and social and religious reform led by both white and black officials.[36] Although Africans could be involved, the prevailing sentiment was that they were not yet ready to take over their own affairs. Given that many Africans in this era already held positions within colonial administrations on the continent, it seems presumptuous of African Americans to argue that they were ill equipped to govern themselves. Yet this idea persisted and was certainly the view of the Jamaican-born Marcus Garvey, a strong voice for African American involvement in Africa in the early twentieth century.

Although not American by birth, Marcus Garvey, like Edward Blyden, greatly influenced African American attitudes toward Africa. Garvey migrated to New York in 1916 from Jamaica. Founder of the Universal Negro Improvement Association (UNIA), his "back to Africa" mass movement allowed African Americans to engage in more significant ways with the continent. The UNIA galvanized blacks in Africa and the diaspora as its founder called for racial unity and Africa's redemption. Garvey "broadened and energized" African American interest in Africa. Like Du Bois, he stressed racial solidarity and pride in African heritage, but he exerted a more populist appeal. His message was well received by working-class, largely urban black Americans, although his reach went far beyond the borders of Harlem, his New York base. Because of his rhetoric and style, he drew "hundreds of thousands of African Americans to the cause of African redemption."[37] He resurrected the issue of emigration, urging African Americans to go to Africa to uplift the continent.

THE CRISIS

A RECORD OF THE DARKER RACES

| Volume One | MARCH, 1911 | Number Five |

Edited by W. E. BURGHARDT DU BOIS, with the co-operation of Oswald Garrison Villard, J. Max Barber, Charles Edward Russell, Kelly Miller, W. S. Braithwaite and M. D. Maclean.

.Egyptian Portrait of One of the Black Kings of the Upper Nile, Ra-Maat-Neb, Builder of Pyramid No. 17. (After Lepsius.)

PUBLISHED MONTHLY BY THE

National Association for the Advancement of Colored People

AT TWENTY VESEY STREET　　　　　　NEW YORK CITY

ONE DOLLAR A YEAR　　　　　　TEN CENTS A COPY

Cover of The Crisis, *March 1911, with a black pharoah illustration.*
(From Wikimedia Commons/Public Domain.)

Garvey incorporated the Black Star shipping line to foster trade and transport migrants to Africa. Although the venture failed, he succeeded in sending two delegations to Liberia in 1924 to negotiate a possible site of settlement for African Americans. Alongside

Garvey was his wife, Amy Jacques, whose pride in her African ancestry rivaled that of her husband. Women played important roles
in the UNIA, and Amy Jacques pushed for the inclusion of women
in all levels of the organization. Like her husband, she called for a
move "back" to Africa, exclaiming: "Africa must be for Africans, and
Negroes everywhere must be independent, God being our helper
and guide. Mr. Black Man watch your step! Ethiopia's queens will
reign again and her Amazons protect her shores and people.
Strengthen your shaking knees and move forward, or we will dis-
place you and lead on to victory and glory."[38]

Garvey believed African Americans had a greater role to play in
the continent's uplift, more so than Africans themselves. While he
enumerated the glories of Africa's past, he did not consider contemporary Africans up to the task of redeeming their homeland. In
the hierarchy of civilization African Americans were ranked higher
than continental Africans. Yet Garvey's movement attracted Africans both on the continent and in the United States. Arguably, of
all the leaders in the United States at that time, Garvey had the
most influence on Africans on the continent, who interpreted Garveyism for their own purposes. His language of liberation resonated with colonized Africans seeking freedom from their colonial
masters just as it did with black Americans battling Jim Crow. Men
and women from across Africa traveled to the United States to be
part of the UNIA, and to learn from the struggles of blacks in the
United States. Branches of the organization sprang up in African
colonies, and Africans in the United States sought out Garvey's
teachings.[39]

Such was the case of the Sierra Leonean George O. Marke, a
staunch supporter of the UNIA's leader. Marke had been the official representative of the UNIA's Freetown division, and he traveled to the United States several times in the early 1920s. He later
settled in the United States, becoming deputy potentate of the
UNIA. Other continental Africans also gravitated to the movement. Garvey's importance to Africa lies in his influence on the
movement for self-determination among colonized populations.
His *Negro World* newspaper, read widely in Africa, influenced nationalists across the continent, prompting some colonial governments to ban the publication.[40]

Garvey's movement succeeded in presenting Africa positively to African Americans, allowing them to take pride in their connection to the continent. It is fair to say that it was a romanticized view. The vision of Africa's greatness that appealed to black Americans was one of great wealth and power, with strong rulers governing large expanses of territory and kingdoms. Given that Africans were living under colonialism in this era, it was an idealized image. Ultimately Garvey did not succeed in galvanizing African Americans to emigrate to Africa en masse, but his rhetoric engendered in them a tremendous pride in their African ancestry. His oratory also gave space for African Americans to make a choice about whether they wanted to leave the United States or claim their American identity. Embracing Africa did not mean rejecting America or their contribution to the United States. "To fight for African redemption," Garvey argued, "does not mean that we must give up our domestic fights for political justice and industrial rights. It does not mean that we must become disloyal to any government or to any country wherein we were born. . . . We can be as loyal American citizens or British subjects as the Irishman or the Jew, and yet fight for the redemption of Africa, a complete emancipation of the race. . . . Why should fighting for the freedom of Africa make the Afro-American disloyal or a bad citizen?"[41] In this language we clearly see African American identification, interest, and involvement with Africa. An embrace of African ancestry did not negate blacks' love for America.

Along with his push for black migration, Garvey promoted a philosophy of self-help influenced by Booker T. Washington, the principal of Tuskegee Institute and spokesman for African Americans. Washington, though not often invoked as a Pan-Africanist, was keenly interested in African issues. Like Garvey and Du Bois, he recognized the ties between African Americans and Africa and called for the uplift of both groups. Booker T. Washington spoke out against immigration laws adversely impacting Africans. In 1915 Washington repudiated a bill proposing that only whites should be allowed to establish permanent residency in the United States. Denouncing the proposal, he made a plea to Congress for "fair play and justice." He characterized it as an "unnecessary slight upon colored people by classing them as alien criminals." Furthermore, it

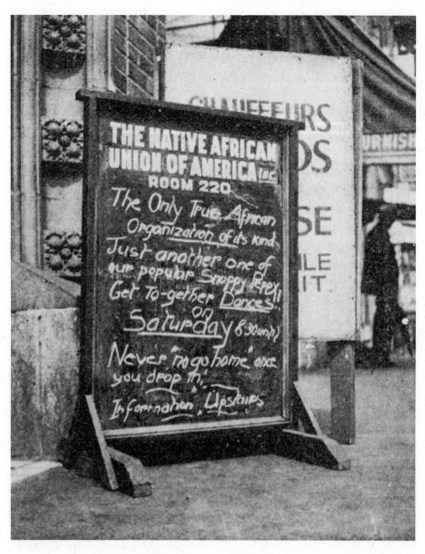

*A Harlem "Back to Africa" announcement, Negro Club, New York City, 1929.
(Jean Blackwell Hutson Research and Reference Division, Schomburg Center for
Research in Black Culture, The New York Public Library. New York Public
Library Digital Collections.)*

would "cripple the missionary and educational work which we are trying to do in Africa."[42] The bill was later defeated in the Senate.

Even though he did not promote emigration, Washington believed African Americans had a role to play in Africa. In 1901 he sponsored a delegation from Tuskegee to the German colony of Togo to explore the possibility of growing cotton. The result, Andrew Zimmerman has shown, was an attempt to use the post-Reconstruction South as a model for creating a cotton economy in the German colony.[43] Furthermore, Tuskegee, over which Washington presided from 1881 until his death in 1915, educated dozens of Africans drawn to his philosophy of self-help and the institution's focus on industrial education.[44]

"Africa is here": Africans in the United States

Throughout the late nineteenth and early twentieth centuries, Africans traveled to the United States in different capacities, influencing and shaping American views of the continent and interacting with African Americans. Between 1891 and 1900, an estimated 350 Africans entered the United States. Many came as students. Some, like George Marke, were driven by political activism. During this time, Africans living in the United States could be found in all walks of life. They were students, visitors, college professors, actors, missionaries, and immigrants. They interacted with Americans, black and white. Like Etna Holderness, who spoke at the 1896 conference, they were received as "authentic" Africans who could serve as examples of the good work missionaries were doing in Africa. Since they came directly from Africa, Americans often believed that these individuals could teach them more about Africa and more fully articulate the needs of the communities from which they came than African observers who stayed in America.[45]

Many of these men and women educated in the United States returned to Africa, galvanized by what they had learned. The South African John L. Dube received high school training at Oberlin and did a theology degree at Brooklyn Theological Seminary in New York in the late 1890s. After completing his studies, he returned to open the Ohlange Institute, often promoted as the Tuskegee of Africa. Alfred Xuma, also South African and influenced by Dube, traveled to the United States to study at Tuskegee. During the summer of 1916 he worked at a pipe shop in Birmingham, Alabama, where he undoubtedly worked with African Americans, before leaving for St. Paul, Minnesota, for further studies. He too would return to South Africa, taking along his African American wife Madie Hall. Others, like Kamba Simango from Mozambique and John Chilembwe from Nyasaland (now Malawi), became leaders in their communities. Chilembwe went to a theological school in Lynchburg, Virginia, and Simango was educated at Talladega.[46]

James Kwegyir Aggrey from the Gold Coast (Ghana) was perhaps the most well-known African in the United States in the late nineteenth and early twentieth centuries. Aggrey came as a student to Livingstone College in Salisbury, North Carolina, in 1898, sponsored by Bryan Small, a Barbadian-born bishop of the African Methodist Episcopal Zion church, who had served as a missionary in the Gold Coast. After graduating from Livingstone in 1902, Aggrey stayed on campus as a professor and administrator, teaching and mentoring students and working with black communities in rural areas surrounding Salisbury. Until his death in 1927 Aggrey was considered the preeminent "African" in the United States. He is best known for his work with the Phelps Stokes Fund, a philanthropic organization that contributed to the education of African Americans, Native Americans, and Africans. In Africa he is remembered as one of the founders of Achimota College, a premier school for young Ghanaians. He spent almost thirty years in the American South.[47]

Aggrey had come to train as a missionary with the understanding that he would return to Africa, but he chose to stay in the United States. In 1905 he married a young African American woman from Portsmouth, Virginia. Rosebud Rudolf Douglass was a graduate of Shaw University. The *Portsmouth Lodge Journal and Guide* described their November wedding as "one of the most brilliant and alluring marriages ever chronicled in the city's history." It noted the prominence of both the bride and groom, described in great detail the bride's dress, and enumerated the illustrious guest list, including out-of-town guests. The piece highlighted the couple's professions—Rose a teacher in the city's public school, James a professor at Livingstone College. Interestingly enough, no mention was made of Aggrey's African origin. This is in contrast to the many newspaper articles that never failed to refer to his connection to Africa, or to describe his dark skin. In 1915 the *Charlotte Gazette* noted Rose's attendance at a Tuskegee conference, describing her as "the accomplished wife of a remarkable man." Aggrey was described as "a native African," who "has been in this country but eight years, graduated at the head of his class, is only 30 years old and is teaching Americans English, besides two dead languages."[48] His views and philosophy of accommodation and racial harmony were particularly palatable to white Americans who believed in the gradual integration of blacks into American society. Like Booker T. Washington, Aggrey stressed self-help and promoted industrial education and Christianity for Africans. He spent his adult years in the United States, coming to understand the role of race in the lives of African-descended people. Lecturing around the nation, he became a poster child for the influence of Christianity's success in Africa.

Like Aggrey, Orishatukeh Faduma came to the United States to study with the hope of returning to his native land, in his case Sierra Leone, as a missionary. However, upon completing his studies at Yale Divinity School, he served as a missionary and teacher in the American South. He married Henrietta Adams, a black American woman from Georgia, taught at the Peabody Academy, a black institution in Troy, North Carolina, for seventeen years, and served as a missionary and educator to African Americans in North Carolina for more than fifty years. Like other Africans in that era, Faduma lived in a segregated South, operating within a world in which by virtue of the color of his skin he was thought to be inferior. He adapted to life as a black man in a racially segregated nation at a time when discrimination, racism, and violence were leveled at men and women of African descent. He lived and worked among less privileged blacks, referring to them as his "kith and kin," deeming it his responsibility and duty to enhance African American lives and improve their situation.

Faduma's contributions were recognized in a 1904 publication lauding him for his contributions to African Americans and for his missionary work: "We question if this native African could have made a better investment of his powers had he remained in Africa. Africa is here."[49] The notion of Africa being in the United States clearly indicated the ties many African Americans continued to have with the continent. Faduma was a strong voice for the emigration movement and worked with Chief Alfred Sam to urge African Americans to settle in Africa. Having lived in the American South for decades, he knew the marginalization faced by those of African descent. In encouraging emigration, he remarked: "It is certainly better for American Negroes to die of African fever in the effort to contribute to Africa's development than to be riddled by the bullets of the White mob who control the local governments of the United States. ... It is better to live even among pagans, where the majority respect their laws and life is secure, than to live in a country where only the minority are law keepers as in the Southern States." Despite this understanding of the trouble blacks faced, he remained in the United States. Becoming a naturalized citizen in 1902, he spent the rest of his life in the United States. He died in North Carolina in 1946.[50]

Simbini Mamba Nkomo from the British colony of Rhodesia also came to study. After receiving his degree from a Christian college in southern Illinois, he became professor of African history at Tuskegee. In 1912, while a student, Nkomo formed an African student organization in hopes of rallying African students in the United States to help with Africa's uplift, and "as a result of his dire need of personal touch with his fellow-countrymen."[51] At Tuskegee, Nkomo succeeded in creating strong ties, exerting great influence on his black American students. Aggrey, Faduma, and Nkomo were just a few of the many Africans who chose to stay in the United States, becoming immigrants and subsumed under the label of "Negro" in a country still racially divided. They served as role models for young black students in a segregated American South and shaped American views on Africa. No doubt their experiences with these men helped black Americans redefine their vision and ideas about Africa, as they recognized it was not the backward, uncivilized place they had understood it to be.[52]

African women also traveled to the United States, where they found common cause with African Americans. Many, like Charlotte Manye and Adelaide Tantsi, South Africans at Wilberforce University in the 1890s, returned home. Some, although their lives are harder to trace than those of their male counterparts, married and remained in the United States. Charlotte Manye, sponsored by

Bishop Benjamin Arnett of the AME church, studied under W. E. B. Du Bois at Wilberforce. He later wrote: "I have known Charlotte Manye Maxeke since 1894, when I went to Wilberforce University as a teacher. She was one of the three or four students from South Africa, and was the only woman. . . . We were interested in Charlotte Manye because of her clear mind, her fund of subtle humour and the straight-forward honesty of her character. . . . She did her work with a slow, quiet determination, that augured well for her future."[53]

Kathleen Easmon from Sierra Leone shared her knowledge of Africa through cultural performances and lectures. Along with her famous aunt, Adelaide Casely Hayford, who visited the United States in 1920, she raised money for a girls' school in their native Sierra Leone. Emma Yongebloed (Zinga) and her sister Suluka, Flora Zeto, Margaret Rattray (Nkebani), and Lena Clark (Vunga), all from the Congo, were brought by missionaries to study at Spelman College. Suluka and Emma married African American men and stayed in the United States, while Flora Zeto married Daniel Malekebu, the adopted son of the African American missionary Emma Delaney and returned to Africa. Lena Clark, referred to as a "Congo girl," returned to Africa with the missionary James Clark, who had adopted her. All these men and women reshaped black American ideas about Africa. They debunked the extreme images of the continent as either a savage wasteland or an idyllic paradise. Their Christianity and Western orientation were illustrations of missionary success, and many of their black American counterparts felt vindicated by their capacity for adopting Western culture.[54]

Yet long-held stereotypes and images were hard to break, and Africa continued to be constructed as remote and backward. Exotic descriptions of the continent and its people persisted. Africans were unhelpful in rectifying these views, for they often presented a vision of the continent in line with what Americans expected. Many of the students and visitors in the United States gave lectures to American audiences that frequently focused on the outlandish and uncivilized nature of the continent. To white Americans their acceptance of Christianity was admirable. For African Americans they served as confirmation of their potential for civilization.

Whether to please their benefactors and sponsors or because, as converted Christians themselves, they held similar views, many

Africans perpetuated the negative stereotypes of the continent. They believed that Christianity was the most suitable religion for the continent's uplift. Those who arrived in America were often sponsored by missionary organizations and had to prove they were good Christians. Educated Africans in the United States therefore accepted the prevailing stereotypes of Africa as the "benighted" continent. "At least in their public discourse through which they represented themselves to Americans," they sought to portray Africa as needing salvation. These men and women were educated within colonial systems, typically in mission schools that had provided them with economic and social mobility. Their Western education allowed them to advance, both in their home countries and in the larger, European-dominated world.[55]

Africans frequently portrayed their homeland in particular ways in order to secure funding for whatever cause they championed. Reliance on American sponsors regularly required them to construct narratives of Africa that would be palatable to their American audiences, which were largely church or other Christian communities. Claudius Clement, brought to the United States by the American missionary Ackrel White in 1881, returned to Sierra Leone after graduating from Hampton University in 1884. He later wrote of the differences between his native home and the United States: "America and Africa—what a world of difference between the two places! Both end with the four last letters alike, but a mighty contrast exists. In America, education, religion and civilization abound; but, in Africa, darkness, intellectual darkness, broods over her millions. May God hasten the time when intellectual light shall be sent to Africa, and other non Christianized settlements."[56] This was the view of many black Americans as well.

As the twentieth century progressed, African Americans interacted with Africa and Africans in more significant ways even as they moved toward greater integration at home. As we have seen, African Americans had limited exchanges with continental Africans until late in the nineteenth century. Contact with African students, visitors, and immigrants in the United States, beginning in this era, provided black Americans with a more diverse picture of their ancestral continent. They frequently hosted Africans during their time in the United States and doubtless had a better opportunity to engage with them in more authentic ways. Africans who made their home in the United States were forced to live in segregated spaces, also encountering discrimination and racism. For that reason, they sought out African Americans who welcomed them into their communities. In turn, these African-born men and women influenced African American views of the continent. While living among Americans, Africans learned about the society they were in but also taught Americans about Africa.

Some Africans resented African Americans who sought to speak for them, believing they were better equipped to defend their homeland from negative representations. The Gold Coast nationalist Kobina Sekyi, although he admired Marcus Garvey and his movement, was critical of diaspora blacks' view of their role in Africa's uplift. In 1922 he chastised those who believed that "we are in such a condition that the only part we can play in the prevailing endeavour on the part of the darker races to attain a better place . . . is to be led by them. That is a very serious mistake, which ought to be corrected as early as possible. . . . We claim that we should be the architects, and that our brethren in America and those in the West Indies should be among the builders of the structure of racial oneness. . . . We contend that we have the controlling forces in our hands, and we in Africa alone understand these forces and can direct them aright for the good of the whole Negro race."[57] George Marke, the former Garveyite, echoed this sentiment: "The American and West Indian Negroes could control things on their side of the water," while "we Africans will run things over here. We hold the trump cards."[58]

Given the number of Africans residing in the United States at this time, black Americans, it seemed, forgot or ignored the fact that Africans were capable of advocating for their own homeland. Despite these tensions, African Americans continued to be a strong voice for Africa and its liberation as its people struggled to end colonialism.

After the First World War some European colonial governments recognized the need to develop education further in order to train Africans to fill certain positions within colonial structures. Alerted to the serious shortage of educated people, some colonies embarked on a project to provide more schooling for Africans. In the early 1920s the British government, in collaboration with the American Phelps Stokes Fund, sent a delegation to assess the state of education in its African colonies. Part of the rationale for partnering with Phelps Stokes was that the foundation had long championed a particular vision of education for African Americans, particularly those in Southern states. The Phelps Stokes Fund was instrumental in funding Tuskegee and Hampton Colleges, both institutions promoting industrial education for African Americans. The commission was motivated by a similar vision of encouraging this type of education in Africa. In fact, one scholar has noted that the fund "played a key role in reinforcing and perpetuating the belief that the educational methods which had been hammered out for the freed slaves in the post bellum period were particularly relevant for black Africans in the twentieth century."[59] Phelps Stokes was already sponsoring African students to study at Hampton, Tuskegee, and other American institutions, anticipating they would return to Africa with the skills they had acquired. The commission set out in 1920 with the African James Aggrey as its only black member.

Aggrey was heartily welcomed by Africans in the colonies he visited. In South Africa he was received as an emancipator by the black population. Returning to Africa for the first time after twenty-two years, Aggrey made interesting observations about the contrasts in African and American life. In a letter to his African American wife he wrote of the warm welcome he received from the Africans he encountered in the colonies. In the Gold Coast he met old friends who were interested in his life in America and in his relationship with African Americans. "When I tell them you are of African descent and not a white woman," he wrote, "their joy knows no bounds." Aggrey also remarked on the differences in attitudes toward race. In Ghana he was treated like the royalty he was; colonial officials provided him with housing during his visit, and he was welcomed among Europeans in the colony. He noted that his black American friends would have wondered "how I stood some things" in the United States.[60] In other words, Aggrey intimated, rather naively, that there were fewer prejudices directed at blacks in the colonies. Although Africans outnumbered Europeans in many colonies, making it difficult to institute segregation practices found in the American South, racial discrimination operated in

Africa in similar ways. Like black Americans in the United States, Africans were excluded from many opportunities, including access to education.[61]

The Phelps Stokes commission's report resulted in changes to education systems in some British colonies, expanding access to colonized subjects. These opportunities gave rise to an African elite whose members challenged the status quo as they pushed for greater representation in their own affairs. During the 1920s John Dube, Solomon Plaatje, and others challenged segregation laws in South Africa, doubtless with their time in the United States in mind. These men, who later played a role in the growth of the South African Native National Congress (SANNC), had either studied or visited the United States and been influenced by African Americans like Carter G. Woodson, W. E. B. Du Bois, and Booker T. Washington. Other young men and women with American college degrees returned to their homelands to effect change. Meanwhile, African nationalists, influenced by Du Bois's Pan-African Congresses, called meetings of their own. In March 1920 the Ghanaian lawyer Joseph Casely Hayford organized the National Congress of British West Africa. Delegates from the four British West African colonies—Sierra Leone, Gambia, Nigeria, and Ghana—attended this conference, where participants petitioned the British government for increased representation in the legislative councils of the colonies. They did not achieve much, getting few or no concessions from Britain, but the congress succeeded in promoting cooperation among Africans in the four colonies.

While Africans sought access to education and political rights, African Americans were fighting their own battles for equality. The historian George Shepperson has explored the long engagement between African Americans and Africa in this era. Organizations and associations were formed aimed at promoting the well-being and unity of blacks all over the world. Africans attended Du Bois's congresses and read the UNIA's newspaper. In British colonies administrators worried about the influence these diaspora movements were having on their colonized populations. Marcus Garvey, for instance, had tremendous influence on Africans who interpreted Garveyism for their own purposes and used it in their nationalist rhetoric to effect change in the colonies. In many colonies Garvey's *Negro World* newspaper was thought to be seditious and banned. As the civil rights movement took off in the United States, and Africans sought to free themselves from colonialism, African Americans and Africans looked to each other for strategies, tactics, and methods to escape oppressive political systems.[62]

CHAPTER SIX

"My Africa, Motherland of
the Negro peoples!"

I n May 1935 the *Baltimore Afro American* reported on a parade
in Harlem, New York. Two thousand people marched to
the Abyssinian Baptist Church in protest of Italy's invasion
of Abyssinia (later Ethiopia). The crowd congregated in the
church to listen to a series of speakers read poems, press for a boy-
cott of Italian American businesses, and urge support for Ethiopia
and its citizens. I. Alleyn of the Workers Forum passionately declared that "when a man in Abyssinia is struck by Italy, it is not that
one man alone who is hurt, but men in the British West Indies, in
America, and in every country where black men are found." Men
and women of African descent around the world were outraged by
Italy's aggression against Abyssinia.[1]

Alleyn voiced a sentiment shared by many of those crowded in
the church that day—that black America and Africa were intimately connected, largely because of the color of their skin. African
Americans saw their plight as inextricably linked with that of Africans and their struggle for liberation. This belief was sustained
until Africans gained independence from colonial rule.

From the 1930s to the 1950s African Americans agitated, advocated, and spoke out on behalf of Africa and its people. During the

Cold War, as the United States began to see the continent's importance, African Americans played a leading role in the new relationship between Africa and the United States. In this era we can see
clear distinctions between African American interest, identification,
influence, and engagement with Africa. There were those who continued to identify with Africa as a source of their heritage and those
who sought to influence events on the continent, advocate on its
behalf, and help shape American policy toward it. As descendants of
Africa they frequently crafted a discourse positing themselves as
suitable consultants and advisers on African issues. However, by the
middle of the twentieth century the voice for Africa in the United
States was no longer solely an African American voice. Africans
were speaking for themselves.

By the early twentieth century European colonizers had consolidated their hold in Africa. Colonialism was characterized by
a racial domination similar to that which existed in the United
States. Strong elements of racism, cultural imposition, and economic exploitation marked the relationship between European colonizers and their African subjects. The historian Christopher Fyfe
has written cogently on racial rule in Africa, pointing out the use of
race as "political control." "Authority in colonial Africa," he observes, "was white authority, exercised through the presence of an
imputed white skin."[2]

Although Africans were a majority in the colonies, they were
subordinated and their resources exploited under the guise of European superiority. African subjects had very limited access to education, although missionaries often set up schools to educate them in
the ways of Christianity. Consequently, there was a small literate
African population in many colonies. Mostly male, literate Africans
had acquired at least a secondary school education, which allowed
them to hold minor positions within colonial structures. But there
were few secondary schools in colonial Africa before the First
World War, leaving many colonies without qualified and skilled
workers. White rule was firmly established in African colonies,
excluding Africans from more than clerical positions. With some exceptions, Europeans were typically hired to hold certain positions
within colonial governments. Hard to attract, these people were ex-
pensive, induced to come to Africa with the promise of high salaries,

subsidized housing, and frequent leave and opportunities to travel. The few Africans qualified to hold these positions resented their marginalization and began to push for change. The 1920s saw colonial governments put more emphasis on education, and by the 1930s they recognized the need for higher education of colonial subjects. Those Africans who could not wait for these developments often made their way to Europe and the United States to gain an education.[3]

The period between the two world wars was the beginning of a nascent nationalism in African colonies. In the 1920s and 1930s local organizations for self-help and improvement were formed in African colonies to protest colonial injustices and inequities. A newly educated class of Africans found work as interpreters, clerks, clergy, teachers, and businessmen. This group would launch an early form of nationalism. Early African nationalists, while not seriously questioning the colonial project or pushing for an end to colonial rule, nevertheless questioned European disregard for their achievements. They were gradualists who used a moderate rhetoric, asking not for an end to imperial rule but for inclusion in the running of their societies, for injustices to be redressed, and for the abuses of colonial rule to stop. Typically, these men had been educated in missionary schools, in colonial metropoles, or in the United States. They were cosmopolitan and inter-regional in their views and values. This educated elite often identified as British or French Africans rather than as members of a tribe or a particular ethnicity. Pan-Africanist in their outlook, they were often the direct products of the colonial system. Many of them took Western names, wore European clothing, and emulated their colonial masters in other ways. Those educated in the United States drew on their American experiences to craft their anticolonial language and strategies. Those who returned to Africa became examples of how to engage their colonial rulers and succeeded in effecting change.[4]

The Italian invasion of Ethiopia angered women and men of African descent throughout the world. As one of only two independent nations in Africa, Ethiopia "represented a potent symbol of African defiance in the face of imperialism and of a renascent Africa."[5] Although Liberia remained independent, its close relationship with the United States made it, to all intents and purposes, if not a colony, then very dependent on the larger nation. Furthermore, in the late 1920s a damning report implicated Americo-Liberian settlers in the use of indigenous Africans as forced labor on rubber plantations and accused them of participating in what was tantamount to slavery by shipping Africans to the Spanish island of Fernando Pó. These accusations soured African American attitudes toward that nation.[6]

Abyssinia, on the other hand, was a Christian kingdom dating back centuries, governed by Africans, and jealous of its sovereignty. African Americans could take pride in the fact that Ethiopia did not fit the typical European stereotype of savage Africa. Italy had long tried to colonize the kingdom but failed in the face of African resistance. Early in 1896 the Ethiopians had fought off Italian attempts to annex their territory. Haile Selassie's coronation as emperor in 1930 also caught the attention of blacks around the world as they watched an African crowned the head of a self-governing African empire.[7] When Italy invaded Abyssinia once again, Africans and African Americans spoke out against this affront to the nation's sovereignty.

The African American press reported extensively on the ensuing war between Italy and Ethiopia. Activists organized demonstrations and protest marches such as the one in Harlem. All over the country organizations helped raise funds for the Ethiopian cause. The Pan-African Reconstruction Association, the International African Progressive Association, the Detroit Committee for the Aid of Ethiopia, and the Association for Ethiopian Independence all raised money. Rallies were organized by groups like the Negro World Alliance in Chicago, the Provisional Committee for the Defense of Ethiopia in New York, and the Ethiopian Relief League in Miami. Black leaders and academics like Ralph Bunche and Leo Hansberry of Howard University formed the Ethiopian Research Council in 1934; the Medical Committee for the Defense of Ethiopia sent medical supplies to the African nation.

Black Americans boycotted Italian American businesses and individuals volunteered to fight in the Ethiopian army. Hubert Julian and John Robinson served as pilots for Emperor Haile Selassie, who years later would acknowledge the contributions of African Americans: "We can never forget the help Ethiopia received from

Negro Americans during the crisis. . . . It moved me to know that Americans of African descent did not abandon their embattled brothers, but stood by us."[8]

At the same time that African Americans spoke out against European occupation of Africa, they pushed for changes within their own communities. Many began to understand their experience in broader and more global terms, seeing parallels between their situation and that of African-descended people worldwide. Black Americans connected Ethiopia's plight with that of the larger African world, and many saw a direct correlation between their situation and events in Ethiopia. An extract from the *Daily Worker* illustrates how some black Americans understood this act of aggression. A strongly worded editorial declared that "the struggle against the projected rape of Abyssinia is inextricably linked with the fight against war and fascism for Negro liberation, for the national independence of the peoples of Africa and the West Indies, for unconditional equality of the Negro people everywhere and for self-determination for the Negro majorities in the Southern Black Belt territories of the United States." The NAACP weighed in, noting, "When all is said and done, the struggles of the Abyssinians is fundamentally a part of the struggle of the black race the world over for national freedom, economic, political and racial emancipation."[9]

African Americans from all walks of life spoke out against Italy's aggression even as they faced similar assaults at home. The enthusiastic response and support of black Americans prompted the editor of the *Chicago Defender* to worry about whether African Americans were losing sight of the need to concentrate on struggles at home. In an editorial he cautioned, "Don't do it, young men and women. There is too much for you to do at home" and wondered if "you suppose your conditions are better than those of the warriors of Ethiopia?" Mrs. Wimley Thompson of New Mexico responded, asking, "Don't we owe them something?" She thought so: "One must remember that we didn't come to this country on our own accord, so why should we battle for something we will never receive? Justice. Ethiopia is our country and as long as there is blood in our veins we should love and respect it as such." She condemned the treatment of black Americans and called on their support for Ethiopia, concluding that "Ethiopia may some day prove to be a place for our future children." Mrs. Thompson clearly recognized that the violence against Africans in Ethiopia warranted as much resistance as the unfair conditions faced by black Americans.[10]

These responses to the invasion of Ethiopia, connecting the predicament of blacks globally, can be characterized as a strand of black internationalism. This idea or movement is described by one scholar as "an insurgent political culture emerging in response to slavery, colonialism, and white imperialism," centered on "visions of freedom and liberation movements among African descended people worldwide. It captures their efforts to forge transnational collaborations and solidarities with other people of color."[11] Black internationalist sensibilities generated activism on the part of women and men of African descent in Africa, Europe, and the Americas into the 1940s and 1950s. In the United States black Americans were particularly sensitive to oppression and discrimination.

African Americans had, after all, entered the twentieth century disenfranchised and subject to increased violence. Though slavery had been abolished, the actual bondage of black Americans continued in the face of discriminatory legislation and practice. Most white Americans believed they were superior to blacks and "the Southern way had become the American way."[12]

Between 1930 and 1950 African Americans experienced many changes. In the South Jim Crow laws hampered their progress, and racial terror, lynching, and other forms of intimidation continued to define their daily lives. Although rapid industrialization had broadened opportunities for many, black people were still regarded as second-class citizens in Northern cities. They faced discrimination in public housing, employment, public accommodations, public transportation, and the workplace. Although strides had been made in the courts, white prejudice and the weight of tradition perpetuated segregation.[13] American blacks who had been in the United States for several generations identified with values shaped by the dominant culture of white America. Many accepted that they were Americans and gave little thought to identifying with Africa.

W. E. B. Du Bois, fresh from the Pan-African conferences, understood this state of affairs. He wrote that young black Americans did not think of themselves as anything other than American. "It is impossible," he wrote, "for that boy to think of himself as African, simply because he happens to be black. He is an American." Yet, Du Bois added, African Americans were a "peculiar sort of American." Because of discrimination, prejudice, and economic hardship, they would be drawn "nearer to the dark people outside of America" than they would to white Americans. He called for people of African descent in the United States and elsewhere to dispel stereotypes they had of each other. Although large numbers of the black population did not or could not identify with Africa, they could still get involved with African issues and advocate on its behalf. Although they may not have been interested in Africa as a potential homeland, many black American citizens recognized that their ancestry impacted their lives. Indeed, a small number continued the practice of linking themselves with Africa and African issues.[14]

Writers and artists during the Harlem Renaissance took up Du Bois's challenge. They embraced Africa, although not always based on accurate knowledge. In this era Americans, black and white, developed a "fascination with the exotic and the primitive."[15] "New Negroes" in the Harlem Renaissance sought to broaden African American conceptions of Africa. As they delved into racial themes, they interrogated what it meant to be black in the United States. In answering this question, they often turned to Africa and its past, one that was frequently romanticized, with emperors, kings, and queens, idyllic landscapes, and welcoming, friendly people. It was in this context that Countee Cullen penned his rumination in "Heritage," idealizing the link between African Americans and Africa. Other writers also explored ways to incorporate African elements and themes in their art and writing. Some were encouraged to do so by white benefactors and sponsors who wanted a particular image of Africa presented.[16]

This movement, often called the New Negro movement or the Harlem Renaissance, served to reverse some of the negative ideas associated with Africa. Writers such as Langston Hughes and Zora Neale Hurston, among others, tried to understand the African roots of their heritage. Langston Hughes carried on an extensive correspondence with Africans, especially writers, and first traveled to the continent in 1923. Hughes struggled to understand his tie to Africa. Throughout his life he would cultivate and develop relationships with Africans. Zora Neale Hurston used anthropology as a lens to explore Africa and studied African cultural retentions in the American South, where vestiges of African worldviews and cultural forms remained. Historian Leo Hansberry, the philosopher Alain Locke, and other scholars presented diverse perspectives on Africa to students at black colleges and universities, allowing them to embrace a positive identity.[17]

Locke, a professor at Howard University between the 1920s and 1950s, mentored African students at Howard, including Nnamdi Azikiwe, the future president of Nigeria. A key figure in the Harlem Renaissance, he urged greater study and understanding of Africa and promoted increased contact between Africans and African Americans. In 1924, urging African Americans to take more interest in Africa, he wrote: "With notable exceptions, our interest in Africa has heretofore been sporadic, sentimental and unpractical. . . . The time has come . . . to see Africa, at least with the interest of the rest of the world, if not indeed with a keener, more favored regard." He believed that "eventually all peoples exhibit the homing instinct and turn back physically or mentally, hopefully and helpfully, to the land of their origin. And we American Negroes in this respect cannot, will not be an exception."[18]

Howard history professor Rayford Logan also mentored African students, publishing books on Africa and its relationship to African Americans and the world. Another Howard professor, Alphaeus Hunton, became a strong advocate for the continent. When a young African American asked why he should be concerned with Africa "when we as a minority group catch hell in this country," Hunton responded:

> First, we have to be concerned with the oppression of our Negro brothers in Africa for the very same reason that we here in New York or in any other state in the Union have to be concerned with the plight of our brothers in Tennessee, Mississippi or Alabama. If you say that what goes on in the United States is one thing, quite different from what goes on in the West Indies, Africa or anywhere else affecting black people, the answer is, then you are wrong. Racial oppression and exploitation have a universal pattern, and

whether they occur in South Africa, Mississippi or New Jersey, they must be exposed and fought as part of a world-wide system of oppression, the fountain-head of which is today among the reactionary and fascist-minded ruling circles of white America. Jim-Crowism, colonialism and imperialism are not separate enemies, but a single enemy with different faces and different forms. If you are genuinely opposed to Jim-Crowism in America, you must be genuinely opposed to the colonial, imperialist enslavement of our brothers in other lands.[19]

Hunton would later settle in Africa.

In the interwar years African Americans developed a new regard for Africa in the face of emerging nationalist movements that liberated most of the continent from colonialism. By the end of the Second World War a new group of African nationalists, more impatient and less tolerant of colonial policies, had emerged. Educated in colonial schools established after the Phelps Stokes report, they pushed for greater participation in their own affairs, for more rapid changes, and for eventual decolonization. Many of them had attended black American colleges.

As African Americans fought for their own civil rights, they drew parallels between their struggle and that of Africans fighting for independence. Black Americans formed organizations and groups purporting to speak for Africa and Africans, similar to ones that had existed before. The difference was that by midcentury Africans were challenging the status quo on their own behalf, demanding a place at the table.

Throughout the centuries, as we have seen, some African Americans were afraid of embracing this heritage, seeing it as a threat to their acceptance, inclusion, and integration in American society. Even while some black Americans presented Africa positively, it was equally marked as tribal, exotic, and idyllic. Africa was still an imagined space for many, but one that was becoming real to some black Americans. In the twentieth century some African Americans traveled to the continent, taking it upon themselves to champion African causes in the face of negative representations. Ralph Bunche took a trip to South Africa and East Africa in late

1937 and early 1938. His diaries are rich with observations on African American and Africa connections.

Langston Hughes expressed joy when he arrived in Africa: "And finally, when I saw the dust-green hills in the sunlight, something took hold of me inside. My Africa, Motherland of the Negro peoples! And me a Negro! Africa! The real thing, to be touched and seen, not merely read about in a book." Yet even then he could not resist the romanticized notion of the continent. As his ship sailed down the West African coast, in words reminiscent of Cullen's musings, he reflected: "It was more like the Africa I had dreamed about. Wild and lovely, the people dark and beautiful, the palm trees tall, the sun bright, and the rivers deep. The great Africa of my dreams."[20] By glorifying the African past, writers like Hughes hoped to create positive association and identity for black Americans. Yet they recognized, as Cullen did, that they were more American than African. Thus Langston Hughes mused: "I was only an American Negro who had lived the surface of Africa and the rhythms of Africa, but I was not Africa. I was Chicago and Kansas City and Broadway and Harlem."[21]

For most black Americans, the continent was an unknown. What they knew of it continued to be filtered through negative depictions in popular culture. Some resented claims of their connections and obligations to Africa. When the virulently racist Senator Bilbo (D-MS) promoted sending African Americans "back to Africa" as a solution to the race problem, African Americans responded with derision. The NAACP published a vocal criticism, citing the words of its Savannah, Georgia, president, Dr. Ralph Mark Gilbert: "Africa is no more the fatherland of the present generation of Negroes than of Anglo-Saxons. Unless your plan is to make a resettlement so as to include peoples of various racial stocks instead of singling the Negro out, I am afraid our people will not get the point. We have no objection to any Negroes who wish to go to Liberia or Egypt or France or Brazil, or any other country to settle, in going ahead and doing it. But, we do not feel that the U.S. Government should single us out to give us help in returning to a land from whence we have never come and concerning which we know nothing by personal contact."[22]

In the 1930s and 1940s African Americans challenged discrimination and disfranchisement with a view to shaping the "representation of black people in American society."[23] This required that they revise the dominant portrayals of Africa as backward, savage, and incapable of self-government. In these two decades images of Africa were still largely derived from narratives of missionaries and explorers and, more and more, from representations in film. In this era "jungle" movies presenting Africans as subservient, obsequious, meek, and cowardly were popular. Films like *Tarzan the Ape Man* (1932), *Sanders of the River* (1935), and *Stanley and Livingstone* (1939), among others, contributed to racist modes of thinking.[24]

Perhaps the most vociferous voice for Africa at that time was that of noted singer, actor, athlete, and activist Paul Robeson. Robeson starred in movies with African settings, often portraying stereotypical versions of Africa and Africans, although he imbued them with dignity. In *Sanders of the River* he was cast in the unflattering role of an obedient and good African in a colonial space who later rejects the civilizing influence of Europeans. The film portrayed the character, once he had abandoned the European way of life, as a savage despot. Such representations in film served to distance African Americans from the continent the way accounts by missionaries and explorers had in the nineteenth century. Robeson, who became an active member of the Communist Party, later disowned the film, criticizing it for justifying imperialism and for showing Africans in a negative light. Although there were other African Americans speaking on behalf of the continent, Robeson, educated at Rutgers University, where he was an All American football player, was one of the loudest and most famous. W. E. B. Du Bois and Carter G. Woodson also continued to study and write about Africa in this period. In fact, Du Bois, who shared many of Robeson's political affiliations, was influential in Robeson's deep interest in Africa, and the men maintained a forty-year friendship.

Paul Robeson became interested in Africa early in his life, but his passionate advocacy began when he lived in England. Years later he would recollect: "I 'discovered' Africa in London. That discovery—back in the Twenties—profoundly influenced my life. Like most of Africa's children in America, I had known little about the land of our fathers."[25] In London Robeson encountered students from the colonies, gleaning a variety of perspectives from the continent. Meeting men like Nnamdi Azikiwe, Jomo Kenyatta, and

Kwame Nkrumah, who would go on to lead independent African nations, he became proud of his connection to the continent. Robeson's passionate fight for civil rights undoubtedly influenced the African struggle for independence. Throughout his life he urged African Americans to learn more about Africa and look to it for inspiration. Although not an advocate of emigration, Robeson believed African Americans had strong ties to the continent and that their future lay in Africa. "For myself," he proclaimed, "I belong to Africa; if I am not there in body, I am there in spirit."[26] The actor traveled to Africa for the first time in 1937—ironically to Egypt rather than sub-Saharan Africa, in order to film a movie.

In 1937, along with Max Yergan, Du Bois, and Alphaeus Hunton, Robeson founded the Council on African Affairs (CAA), becoming the organization's chairman. Max Yergan, educated at Shaw University in North Carolina, went to Africa in 1916 under the auspices of the YMCA. He spent two years in Tanganyika and fifteen years in South Africa. While he worked for the YMCA, Yergan also became politically active, working with black South Africans. Upon his return to the United States he became involved with the Council on African Affairs.[27] Hunton left his position at Howard University to concentrate full-time on his activism and work with the CAA. Many of the organization's members had an abiding interest in Africa, believing the continent and its people needed uplift and liberation from European dominance.

Centered in Harlem, New York, the Council on African Affairs' major purpose was to support anticolonial struggles in Africa, with its stated mission to serve the "interests of the peoples of Africa." Throughout its existence (it dissolved in 1955), the CAA drew attention to African issues. It especially condemned apartheid and racial segregation in South Africa, no doubt because it saw parallels between that country and the American South. The CAA counted many prominent African Americans among its members and supporters. E. Franklin Frazier, Ralph Bunche, Mary McLeod Bethune, Rayford Logan, and Adam Clayton Powell Jr. were among its prominent members. CAA members supported the organization's goal of ending colonialism in Africa.

The CAA's monthly newsletter, *New Africa*, published in-depth human-interest stories and news from the continent. The group was a conduit between Africans and Americans, raising money to assist African students facing financial difficulties in the United States. Most important, the organization took as its major function "providing Americans with the TRUTH about Africa." Given the lack of knowledge and prejudices persisting among Americans, this was no small task. Furthermore, many of its members knew little of the continent. Nonetheless, they advocated strongly on its behalf. In a 1945 fund-raising letter, Robeson proclaimed that "the need in Africa is to free its millions from political and economic handicaps, some expressions of which are poverty, illiteracy, insufficient hospitals, and barriers to cultural development. The task is to bring the need strongly enough before the American people and their representatives."[28] The Council on African Affairs, he stressed, had been doing just that.

Throughout the 1940s and 1950s Robeson championed African causes even as he continued to work in the arts. In 1952, accused of being a Communist, he was put under FBI surveillance and had his passport seized. His American critics tried to discredit him among Africans. The Russians used him for propaganda purposes to personify how American blacks suffered from racial persecution, which they presumably implied did not exist in Russia. Regardless of how others sought to use him for their own purposes Robeson was focused on black emancipation. Robeson and his family lived in Europe for many years and upon returning to the United States he continued his activism on behalf of African Americans and Africans.

No less than her husband, Eslanda Robeson was a staunch advocate for Africa. She preceded her more famous husband to Africa, traveling to East and Southern Africa with their young son Pauli in 1936. Ten years later she published *African Journey*, a chronicle of the months she spent on the continent doing research for her anthropology degree. She acknowledged her African roots, expressing her long-held desire to visit the continent: "I wanted to go to Africa. . . . Africa was the place we Negroes came from originally." Like the many American immigrants who, when they could, visited their original homelands, "I remember wanting very much to see my 'old country.' "[29] Observing the lack of interest in Africa in the United States, Eslanda, like her husband, acknowledged that living in England had raised her awareness of African issues. She identified with the continent, serving, like her nineteenth-century predecessors, as a vindicator for Africa and its people.

She argued that merely recognizing one's ancestry was not enough. Long before widespread usage of "African American" as a designation for black Americans, Eslanda Robeson mused on its use. "The term African American," she wrote, "can provide then only an artificial sense of homeland or nationality, for Africa is not a nation but a huge heterogeneous continent." She recognized that the "Africa" of her childhood was an "imagined community." In *African Journey* she meditated on many aspects of the communities she visited, illuminating their diversity and difference, even commenting on the strangeness of some of the customs. This was a firsthand view of Africans in their own milieu. She voiced her opinion on the need for education in Africa, arguing for the benefits and advancement this would bring. Most of all she articulated the idea that Africa was coming into its own. In the postwar period, "the people of the world will have to consider the *people of Africa.*" "Africans," she concluded her book, "are people."[30] This was an idea that bore repeating in the United States, despite growing knowledge about the continent. Eslanda would return to Africa in 1946 and again in 1958 for the All Africa People's Conference in the wake of Ghana's independence. In 1953 the House Un-American Activities Committee (HUAC) questioned Robeson about her books. She defended her patriotism and expressed her pride in being Paul Robeson's wife. Her commitment to Africa did not prevent her from embracing America.

Forced to engage with Africa in multidimensional ways, African Americans sought different paths. The assortment of views historically characterizing African American attitudes to Africa persisted. Some, like the Robesons, chose to identify with the continent and its people. Others rejected any notion of an affinity to it. Though not identifying strongly with Africa or expressing any desire to connect in any way with the continent, they still believed in the right of Africans to self-determination. The noted sociologist E. Franklin Frazier, for example, had long argued that the experience of slavery had eradicated the African cultural heritage in African American life and culture. He maintained that there were few African antecedents in the structure of the black family in America, believing that

Eslanda Goode Robeson speaking at an Africa Women's Day gathering, n.d. (Photographs and Prints Division. Schomburg Center for Research in Black Culture, The New York Public Library, Astor, Lenox and Tilden Foundations. New York Public Library Digital Collections.)

"memories of the homeland were effaced, and what they retained of African ways and conceptions of life ceased to have meaning in the new environment."[31] Yet even he recognized the integral connections between the fate of Africa and African Americans. Along with Rayford Logan he pushed for African studies programs at Howard University.

As the Cold War intensified, black Americans went to great pains to show loyalty to the United States, wary of embracing anything that might call their patriotism into question. Unfortunately, cries against colonialism were often construed as disloyalty or split loyalty. More and more African Americans eschewed anticolonialism. Yet even those who believed their attention and energies should be focused on the plight of African Americans allied themselves with the anticolonial movement. Men and women in the labor movement, for instance, saw commonalities between their issues and those of Africans. A. Philip Randolph and Maida Springer best exemplify this.

Yevette Richards has shown how Springer's work with the international labor movement brought her into contact with African labor leaders in the 1950s. Working closely with Randolph, they promoted Pan-African labor struggles and were defenders of nationalist and labor movements on the continent. Springer, she notes, "expressed longing to visit Africa."[32] She was able to do so in 1953. In 1959 she also worked in Tanzania and Kenya. A. Philip Randolph, though largely focused on labor issues in the United States, also spoke out against colonialism in Africa. He corresponded with African labor leaders and helped develop labor movements on the continent. Randolph piloted an American Federation of Labor and Congress of Industrial Organizations' (AFL-CIO) program to train African labor leaders.[33]

By the 1950s activism on behalf of Africa had given way to a more conservative and cautious approach toward the anticolonial struggle and identification with Africa. Where in the past disparate groups had agreed on the issue of colonialism, engaging in anticolonial activity, a split now occurred. A strong anti-Communist strand also emerged in the rhetoric of some black leaders as they distanced themselves from African issues. Many turned to support American foreign policy, which often meant backing European colonial powers. Fearing accusations of disloyalty to their country, some backed away from active engagement with issues putting them in conflict with the U.S. government. Hesitant to criticize their government and its policies, black Americans embraced their American identity. The CAA soon dissolved over conflicts between members like Robeson and Du Bois, who continued to link African and African American problems, and others, including Max Yergan, who became more conservative. Yergan turned against the group around 1948.[34]

The NAACP, which under Du Bois's leadership had linked the plight of blacks globally, now increasingly focused on American concerns. "Negroes are American," Walter White of the NAACP asserted. In 1956 Kwame Nkrumah criticized the NAACP for being "exclusively concerned" with race policies domestically, at the expense of a broader vision for black liberation. Recently the historian Carol Anderson has made a case that the NAACP, contrary to Nkrumah's criticism, was in fact very much engaged with African issues. Although this was indeed the case, this commitment was, arguably, part of a larger agenda of anticolonialism worldwide. Nonetheless, nascent African nations recognized their debt to the organization. In 1959, on the occasion of the NAACP's fiftieth anniversary, Nnamdi Azikiwe, once a student at Lincoln and Howard, expressed his gratitude for its influence:

> The NAACP has been an inspiration to me and to my colleagues who have struggled in these past years in order to strengthen the cause of democracy and revive the stature of man in my country. As a student in this country from 1925–1934, I had the opportunity of being fed with my American cousins what Claude McKay called the "bread of bitterness." But I have also had the unique honour of sharing with these underprivileged God's own children the challenge to conquer man-made barriers and to forge ahead to the stars, "in spite of handicaps." This spirit of the American Negro, as exemplified in the constitutional struggles of the NAACP, has borne fruits of victory in the course of the years. It has given the United States a fair chance of reconciling the theory of democracy with its practice in America. It has also fired the imagination of the sleeping African giant, who is now waking up and taking his rightful place in the comity of Nations. What a glorious victory for the American Negro![35]

For leaders of the NAACP who sought to be included in U.S. foreign policy decisions, Africa seemed a logical pathway. Many African Americans embraced anti-Communism in a bid to show their patriotism, highlighting the differences between African Americans and Africans. They often became the accepted and acceptable spokespeople for black Americans as they shaped the discussion of Africa and anticolonialism. African Americans had become more demanding of the rights due to them and wanted to have a greater voice in discussions of America's relationship with Africa. While some black Americans distanced themselves from Africa, others took advantage of a new strand of interest in Africa emerging in the 1940s and 1950s. Even as African American identification with Africa diminished, the U.S. government and other mainstream organizations turned their gaze toward the continent. It became a foreign policy focus as the American government, within the context of the Cold War, found it had strategic interests in some parts of the continent.

Greater interest in African resources prompted funding of organizations that could produce knowledge of the continent. Organizations such as the American Committee on Africa (ACOA), founded by the white American George Houser in 1953, attracted black members. ACOA was a national organization founded to support the liberation struggle against colonialism and apartheid. It emerged out of a smaller organization, Americans for South African Resistance (AFSAR), which had formed to support the Campaign of Defiance against Unjust Laws spearheaded by the African National Congress (ANC). Other black-led organizations also emerged in this era. African American luminaries like Springer and Randolph were members.[36]

As always, black Americans tried to speak for Africa. In April 1954 the Council on African Affairs held a "Working Conference in support of African Liberation" at the Friendship Baptist Church in New York City. W. E. B. Du Bois and Alphaeus Hunton were included in the roster of speakers. Long before the anti-apartheid movement of the 1970s and 1980s, participants at the conference called for protest against racial injustice in South Africa. They drew parallels between lynching in the United States and the exploitation of black South Africans, condemned the brutality of the South African government in its response to striking miners, and criticized the pass laws system that restricted the movement of blacks. The treatment of Africans in "native reserves" was highlighted as horrendous, and the CAA pledged to send money to help "starving Africans." Among the resolutions at the conference was a call for protests at the South African embassy in Washington, DC, and a decision to urge President Harry Truman and other officials to protest discrimination.[37]

Some African Americans at this time posited themselves as experts on African issues, history, and "problems," and policy makers with growing interests in Africa often called upon them. Perhaps for the first time we see the rise of a class of black American "consultants" on Africa, men and women turned to for their knowledge of the continent. Although in smaller circles a less visible and vocal group of African Americans continued to promote the idea of Africa as diverse, there was a general disinterest in Africa and its people. There was less coverage of Africa in the black press. Reporting was scanty and presented the continent as exotic.

Yet more than ever African Americans were traveling to Africa. Claude Barnett, founder of the Associated Negro Press (ANP) in 1919, engaged extensively with Africa. Barnett and his wife, the actress and singer Etta Moten, traveled to West Africa in 1947, visiting Liberia, Sierra Leone, Nigeria, and the Gold Coast under the auspices of the Phelps Stokes Fund. In explaining the reason for the Barnetts' trip, Channing Tobias of Phelps Stokes observed that "with Mr. Barnett's access to a large number of publications in the United States, it is believed that the knowledge which he may gain of the people of West Africa, their conditions and aspirations, etc., will enable him to present a statement to the American public which will improve their understanding of West Africa. Also he should be able to give a picture of the American people and institutions which may be helpful to the people of Africa."[38]

On their return the Barnetts wrote "A West African Journey," in which they chronicled their experiences in West Africa. In Liberia they visited the Booker Washington Institute. Among those they met in Sierra Leone were individuals with American connections: Adelaide Casely Hayford, the "distinguished and cultural elder citizen" who had visited the United States in the 1920s, along with some of her Easmon relatives, S. M. Broderick and Solomon Caulker, who had studied in the United States and were both now at Fourah Bay College. The Barnetts were met at the airport by Caulker, who had received his degree in education from the University of Chicago in 1945, and his wife, Olive, "an American girl, daughter of Dr. E. A Selby of Nashville." Olive had met her husband at the University of Chicago, where she received her master's degree in education. In this union between an African and an African American, the couple saw great potential: "The romance which developed on the campus blossomed into marriage and these two fine young people are now both members of the faculty of Fourah Bay College in Freetown."³⁹

Claude Barnett was impressed by the West African press, which he described as "almost totally organs of protest." Azikiwe's newspaper in particular was labeled an agitator. In Nigeria Barnett met Mbonu Ojike, who had received his degree from Chicago in 1945 and was now a devotee of Nnamdi Azikiwe, serving as the general manager of the *Zik Papers*, a reference to the newspaper started by Azikiwe. Barnett also met Prince Nwafor Orizu, "another American trained Ibo," a founding member of the African Students Association now back in his homeland.⁴⁰ Upon his return Orizu started a scholarship program to send Nigerian students to the United States. Like Ojike, he admired his fellow American-trained leader Azikiwe.

Although they were invited to events where whites mingled with Africans in the colonies, the Barnetts also saw examples of segregation (the hospitals in Accra and the whites-only YMCA). They observed that the mixed-company events were those where "people wanted to let their hair down and the topic of conversation was 'the race problem.'" Africans were interested in African American life and experiences and questioned Mr. and Mrs. Barnett about lynching. They expressed hope that black Americans would make a contribution to the "upward progress of Africans."⁴¹

On the return trip Barnett met with Creech Jones, British secretary of state for the colonies, who "reacted favorably toward the idea of using American Negro teachers in West Africa." He followed up with a letter to W.E.F. Ward, the deputy adviser in education at the Colonial Office, expressing the idea of promoting African American teachers and missionaries in Africa who, he argued, would be helpful in explaining Africa to Americans. He asked for more information on Africa and stressed the need for training more Africans at institutions like Tuskegee and Hampton. Barnett believed that Africans would be receptive to African Americans in this role, declaring: "Finally, the growth of interest on the part of American Negroes in Africans and of Africans in their kin across the sea through such a program, could prove a most helpful and useful relationship during the years to come. Such an achievement would pay big dividends in the development of understanding, progress and good will."[42] Claude Barnett maintained ties to the continent, visiting several times over the next decade or two. Those who had direct experience with the continent strove to present it as diverse, modern, and progressive. The growing number of Africans living in the United States supported this image.

There was a small but vocal group of Africans in the United States who considered themselves equipped to be spokespeople for Africa. Increasingly, Africans began to speak on African issues, form groups, push for greater attention to Africa, and call for changes in their homeland. In the 1940s and 1950s more Africans were studying in the United States, engaging with African Americans and sharing their history and culture. Housing discrimination meant they could not find living spaces in nonblack neighborhoods. African students often lived with black American families in black neighborhoods. Harlem, for instance, served as a safe haven for black immigrants in the era of segregation. Africans created ties with African Americans in this milieu as they observed what life was like for people of African descent. Having rubbed shoulders with their African American classmates, landladies, and hosts, they learned firsthand of discrimination and segregation, and witnessed challenges to the status quo.

Some of the first leaders of independent African nations studied in the United States, often in black colleges and universities. Kwame Nkrumah of Ghana studied at Lincoln University; Nnamdi Azikiwe from Nigeria studied at Howard and Lincoln. In their autobiographies both men noted the great influence Lincoln and its black American students and faculty exerted on them. Hastings Banda from Malawi studied at Central State University, a historically black college in Ohio. All three went on to lead their countries at independence. Many others took leadership roles in nationalist movements and later in newly independent governments.

African students sometimes gave accounts of their African and American experiences and their observations on American life. Mbonu Ojike wrote *My Africa* and *I Have Two Countries*. The first was billed as a book in which "a Native Son tells the true story of Africa." The promotional pamphlet dramatically declared, "Africa speaks": "The truth about the 'Dark' Continent; the explosion of outmoded ideas of Africa as a sort of museum piece or zoo; a true

picture of the continent—a mixture of the primitive and modern—
but entirely contemporary with the rest of the world in hope, effort and aspiration toward peace and a co-operative security."[43]
Some students and visitors depicted the United States as hospitable
to Africans, but their observations of American life were not always
flattering.

A few women helped shape American views of the continent.
Female students showed African Americans a different side of Africa. In February 1945 the *Baltimore Afro-American* reported the
conclusion to the case of the "daughter of an African King." Princess Fatima Massaquoi won a lawsuit over who had the right to
publish her autobiography, begun as a class paper at Fisk University and completed in 1946 at Boston University. Fatima filed the
suit against parties at Fisk who, she argued, had appropriated her
work. The biography gave glimpses into Vai culture and customs,
as she understood them, describing childbirth beliefs, marriage
practices, and funeral and food customs. It was clearly directed at
an audience with stock images of Africa, and Fatima took pains to
present an Africa with cultures, civilizations, and values equal to
those of the West. Fatima's father, Momolu Massaquoi, had studied
at Central Tennessee University in 1892, becoming one of the first
Africans to study at American institutions. While in the United
States he was a frequent lecturer on Africa. Welcomed by African
Americans, many of whom were friends of her father, Fatima remarked upon the kindness she received from black Americans.

Yet stereotypes about Africa prevailed. Fatima poignantly
writes of her experiences of being portrayed as exotic. Those she
encountered sought to place her within a context of an Africa they
had imagined. One of the more disquieting episodes she describes
illustrates the beliefs African Americans had imbibed. When
Fatima arrived at Lane College, a historically black institution,
some of the female students, seeking to make the new girl from Africa feel welcome, painted their faces and decorated their hair with
feathers. Given the prevailing images of Africans abounding at the
time, they expected to see a young woman just snatched out of the
wilderness. The "savage" turned out to be the poised, cosmopolitan, well-educated daughter of a diplomat, a young woman who
had been schooled in Germany, traveled widely in Europe, rubbed

shoulders with dignitaries, and spoke several languages. In her autobiography she hoped to give Americans a more realistic view of
her homeland. Explaining why she fought so hard for the rights to
her own story, Fatima told the *Afro American*, "My autobiography
is my soul and my heritage, and I couldn't go home to Liberia and
look my family in the face after selling my culture and heritage for
a mess of pottage."[44]

African students, though small in number, were forceful in
drawing attention to African issues. In fact, African students in the
United States had formed organizations as early as 1919 when
Simbini Nkomo organized a conference in Chicago.[45] Students
concerned with the welfare of their compatriots from all over the
continent founded the African Students Association in 1941. Its
student creators, John Karefa Smart from Sierra Leone and Prince
Nwafor Orizu from Nigeria, recognized that the war had made it
difficult for many to get financial aid from families back home. The
group came together as a source of support for students in the
United States and as a resource on Africa and African concerns.

The African Academy of Arts and Research, designed to teach
Americans about Africa, was an offshoot of the student association.
The academy published a monthly newsletter with articles directed
at Africans on the continent and news about international events
affecting them. The organization frequently put out pieces meant
to inform its members of their duty to the continent. These young
men and women helped shape American views of Africa, although
they more often than not reinforced stereotypes of the continent by
making sweeping generalizations. Wherever possible they strove to
illustrate Africa's diversity, but recognized that Americans were
largely ignorant of the continent and its diverse populations. For
example, the author of the academy's February 1942 newsletter
made a point of clarifying his use of the term *Africa* as an "ideologi-
cal whole, as the symbol, the concentration, the whole dimensional
range of all his best wishes, dreams, and hopes. He means the continent—home, the fatherland. Mother Africa."[46] This explanation
would hardly have clarified how heterogeneous Africa was.

Arguably, African students in the 1940s used the term *African*
much as African Americans had for centuries, symbolically to embrace the continent of their ancestors. The students were clear that

each of them used it denote his or her specific place of origin on the continent: "And what is so incomprehensible about the thought of an African visualizing the whole of Africa, while really talking about Nigerian schools or about chieftaincy in Basutoland? Does Maine speak for Mississippi, even though both believe in an American ideal termed democracy?"[47] The organization embraced a Pan-African ideal of African unity while indicating to American readers the continent's diversity. American interest in Africa surged after the Second World War, and the various organizations with an Africa focus looked to African students for expertise on their countries. The African Studies Association and the African Academy of Arts and Research provided that knowledge base, and continental Africans increasingly became the voice of Africa. Called upon to give their views on the continent's readiness for independence, many spoke out against colonialism and lobbied for U.S. involvement.

Africans who had studied in American universities returned with nationalist fervor, politicized and pushing for change. As independence movements took off in African colonies, leaders of nationalist parties often reached out to African Americans for support. Interaction between the two groups intensified as they sought a closer relationship. In 1958, for example, the New York chapter of the National Negro Business League, an organization founded by Booker T. Washington in 1900, invited Madam Ella Koblo Gulama, a member of Parliament and paramount chief from Sierra Leone, to provide "the first opportunity for business people in our community to hear about economic development in Sierra Leone, one of the several countries of Africa now readying itself for self-government."[48] Indeed, the small but active Sierra Leonean population in New York celebrated when the country finally gained independence in 1961. The Sierra Leone Society of Greater New York and Vicinity put together an independence celebration, highlighting the country and its potential. The souvenir journal, complete with pictures, maps, and advertisements, also showcased the musician Babatunde Olatunji and his "drums of passion," calling for readers to "come on a safe safari to musical Africa." Mrs. Gulama, upon arrival, noted her interest in seeing "how Negroes live in the United States," and in observing the "development of the relationship between the races."[49]

Artists and musicians were often instrumental in shaping American views of the continent and its people. Babatunde Olatunji (mentioned in Bob Dylan's 1963 song "I Shall Be Free") performed and gave lectures and demonstrations of African music. The Sierra Leonean Asadata Dafora Horton, long resident in the United States, influenced American understanding of the musical and dance traditions of "Africa." Dafora, son of an illustrious Sierra Leonean family, had come to the United States to study in the 1920s. Abandoning his graduate career, he began his life as an artist in 1934 when he performed his first "African Dance Drama," *Kykonkor,* in New York. Receiving rave reviews, the play established Dafora as a preeminent translator of African dance and culture to an American public. He would continue to perform for more than thirty years, traveling across the country with his version of African dance and drama.

An early member of the African Academy of Arts and Research, Dafora was featured on the cover of its informational brochure when the academy hosted its first big event, an African Dance Festival, at Carnegie Hall in December 1943. He collaborated extensively with African American artists, including them in his productions. Among the artists he worked with were Esther Rolle, later known for her role as Florida Evans on the television series *Good Times,* and Pearl Primus, the African American choreographer. When Nkrumah visited the United States in 1958, Dafora put on a performance of his famous play *Zunguru,* described as a "native African Dance Drama" at the United Mutual Auditorium on Lenox Avenue in New York City. Among those featured were Babatunde Olatunji and Rolle.[50]

Recognizing that popular culture was an important avenue through which Americans could understand the continent, the academy focused on dance and music. It garnered support from and established relationships with key African American figures such as Mary McLeod Bethune, one of the festival's major patrons, along with Eleanor Roosevelt and several prominent black American sponsors, including Walter White of the NAACP. Alain Locke also served as an officer of the academy. Kingsley Ozuomba Mbadiwe, the founder and president of the academy, wrote frequently to Bethune, apprising her of events and initiatives. In a letter thanking her for her

Dancer and choreographer Asadata Dafora with Musu Esami (Frances Atkins),
as the bridegroom and bride, in his dance-musical production Kykunkor, *1934.*
(Photographs and Prints Division. Schomburg Center for Research in Black
Culture, The New York Public Library, Astor, Lenox and Tilden Foundations.
New York Public Library Digital Collections.)

support of the festival, Mbadiwe reminded Mrs. Bethune of the deep connections between African Americans and Africa, stressing Africa's need for African American support: "We cannot do these things alone, we must draw spiritual energy from our sons and daughters who though many generations removed, but still wear that badge." Mbadiwe reminded Bethune of the speech she had made at Carnegie Hall asserting her relationship with Africa: "You can well remember your speech at Carnegie Hall when you said 'I did not know that this day will come, but here I stand saying without apology that the queenly blood of Africa runs through my veins.'"[51]

Mary McLeod Bethune had always expressed pride in her African ancestry and shown interest in the continent. Her desire to help Africa and Africans, Paula Giddings has explained, "was inspired both by religion and by a special feeling regarding her heritage." She tried unsuccessfully to go to Africa, soon recognizing that her "primary mission was in America."[52] Bethune remained engaged with African issues, donating money and time to the cause of the academy and other initiatives. She received many letters from African students requesting her help and sending her information on what was going on in their countries.

In 1950 Bethune was asked to be on the advisory board of a proposed college in the Gold Coast. The "Afro-College" was to be supported by "Americans of African Descent." Resonant of Booker T. Washington's philosophy, it would provide a curriculum adapted to the needs of Africans, with less stress on classical education and more on vocational and technical skills. It called for an improvement in the education of girls. The proponents of the Afro-College, complaining that Africans educated in the United States were marginalized upon their return, hoped the college would use them to greater effect to "correct those mistakes which the present West African educators have made." Such an institution would have African and African American faculty, be led by an African president, and would "bridge the gap between the American Negro and the African."[53]

In 1954 Bethune was asked to be a board member of the African Cultural Society, whose focus was on education and culture with the aim of promoting goodwill and friendship between Africans and Americans. The society's motto, "To know each other—to

learn from each other—to understand each other," must have resonated with her. Bethune expressed her continuing regard for the
continent and its people by noting in the margins of the letter, and
in her response to the invitation: "I am much interested in Africa."[54]

Africans on the continent communicated frequently with African Americans, asking for help, urging cooperation and unity. Henrietta Peters, headmistress of the West African Industrial Academy
in the Gold Coast, wrote to Sallie Wyatt Stewart, who succeeded
Mary McLeod Bethune as president of the National Association of
Colored Women, asking for collaboration. She informed Stewart
that the West African Women's Union had been formed and asked
for a "proper person to instruct us." All the union's members were
Africans, but "our membership will include any women of African
descent resident in West Africa, if more foreign-born women of colour come to our coast." Peters asked for literature and material to
be sent to her organization "for our women to study the activities of
the women in America that it may inspire these here." She also
asked for information on more African American organizations with
which to correspond. Africans on the continent, who for centuries
had kept abreast of the activities of African Americans, were now
able to directly communicate with them more frequently.[55]

African American academics and intellectuals also wrote extensively about Africa in this era. Scholarly writing about the continent
proliferated in the American academy. Although many of those writing about the continent were white Americans, black American academics also took the mantle of writing about Africa. Elliott Skinner,
St. Clair Drake, and John Henrik Clarke, among others, sought to
shape a positive narrative of the continent. As we have seen, there
was a long tradition of African American intellectuals like Du Bois
and Woodson producing scholarship on Africa, challenging the idea
of Africa as a "Dark Continent."[56]

The 1950s and 1960s saw greater African American engagement
with Africa as the civil rights movement in the United States paral-
leled liberation struggles in Africa. James Meriwether has illustrated
quite persuasively how African nationalist movements influenced
black Americans, shaping the discourse on civil rights. African Americans often drew their government's attention to the fact that while
black American citizens continued to live under discrimination and

segregation, their counterparts in Africa were achieving gains under colonialism. Sometimes to get this point across they resorted to negative representations of the continent. There was a return, in some quarters, to depicting Africa as primitive, with some arguing that Africans were not ready for independence. This was the view of George McCray of Chicago, who argued that although Africans sought Westernization and inclusion in their own affairs, they were not ready for self-government. He believed Europeans should stay on the continent for a while longer and that Africans should be told about black American achievements. "I think American Negroes," he ruminated, "can do a great deal on behalf of a sound African point of view."[57]

Africans, however, did not wait on African Americans to seize their freedom. Many of the young men and women who had studied in the United States and returned to Africa were frequently at the forefront of movements demanding changes, however gradual. Joined by compatriots on the continent who had been challenging colonialism on the ground, the nationalist movement gained ground. By the mid-1950s it was clear that colonialism was on the wane in Africa. As Africa gained its independence, black Americans had to figure out the nature of the relationship they would have with the continent's new nation-states.[58]

CHAPTER SEVEN

"I wanted to see this Africa"

In 1953, on the eve of Ghana's independence, the black American novelist Richard Wright reflected on a version of Countee Cullen's question. When someone suggested he visit the continent, Wright incredulously responded, "Africa?" He went on to muse: "'Africa!' I repeated the word to myself, then paused as something strange and disturbing stirred slowly in the depths of me. I am African! I'm of African descent." Like Cullen, Wright pondered his relationship to the continent. He felt a kinship, he admitted, "yet I'd never seen Africa; I'd never really known any Africans; I'd hardly ever thought of Africa."[1] Despite these misgivings, Richard Wright made the journey. During his eleven-day stay in what was still the Gold Coast, Wright commented on its strangeness, the naked bodies and bare-breasted women, the mud huts, the poverty, and the landscape. He expressed surprise that Ghanaians did not disfigure their bodies, practice female circumcision, or manifest any of the barbaric traditions he had been led to believe were prevalent on the continent. He also pointed out the cultural similarities, or lack thereof, he saw between African Americans and Africans. The writer reflected on the slave trade and slavery, including African complicity in its perpetuation.[2]

Wright's aim in visiting Ghana was to see the continent first-hand and to get answers to questions that, as an African American, he had asked about his relationship to the land of his ancestors: "I wanted to see this Africa that was posing such acute questions for me and was conjuring up in my mind notions of the fabulous and remote: heat, jungle, rain, strange place names like Cape Coast, Elmina, Accra, Kumasi. . . . I wanted to see the crumbling slave castles where my ancestors had lain panting in hot despair. The more I thought of it, the more excited I became, and yet I could not rid myself of a vague sense of disquiet."[3] At once exoticizing and denigrating the continent, Wright, like Cullen, had formed his view of Africa from prevailing stereotypes. Wright's 1940 novel *Native Son* had briefly featured Africa. The book's protagonist Bigger Thomas goes to the movie *Trader Horn* where he "saw pictures of naked black men and women whirling in wild dances and heard drums beating."[4] The way the continent is represented in the film epitomized the negative images African Americans were exposed to. *Trader Horn* came out in 1931, and a trailer for the film billed it as "the most amazing and the greatest adventure picture of all time" that "reveals the long hidden secrets of the Dark Continent." The plot featured a white adventurer and trader searching for the long-lost daughter of a missionary in the jungle. In Africa they encounter wild animals—lions, elephants, leopards, and crocodiles. But even "more dangerous than the herds of animals are the hordes of blood-thirsty cannibals," the trailer informs. The film's representation of Africans as savage, cruel, and wild buttressed many of the prevailing misrepresentations of the continent and its people.

It is safe to say that Richard Wright had encountered many images of the continent like the ones portrayed in the movie. Once on the Gold Coast, however, Wright amended some, if not all, of his preconceptions. He wrote of his encounter with Kwame Nkrumah, who became the leader of an independent Ghana. He observed first-hand the birth of an independent African nation, led by someone with black skin. Whatever assumptions he might have had before arriving in the Gold Coast were quickly dispelled. In opposition to the argument made by European colonizers that Africans could not govern themselves, Wright's *Black Power* illustrated African capacity and capability. His interest in Africa reflected a growing awareness on the part of African Americans that Africans, in achieving liberation from white domination, did not need a guiding hand from African

Richard Wright, June 23, 1939. Photograph by Carl Van Vechten.
(Library of Congress, Prints and Photographs Division.
From Wikimedia Commons/Public Domain.)

Americans. They were the leaders in shedding the yoke of white
domination, so to speak.[5]

By the 1960s and 1970s a new shift occurred in the relationship
between African Americans and the continent. In the 1960s black
Americans struggled to reconcile the real issues facing new African
countries with their imagined idea of the continent, often a difficult task. No longer were African Americans the vanguard in the
struggle for African liberation. African nations, now independent,

were dealing as equals with Europe and the United States. African Americans, although they had made great strides, were still fighting for equality and civil rights.

When Ghana gained its independence in 1957, civil rights legislation outlawing racial discrimination and giving African Americans voting rights had yet to be passed. That year federal troops had to be deployed in Little Rock, Arkansas, to protect nine black children attempting to desegregate a public high school. Africans were now the leaders in the quest to attain freedom and equality. Ghana's independence led the path to widespread decolonization in Africa. By 1965, the year the Voting Rights Act was passed in the United States, most African countries had gained independence from European colonialism.[6]

Yet even as African countries became self-governing, stock images of their backwardness pervaded American thought. Despite this, leaders of new African nations often caught the attention and stoked the pride of black Americans. So it was that the scholar St. Clair Drake began a piece he wrote in 1967 with the epigraph "Africa, Mother of Us All." Drake went on to say that although Africa was indeed the origin of humanity, for black Americans the continent was special:

> But, Africa is Mother Africa to 18,000,000 Americans in a very special sense—Mother, whether they recognize her as such or not,—for, by law and custom in this country, anyone known to have any African ancestors is considered a "person of African descent." Identification with Africa is forced upon those called "Negro" whether they like it or not. In the words of the old spiritual, "There's no hiding place down here." A few Negroes reject the African identification completely and vehemently. A few Negroes adopt the African identification joyously and enthusiastically. Most American Negroes just take it for granted and are ambivalent about it—sometimes feeling ashamed over what they feel are embarrassments from being identified with a people who have been looked down upon and ridiculed for over 400 years; sometimes feeling very proud about people like Lumumba and Kenyatta; and usually being very interested and curious

about African music and dancing, and always having a
feeling that these are our "kinfolks," "our people"—even
"our brothers."[7]

For centuries African Americans struggled with their duality, or
"double consciousness," recognizing their link to Africa but understanding that they were too far removed from it to claim any
meaningful relationship. But as St. Clair Drake so eloquently observed, the connection was there. In Ghana, Wright's certainty that
he was not, in fact, African was confirmed. Even so, the author acknowledged his ties to the place. Echoing earlier writers, he wrote
that his desire to visit Africa was largely due to his ancestry.

Wright's ties with the continent, like those of the millions of
African Americans who had ended up in the United States, originated in slavery. This made him ambivalent about his relationship
to Africa—indeed, he comments on the dualism felt by African
Americans: "The American Negro's passionate identification with
America stemmed from two considerations: first, it was a natural
part of his assimilation of Americanism; second, so long had Africa
been described as something shameful, barbaric, a land in which
one went about naked, a land in which his ancestors had sold their
kith and kin as slaves—so long had he heard all this that he wanted
to disassociate himself in his mind from all such realities."[8] Because
of these feelings he had an interest in and identified with Africa,
but he recognized that he was not of it. Richard Wright's assessment of Africa was shared by many of his contemporaries.

This was certainly true of Pauli Murray, who came to embrace
her Americanness with all its faults during her time in Ghana. A lawyer and writer, Murray lived in Ghana in 1960. There, encountering
criticism of the United States and its treatment of black Americans,
she found herself defending American values. Murray reflected on
Cullen's question, and over time "she found herself given increasingly hostile answers." After seven months in Africa she remarked: "I
am not African and have little feeling of kinship with things African
per se." Yet she did not reject her African ancestry; calling for white
Americans to accept her "as an American, as a Negro," she also insisted that they "respect my African background."[9] If nothing else,
her time in Ghana allowed her to recognize her roots.

Pauli Murray, July 5, 2007.
(Carolina Digital Library and Archives, UNC University Library. Accessed
*8 April 2011. http://dc.lib.unc.edu/cdm4/item_viewer.php?CISOROOT=/vir_*
museum&CISOPTR=431. Carolina Digital Library and Archives [Creative
Commons License; Attribution-ShareAlike 2.0 Generic (CC BY-SA 2.0)].)

Murray remained engaged with African issues long after she left the continent. Many years later in an interview, when asked about her love for America, she responded: "Well, I mean by saying that 'I love America,' that first, it is home. No one can be more native to America than America's black population, because America's black population biologically is all of the great streams of mankind that make up America. The first American, the indigenous American, by this time there has been so much recirculation of genes that we are all mixed up. We all have Indian, European and African ancestry. Secondly, traditionally, black Americans go back to the very beginnings of America. Our blood and our sweat and our tears and our memories are built into the country and I maintain that Africa has already made her contribution to America, that America is as she is today, culturally, because of the presence of black Americans. The impact upon speech, the impact upon customs in the South.

America would have been a different country without the presence of blacks."[10] Murray was expressing the sentiment of African Americans before her, like David Walker and Frederick Douglass. It is clear from this interview that despite her criticism of some African leaders, she remained engaged with the continent and its people.

By the middle of the twentieth century blacks, with their long history in the United States, were more American than African. Even so, they were not accepted as full citizens, and this continued rejection ensured that their gaze would occasionally stray to Africa, especially during moments of crisis. Wright's observations were made on the eve of the Gold Coast's independence from British colonialism. Kwame Nkrumah was poised to take over the reins of government, changing the name of the new nation to Ghana after the medieval empire that had flourished many centuries before. A region long dominated by trade relations between Africans and Europeans, the Gold Coast had sent millions of Africans across the Atlantic into slavery in the Americas. Trading forts like Elmina and Cape Coast along the West African coastline provided storage space and prisons for the many African men and women who would end up on ships bound for enslavement. With the slave trade abolished, Britain moved to engage in "legitimate commerce" with rulers and traders in the region. When the continent was carved up at the end of the nineteenth century, Britain and France emerged as the colonial powers on the West African coast. The English-speaking West African countries serve as an example.

Early resistance had begun almost from the moment of colonization, as Africans rejected foreign domination. The nationalist movement emerging in the early twentieth century relied greatly on a vibrant press, which frequently published articles drawing comparisons between the plight of Africans in the Gold Coast and people of African descent elsewhere. In 1917 the *Gold Coast Leader* printed an invitation to Africans in the four British West African colonies (Nigeria, Gambia, Gold Coast, and Sierra Leone) to send delegates to a conference to discuss issues affecting colonial subjects. This conference resulted in the formation of the National Congress of British West Africa. No doubt influenced by Du Bois's Pan-African conferences, the gathering addressed issues of unity, greater participation of Africans in their own affairs, and an end to discrimination. Such activism laid the groundwork for more vocal nationalists like Nkrumah.[11]

Kwame Nkrumah, regarded by some as the father of an "Africanized" Pan-Africanism, was greatly influenced by his time in the United States and by the African American civil rights struggle. Nkrumah, as we know, had studied in the United States and been involved in the Pan-African movement. He championed the rights of African workers and peasants to reclaim their independence and advocated the use of force if necessary. Nkrumah also urged Africans not to look to outside powers for support, arguing that foreign economic and political forces eroded their values. Nonetheless, he disagreed with the idea, promoted by some nationalist leaders, of returning to some sort of "African tradition." Rather, he called for a new African identity created out of Islam, Christianity, and indigenous cultures. In this vision he was clearly influenced by the diasporan blacks and African nationalists who had come before him. Nkrumah also urged Ghanaians to abandon strong ethnic and religious identities, simply identifying as black or African. He promoted a vision of a United States of Africa, making him popular among those influenced by the Pan-African philosophies of Du Bois and others and drawing the attention of African Americans.

Nkrumah played a prominent role at the Fifth Pan-African Congress held in Manchester, England, in 1945. This was the first of the conferences led by continental Africans, and the discussion about the struggle for independence focused on the African continent. Nkrumah had studied in the United States from 1935 to 1945, and had served as president of the African Students Association, conveying knowledge about Africa to Americans. As a student at the historically black Lincoln University, he befriended African Americans. During summers he worked alongside black Americans at a shipyard, attended and spoke at black churches, and lived in black American homes. In his autobiography he remembers his first girlfriend, an African American, his experiences of "religious gatherings and revivalist meetings," and preaching in black churches. He reminisced that in Philadelphia he "carried out an intensive survey of the Negro from a religious, social and economic standpoint," allowing him to understand the "racial problem in the United States."[12]

Consequently, he had an opportunity to observe firsthand the struggles of African-descended people in the United States. Thus a proud black American community heralded Nkrumah when he visited the United States in the wake of Ghana's independence in 1958. African American newspapers covered the visit widely, and Nkrumah met with black leaders. In Harlem, where he had lived while a student, "people lined his parade route and greeted him with adulation."[13] Likewise, newspapers in the newly independent Ghana reported on the warm welcome their leader received in the United States, especially in New York City. *Ghana Today* reported that in Harlem Nkrumah received "one of the most remarkable receptions of the whole tour." The Harlem Lawyers' Association organized a reception where "he appeared before some 10,000 wildly cheering Negroes, several of them carrying placards reading: We Love Africa and We Want To Come Home."[14]

Prominent black Americans welcomed him, honoring him for the pride he instilled. Ralph Bunche, then at the United Nations, observed that the prime minister represented "all of us whose skins are pigmented." Bunche is quoted in *Ghana Today* as saying: "We salute you, Kwame Nkrumah, ... not only because you are the Prime Minister of Ghana, although this is cause enough. We salute you because you are a true and living representation of our hopes and ideals, of the determination we have to be accepted fully as equal beings, of the pride we have held and nurtured in our African origin. ... We embrace you because you and we are brothers." Among the many black Americans he met was thirteen-year-old George Miller from North Carolina, who had Nkrumah autograph his copy of the leader's autobiography.

Likewise, when the new leader of independent Guinea, Sekou Toure, made an official visit to the United States in 1959, he asked to visit Harlem. Once again crowds of African Americans came out to greet him. One news reporter remarked that it was "difficult picking out the Africans from the 125th Street Africans." Another described Toure as "handsome and apparently fireless. President Toure seemed to have thrived on his New York trip. Committed to a tight schedule, he has been at all times affable, charming, direct and cooperative. He was as attractive in 'American' garb as he was in his colorful ceremonial robes. And he carried with him at all times an aura of tremendous pride in his people, his race and his heritage. This, he has been able to communicate, to the great discomfort of many Americans."[15]

Both men served as a source of pride to African Americans still struggling to achieve equality. Toure and Nkrumah were symbols of black potential and examples of the capacity of African-descended people given a chance to govern themselves. Likewise, African Americans took an interest in liberation struggles in Kenya and Congo, with the charismatic Jomo Kenyatta and Patrice Lumumba leading the struggles. When Eslanda Robeson was asked to defend herself before the House Un-American Activities Committee, she was working on an article on the "Mau Mau" resistance movement in Kenya, and balked at having to interrupt her work: "I resent interference with my work and my life. I can now [illegible] back home to finish the article on Mau Mau," she wrote.[16] Lumumba, the handsome young nationalist leader from the Congo, visited the United States in 1960 to secure assistance with negotiating peace in the Congo. Among the many people he met was a young African American woman, Yvonne Reed (later Seon), who went to Congo to work for the new prime minister.[17]

Lumumba was murdered a year later, engendering protests around the world. African Americans responded to his death with protests in front of the United Nations. The rally drew crowds of African Americans, who linked Lumumba's death with their own struggle. In an article entitled "UN Riot Symbol of Black Unrest," the *Chicago Defender* reported on the large numbers of demonstrators. James Hicks, a black journalist interviewed for the piece, clearly tied the two struggles together: "But when I heard about Lumumba's killing, the first thing I thought about was Sheriff McCall down in Groveland, Fla. It was the same old story—a Negro killed while escaping. They are always escaping. To me, it was another lynching in the dead of night." In his view, "So far as the average American Negro is concerned, the whole Congo affair is a racial question not a political one."[18]

For their part, African nationalist leaders looked to African Americans for support in their struggles, recognizing the benefits of collaboration between Africans and African Americans. On the eve of Nigeria's independence, Nnamdi Azikiwe, lauding the

NAACP for its role as "one of the watch-dogs of the less privileged people," stated: "I am convinced that developments in my native land will do much to enhance the prestige of peoples of African descent who are scattered all over the world. Your kindness in inviting me to speak today underlines the basic community of feeling between coloured Americans and their brothers in Africa. We struggle towards the same ultimate objective: to revive the stature of man so that man's inhumanity to man shall cease. Your success shall be our success and your failure shall be our failure. In this basic unity lies the promise of great advancement for the black race throughout the entire world."[19]

As African countries gained independence, the new challenges they faced often shaped African American perceptions and influenced their engagement with the continent. So long accustomed to embracing an imagined "Africa," many found it difficult to identify with individual African countries. Furthermore, with the end of colonialism, the anticolonial activism that had characterized the relationship between African Americans and their African counterparts no longer seemed pertinent. In the aftermath of decolonization some black Americans sought roles as advisers and experts on Africa to the U.S. government. Some took a genuine interest in events unfolding in the new nations on the continent. As the U.S. government decided what its relationship would be with countries previously governed by European nations, African Americans came forward to serve as a resource, using their historic ties to the continent as credentials. As Brenda Gayle Plummer has noted, African American leaders sought to "project their own influences into the new relationship that Africans would have with the United States."[20]

As more African countries became independent, a new relationship developed between the United States and African countries. Indeed, the article on Sekou Toure's visit observed that "THOSE AMERICANS who are inclined to view Africa and its grasp for independence as just another fight that's going on in a faraway land are taking a second look at the 'dark continent.'"[21] Many African Americans reached out in various ways to new leaders of African nations. As they learned more about Africa and encountered men and women from the continent, debates about black cultural unity and unified political organization emerged.

During the 1960s much of black America's focus was on internal issues. In the late 1950s and early 1960s the civil rights struggle intensified. Often characterized as the Second Reconstruction, this era saw African Americans engaged in a struggle for self-determination, equal access, economic security, and voting rights, among other things. Scholars of the American experience have illustrated the diverse ways black Americans approached the struggle. Martin Luther King Jr. called for a nonviolent and peaceful movement. Many opposed this gradualist approach, calling for armed struggle. Malcolm X, and later young nationalist groups like the Black Panthers and the Student Nonviolent Coordinating Committee (SNCC), advocated the use of violence when necessary.

While Africa did not feature prominently in civil rights discourse, it could be found in the symbols and motifs of some of the nationalist groups that emerged in the 1960s. Some raised the continent up as an example of what liberation struggles could achieve, particularly armed movements. Others argued that if a less developed population in Africa could achieve independence, it was a travesty that African Americans remained unfree. So it was that the Reverend Douglas E. Moore of Durham, North Carolina, was quoted as saying in 1960: "The young Negro is embarrassed because the backward natives of Africa are standing up for freedom but we are moving so slowly here." The SNCC students, however, expressed it more positively: "If they can do it, so can we."[22] Others tied their experiences to that of Africans who had struggled for liberation and achieved it, even reaching out to newly independent nations on the continent. Furthermore, Africa served as a refuge to some radical African Americans in trouble with the American legal system, and as a haven for those who saw no future or chance of equality in the United States. As African countries gained independence, black Americans traveled more frequently to the continent.

Several African Americans attended Ghana's independence celebrations. Among the attendees were those who had maintained connections with Africa and African issues and others engaged in the civil rights movement. Many prominent American activists, politicians, and educators were present, including A. Philip Randolph, Ralph Bunche, Mordecai Johnson, Maida Springer, Horace Mann Bond, Congressman Charles Diggs Jr., and Congressman Adam

Clayton Powell Jr. Although Du Bois was denied a visa on the grounds that his "leftist views" posed a threat to the security of the United States, Martin Luther King Jr. attended.[23] Ghana became a symbol for the liberation of people of African descent worldwide, and African Americans used the country's independence to point out deficiencies in their own nation. As Kevin Gaines has argued, "Ghana stood as the realization of traditional African-American aspirations for African nationhood dating back to the origins of the Pan-African movement, Garveyism, and the Italian invasion of Ethiopia."[24] If Ghana could gain its freedom from British colonialism, surely African Americans could achieve equality in the United States. "The birth of this new nation," Martin Luther King Jr. remarked, "renewed my conviction in the ultimate triumph of justice."[25]

In the wake of Ghana's independence a number of African Americans settled there, attracted by its charismatic leader and hoping to escape American racism. They couched their migration in terms of helping to develop Ghana and finding a place where they could achieve total freedom and equality. Professional and blue-collar African Americans alike brought their skills to the new nation. Among those who moved to Ghana either temporarily or permanently were the writer Maya Angelou, novelist Julian Mayfield, art historian Sylvia Boone, and later W. E. B. Du Bois and his wife Shirley. Others, like the dentist Dr. Robert Lee and his family and plumbing contractor Lou Gardner, also chose Ghana as their home.[26]

Many young civil rights leaders and organizers looked to Africa's anticolonial successes for inspiration. As one scholar has noted, "Africa's sweep toward independence lifted the morale and strengthened the resolve of U.S. civil rights activists disappointed with legal victories that failed to transform day-to-day realities for black southerners."[27] The SNCC was one such group, and its members mobilized against indignities toward blacks in America and Africa. In 1960 members organized a conference with the Zambian nationalist leader Kenneth Kaunda as its main speaker. Members had also spoken out against the Sharpeville Massacre in South Africa where many blacks had been killed.

SNCC members James Forman, John Lewis, Julian Bond, and Dona Richards traveled to Guinea in 1964. Accompanying them was Fannie Lou Hamer, the dynamic civil rights leader and founder of the Mississippi Freedom Democratic Party. Guinean president Sekou Toure, who had been welcomed in Harlem several years before, hosted the group. The Americans took pride in being of African descent and were bowled over by a nation governed by Africans. Mrs. Hamer was especially impressed. Stokely Carmichael, the former SNCC and Black Panther member who would later take his name from Kwame Nkrumah and Sekou Toure, calling himself Kwame Toure, later recalled Fannie Lou Hamer's "elation and joy when she returned from Africa in 1964. Here was this daughter of Southern sharecroppers, speaking neither French nor any of the African languages yet talking on and on about how completely at home and connected she had felt. She had been thrilled and couldn't stop talking about black folks running things."[28] Likewise, SNCC organizer James Forman remembered that "the trip was a culmination of my life in several ways. Africa was a black continent; as our homeland, it had always been on my mind. I had also dreamed for years of helping to build an organization to achieve political power in the United States and then to relate it with one or more African countries for common revolutionary purposes."[29]

African Americans became interested in traveling to newly independent African nations as a tourist destination. Freddye and Jacob Henderson opened the African Travel Agency to encourage African Americans to visit the continent. They chartered the plane that flew many of the prominent black Americans attending Ghana's independence ceremony in 1957. In March 1962 *Ebony* magazine published "Travel—The New Status Symbol," pointing to Africa as a "travel goal" for black Americans. The article remarked on the new interest in travel among African Americans and the boon to the tourist industry. "Africa is calling," one paragraph began, continuing, "Negro Americans, proud that the land of their fathers is coming of age, are flying to the continent to attend independence celebrations and anniversaries."[30]

Young African American men and women sought these ties with Africa and Africans during the 1960s with the aim not of going "back to Africa" but of building networks and organizations. Upon their return from Africa, SNCC leaders set about developing the African Bureau within the organization. Dona Richards took responsibility for the Africa Project to educate members about

Africa. The goal, she maintained, was to "make the long overdue link between the struggle for self-determination of Black people abroad and the struggle of Black people in United States against exploitation."[31] Part of the project was also to lobby the U.S. government for economic sanctions against South Africa's apartheid regime.

In the wake of decolonization African Americans sustained an interest in the continent and its affairs. Meriwether has argued that in the late 1950s and early 1960s African Americans saw Africa "as their special foreign policy concern," which afforded them an opportunity to illustrate their expertise and connection to the continent.[32] Many acted in an advisory capacity to the U.S. government as it interacted with newly independent nations in Africa. Some organizations, such as the American Society of African Culture (AMSAC), founded in 1957, promoted cultural exchange and awareness between Africans and African Americans, in the process educating Americans about Africa and exposing black Americans to their African heritage. The organization published the journal *African Forum*, which informed Americans about African issues.

The many Africa-related interest groups emerging in this era posited themselves as experts as they continued to engage with African issues. In December 1958 many prominent black Americans attended the All Africa Conference in Ghana. Among those in attendance were Congressman Charles Diggs Jr. (Detroit), the journalist Claude Barnett, Horace Mann Bond, president of AMSAC, political scientist Mercer Cook, and civil rights activist John Davis of AMSAC. Also at the conference were labor activist Maida Springer of the AFL-CIO, Robert Keith of the African American Institute, Eslanda Robeson, Shirley Graham Du Bois, Alphaeus Hunton, and James Lawson of the United African Nationalist Movement, a remnant of Garveyism. These groups and individuals occupied different parts of the political spectrum, but their concern for Africa was a common interest. Two years later, on a visit to New York for a United Nations meeting, Nkrumah attended a rally in Harlem organized by black nationalists. Among them was Malcolm X of the Nation of Islam; he would visit Ghana a few years later.

In 1962 AMSAC hosted a festival in Lagos, Nigeria, drawing prominent black Americans such as the writer Langston Hughes,

Horace Bond, the dancer Geoffrey Holder, the singer Odetta, and the actor Brock Peters. One attendee is said to have exclaimed upon disembarking the airplane, "Well it only took about 300 years, but we're back home at last."[33] Civil rights activists, both prominent and lesser known, also visited Africa in the wake of decolonization. Black American expatriates in Ghana welcomed Malcolm X in 1964.[34] Bob Moses and his wife Dona Richards eventually settled in Tanzania, another attractive destination for African American expatriates in the wake of decolonization. Alphaeus Hunton, active for many years with the Council on African Affairs, eventually settled in Africa, first in Guinea, then in Ghana. Some African Americans sought refuge in newly independent countries in the aftermath of civil disobedience. Peter O'Neal from Kansas City, Missouri, fled to Tanzania with his wife Charlotte in 1970 after a 1969 conviction for gun possession. He settled in the East African country, becoming an active member of the community, later establishing the United African American Community Center.

African American experiences in Africa were not always as romantic as people had imagined they would be, as Wright's rumination shows. American blacks faced adjustment problems. They were not always welcomed with open arms by Africans, and sometimes were viewed with suspicion. Maya Angelou writes poignantly about her need to be accepted fully as an African, only to recognize that she could never be. In the end Angelou conceded that "it seemed that I had gotten all Africa had to give me." She wrote in romantic words of what the continent had given to her: "I had seen the African moon grow red as fire over the black hills at Aburi and listened to African priests implore God in rhythm and voices which carried me back to Calvary Baptist Church in San Francisco. If the heart of Africa still remained allusive, my search for it had brought me closer to understanding myself and other human beings." In the end Angelou recognized that although Africa had been the homeland of her ancestors and had welcomed her for a time, her home was in the United States: "My mind was made up. I would go back to the United States as soon as possible."[35]

Perhaps no one in the twentieth century could answer Countee Cullen's question and explicate the connection to Africa more lyrically than Angelou. Explaining what her time in Ghana had done

for her, she writes: "I had not consciously come to Ghana to find
the roots of my beginnings, but I had continually and accidentally
tripped over them or fallen upon them in my everyday life. Once I
had been taken for Bambara, and cared for by other Africans as
they would care for a Bambara woman. . . . And here in my last
days in Africa, descendants of a pillaged past saw their history in
my face and heard their ancestors speak through my voice. . . . Despite the murders, rapes and suicides, we had survived. The middle
passage and the auction block had not erased us. Not humiliations
nor lynchings, individual cruelties nor collective oppression had
been able to eradicate us from the earth. We had come through despite our own ignorance and gullibility, and the ignorance and ra-
pacious greed of our assailants. There was much to cry for, much
to mourn, but in my heart I felt exalted knowing there was much
to celebrate."[36]

Unlike many of the nineteenth-century settlers going to Liberia, later emigrants had the choice to return, and many did so, expressing hope for a better future in the United States. In contrast to
earlier emigration movements that occurred "during periods of
conservative retrenchment, when prospects for black citizenship
seemed bleakest," the 1960s was a "period of political resurgence."[37]
Those who migrated to Africa, therefore, left a country on the
brink of significant civil rights gains. While many of these expatriates, including Angelou, would return to the United States, their
experience in Africa had changed them. Living for a time in countries with large or all-black populations gave them a sense of pride
in their heritage. Thus Maya Angelou penned an ode to Africa,
chronicling the suffering and enslavement of its people, but ending
hopefully with its liberation:

> Now she is rising
> remember her pain
> remember the losses
> her screams loud and vain
> remember her riches
> her history slain
> now she is striding
> although she has lain.

In contrast, her vision of America, in a poem with that title, was bleaker: "The gold of her promise / has never been mined."[38]

Many former expatriates became radicalized politically, continuing to champion African issues even as they looked to concerns affecting African Americans at home. Women often advocated for women's issues as they pointed out gender discrepancies within the civil rights struggles and criticized the marginalization of women in many organizations. Other African American activists back in the United States championed African issues. In 1962 the American Negro Leadership Conference (ANCLA) drew prominent African Americans from diverse backgrounds and political inclinations to raise awareness of issues and events in Africa and to influence their country's policy toward the continent.[39]

In September 1972 the African Liberation Support Committee (ALSC) was formed at a conference in Detroit. A black activist organization supporting a Pan-Africanist philosophy emerged in the wake of the first African Liberation Day (ALD), held on May 27, 1972, which drew black activists in the United States and Canada to show support for African liberation struggles.[40] AMSAC stopped operations in 1969, but other organizations with interests in Africa continued to draw attention to the continent. The Cultural Association for Women of African Heritage, which counted among its members Maya Angelou, actress and singer Abbey Lincoln, and writer Rosa Guy, staged a protest at the United Nations after Patrice Lumumba was murdered.

The tenor of black Americans' relationship to Africa in the late 1960s and early 1970s changed as the strong identification that had characterized earlier relationships often became an interested engagement—that is, while not necessarily interested in embracing Africa as a homeland, they recognized the continent as part of their history, and for that reason showed interest in Africa and its people. A small corps of African Americans in the foreign policy arena and in government continued to push the U.S. government on African issues. In 1976 the Black Leadership Conference, organized by the Congressional Black Caucus, concluded that there was a dearth of African Americans in high-level international affairs positions. They also argued that U.S. foreign policy generally neglected African and Caribbean issues. To solve the problem, the members of the caucus suggested the formation of a foreign policy advocacy organization.

Soon after this conference TransAfrica was born. Its first director and one of its founders, Randall Robinson, recalled: "The idea for TransAfrica grew out of the broadly recognized need for an institutional mechanism through which African-Americans could be informed, galvanized, and moved to a focused, thoughtful participation in the formulation of U.S. foreign policy toward Africa and the Caribbean. It would prove to be a difficult challenge. Americans (unfortunately including African-Americans) knew little about Africa and the Caribbean. They knew even less about their nation's tradition of shameful attitudes and actions in these areas, a tradition often belied by the much ballyhooed image of America as a beneficent, compassionate, and freedom-loving superpower." The organization was perhaps best known for its activism against the racist regime in South Africa and championing liberation for Namibia and Zimbabwe in the 1980s.[41] Robinson later wrote of his political action on behalf of Africa, chronicling African American interest in the continent during the 1970s. He notes, for example, the 1972 March on Washington organized by the African American Owusu Sadauki to protest U.S. policy in Southern Africa. Among the many speakers at the event was Congressman Diggs, long active in Congress as a spokesperson on behalf of Africa.[42]

Cold War politics framed African American engagement with Africa throughout the 1970s and 1980s. Those who continued to be engaged with Africa focused on political developments in Southern Africa, particularly the apartheid regime in South Africa. African Americans, seeing parallels between segregation as it had existed in their nation and South African apartheid, were often at the forefront of the movement to end this oppressive system.[43] African Americans like the Reverend Leon Sullivan lobbied the U.S. government to amend its policies toward the white-dominated South African government, and pressured American companies to divest their holdings in the country. The Reverend Sullivan is best known for his "Sullivan Principles," through which he worked cooperatively with American corporations in South Africa to improve their employment practices. Originally developed in 1977, the principles were intended to put economic pressure on South Africa to encourage it to end apartheid. They also provided guidelines for American companies doing business in South Africa, urging them to hire black South Africans and to work toward ending racial segregation. Artists and musicians boycotted the country, refusing to perform in segregated spaces in South Africa. Across the country, African American students also lobbied their universities to disinvest in the country.[44]

The images of Africa on American television screens included emaciated children dying of starvation, safari and wild animal reserves, violence, and apartheid. The mainstream media frequently portrayed African governments as incompetent, incapable of taking care of their populations and in need of outside assistance. These prevailing images galvanized Americans, black and white, into action. Celebrities once again took up the mantle of uplifting Africa. Although this was an interracial effort, black celebrities often took the lead. In 1985, for example, a group of singers came together to produce the song "We Are the World" in aid of famine relief in Ethiopia. The song was written by Michael Jackson and Lionel Ritchie, both African Americans, based on an idea from singer and activist Harry Belafonte, also of African descent. Returning from Africa in August 1985, Belafonte expressed his distress at the situation in Ethiopia: "'I dream about it every night,' he said softly. 'I still smell the camps, I taste them. I hear the moans.'" His organization, United Support of Artists for Africa (USA for Africa) attracted top names in the music industry. The singer charged the U.S. government with ignoring the famine because it was in Africa rather than Europe. Criticizing then President Ronald Reagan, he asked, "How often have you heard Ronald Reagan discuss that there will be 7 million deaths this year in Africa? ... Where on his agenda does Africa even equate, except in his own interest in supporting apartheid in South Africa?"[45] The organization has continued to support efforts to eradicate poverty and has raised $100 million to ease poverty in Africa and the United States.

Harry Belafonte and other African Americans championed the anti-apartheid movement of the late 1980s and early 1990s, although Belafonte's activism on South African issues dates back to the 1950s, when he was a national committee member of the American Committee on Africa (ACOA). In the 1960s he had met and recorded music with the exiled South African singer Miriam Makeba, further strengthening his commitment to the anti-apartheid cause. Often at the forefront of the movement, he challenged and shamed American companies and the U.S. government into ending their relationship with South Africa.[46]

In November 1984 activists staged a sit-in in front of the South African embassy in Washington, DC, sparking a protracted movement to dismantle the system of apartheid and free Nelson Mandela from prison. Threatening not to leave until their demands were met, prominent African Americans such as Randall Robinson, executive director of TransAfrica; Professor Mary Frances Berry, a U.S. Civil Rights commissioner; Congresswoman Eleanor Holmes Norton; and Congressman Walter Fauntroy participated in the demonstration. Some were arrested. Representatives later met with the South African ambassador in Washington, DC, to ask for the release of political prisoners, including Nelson Mandela, who had been imprisoned since 1964.

Out of this meeting the Free South Africa Movement emerged, led by the author Sylvia Hill. Hill was a founding member of the grassroots Southern African Support Project. In December 1984 a rally in Detroit called for support of those demonstrating in Washington and in support of trade unionists in the United States and South Africa. The flier for the event called for Americans to "resist this obnoxious system and demand the release of all prisoners and pressure the South African regime into ending its apartheid system." Among the many advertised speakers was Rosa Parks, billed as "Mother of the Civil Rights movement."[47] Prominent African Americans joined the cause, volunteering to be arrested as they staged civil disobedience. The movement inspired similar action across the country and the world, including on college campuses. Colleges and universities, urged on by their students and faculty members, began to slowly disinvest from companies doing business with South Africa, and corporations followed suit. The Anti-Apartheid Act of 1986 imposed economic sanctions against South Africa. Among the five conditions listed for ending sanctions was Nelson Mandela's release, which happened in 1990. Apartheid formally came to an end, culminating in his election to the presidency in 1994.

Nelson Mandela continued to be a symbol for African Americans until his death in 2014. He visited the United States and met with African Americans in South Africa. Oprah Winfrey has perhaps been most vocal about Mandela's influence in her life. In 2007 Winfrey opened the doors to the Oprah Winfrey Leadership Academy for Girls. Asked what motivated her to open a school for girls in South Africa, she replied: "The dream to build my school began with Nelson Mandela because of my love and respect for a man who spent 27 years in prison and became the first freely elected President of South Africa. He is a great citizen of the world. I was humbled by his humility."[48] Maya Angelou, who had first met Mandela in Egypt in 1962 before he was imprisoned and attended his presidential inauguration in 1994, wrote a poem in his honor when he died. "His Day Is Done," written "on behalf of the American people," paid tribute to Mandela's struggles for justice and the impact he had on the world.[49]

Yet even as political activism surrounding South Africa and its apartheid system intensified, old images of Africa remained. In the 1980s African Americans appropriated what they understood as African symbols and cultural elements. The kente cloth, often used as a sash by black college graduates, African fabrics used as head wraps or caps, and the map of Africa on chains and neckwear worn by hip-hop artists all demonstrated pride in African ancestry. Rap songs occasionally invoked Africa, and Afrocentric images often graced album covers and music videos. Arguably, this was part of a long tradition of incorporating Africa and African symbols into the art, music, and literature produced by black Americans. For centuries, after all, elements of African cultures had made their way into black American life.[50]

These representations and use of symbols were more often than not based on an imagined and often exaggerated idea of Africa. For example, the 1988 film *Coming to America* portrayed Africa and its people in stereotypical, albeit positive, ways. The story of a prince arriving in the United States disguised as a poor immigrant presented stock images of Africa and Africans. The film used tropes recognizable to American audiences to portray an African community, juxtaposing Western influences with imagined "African" customs. The royal family is dressed in Western clothes, while servants typically appear in "African" dress. The royal palace is depicted as modern, wealthy, and opulent, with Western furnishings and decorations, but dancers and entertainers are scantily clad with grass skirts. The song "Wimoweh," recognizable to many Americans, accompanies the opening scenes of the film. Bare-breasted women wait on Prince Akeem as servants play classical music on violins.

It was perhaps in this context that the playwright August Wilson, whose work chronicled the black experience in America during the twentieth century, observed: "There is an Africa in each of us that we have to get in touch with to understand our relationship to this society. . . . But all we have to do is to claim that part of ourselves which I think is the strongest part—our Africanism. It has nothing to do with putting on beads or dashikis. It's simply understanding who we are in the world, understanding our relationship to this society and claiming a responsibility for ourselves and our salvation instead of letting other people claim that for us."[51] Wilson, whose plays often highlighted the African elements of black American culture, frequently embraced the African part of his heritage, declaring, "We are African people. And we have a culture that's separate and distinct from the mainstream white American culture."[52]

This mix of pride and hesitation in engaging with Africa was reflected in what "African" causes African Americans chose to take up. The injustice of apartheid and famine on the continent were causes any American, black or white, could stand behind. Incompetent governments, military dictators, and corrupt politicians were less likely to engender expressions of ancestral ties. Furthermore, the 1980s and 1990s saw African economies go into crisis as national debts incurred in the 1970s and 1980s resulted in the World Bank and International Monetary Fund (IMF) imposing Structural Adjustment Programs that forced governments to cut back on services to their citizens. The global debt crisis impacted African nations as leaders struggled to provide health care, education, and even food to their populations. As indebted African countries struggled to maintain their economies, their citizens sought alternatives.

By the 1990s Africa was a net exporter of its wealth to Europe and North America, including what the economists call human capital. Taking a long view, one can argue that this net exporting of the continent's wealth dated back to the transatlantic slave trade. As Ger-

ald Horne has noted, Africans, "because of the devastation and inhumanity of the transatlantic slave trade were an early form of capital
itself."[53] Large numbers of Africans sought greener pastures in the
cities of Europe and the United States. Just as wealth was measured
in people in precolonial African societies, wealth was now being
exported in the form of professional and educated African citizens.

This "brain drain" from Africa produced large immigrant populations in the United States. Where once Africans who studied in the
United States returned to contribute to their nations' development,
by the 1980s they sought to stay. Between 1961 and 1980 the U.S.
Immigration and Naturalization Service recorded approximately
110,000 African immigrants, and nearly five times that number between 1981 and 2000.[54] African-born migrants numbered 363,819 in
1990. By 2005 African-born U.S. residents numbered a little over a
million.[55] In 2009, the Migration Policy Institute reported 1.5 million African-born immigrants in the United States. In 2015 there
were an estimated 2.1 million African immigrants in the United
States, making up about 4.8 percent of the immigrant population.[56]

The Immigration Reform and Control Act of 1986, the Diversity Visa Program ("the lottery") of the Immigration Act of 1990,
and the Refugee Resettlement Policies have boosted African immigration. Both skilled professionals and unskilled workers took advantage of these programs. Increasingly, Africans in the United
States seek to make their status legal. The Department of Homeland Security Office of Immigration statistics show that in 2002,
60,269 immigrants from Africa had acquired legal permanent residence status.[57]

African immigrants no longer settle exclusively in large urban
centers, where they are likely to live among black Americans, but
increasingly seek suburban and rural areas. Nonetheless, urban
areas remain important destinations for black populations, as they
did in earlier years when segregation prevented blacks, both native
and immigrant, from living in certain areas. These spaces allow African immigrants to create communities with black Americans.
Black immigrants recognize their minority status and the particu-
larities of race and ethnicity issues in the United States, frequently
choosing to settle either in areas with significant black populations
or in largely nonblack neighborhoods and communities. Black

migrants "face an entirely different set of issues [and] ... must reconstruct and redefine their identity in terms of the American society's system of race relations and hierarchies." Despite the lack of acceptance and the prevalence of racial stereotypes, some African immigrants prefer to settle among mixed or largely white populations. They often choose not to settle in African American neighborhoods, fearing it might hinder socioeconomic advancement and accelerate loss of ethnic identity.[58]

African immigrants are becoming more vocal, telling their own stories. The widespread success of the Nigerian novelist Chimamanda Adichie, particularly with the publication of the novel *Americanah*, is representative of this. Among other things, the book portrays the experience of a young immigrant woman as she comes to understand race in her interactions with black and white Americans. Ifemelu, the protagonist, records her observations in a series of blogs with titles like "Traveling while Black," "Job Vacancy in America—National Arbiter in Chief of 'Who Is Racist,'" "Is Obama Anything but Black?" and "Understanding America for the Non-American Black." Throughout the novel the character seeks to understand the experience of black Americans. Her black American lover Blaine is portrayed as equally sensitive, defensive, combative, and hopeful, while the young African woman recognizes that "there were things that existed for him that she could not penetrate." One scene in particular exemplifies those differences. An African American woman, commenting on Ifemelu's blog, argues that only an African could comfortably write as she does on issues of race: "Because she's African. She's writing from the outside. She doesn't really feel all the stuff she's writing about. It's all quaint and curious to her. So she can write it and get all these accolades and get invited to give talks. If she were African American, she'd just be labeled angry and shunned."[59] African Americans have recognized these differences, and it has sometimes resulted in tense relationships between the two groups.

The growing number of immigrants from Africa has led to debates and discussions about who can embrace the label "African American." After a few years in the United States, many African immigrants often refer to themselves as African Americans, much as Irish or Italian immigrants might attach "American" to their self-identity. American-born children of African migrants are more likely to identify themselves as African American (while acknowledging that their parents hail from a particular country in Africa). Settlement in black neighborhoods tends to increase their identity as African American. However, black immigrants who settle in areas with few African Americans are more likely to identify themselves ethnically rather than in racial terms. Thus, "blackness among Black immigrants in the African Diaspora is lived in many different ways. These include assimilation into African-American culture, adherence to an ethnic culture or choosing an 'immigrant identity.' "[60]

By creating an identity distinct from native-born African Americans, African immigrants hope that they are protecting their children from racialization in American society. While retaining some aspects of their cultural heritage, some Africans make a concerted effort to assimilate into American society, involving themselves in local politics, business, and professional sports (for example, basketball and football). Because most choose to settle in urban areas, they are more likely to be in close proximity to African Americans, resulting in some friction but also affording an opportunity for the groups to learn about each other, and in some instances to work together for both social and political causes.

Native-born blacks often perceive the black immigrant population as a threat or competition for jobs and other resources, resulting in cultural clashes and misunderstanding between Africans and African Americans. The two groups often have little cultural connection. Commonly claiming not to experience racism, African immigrants often believe that black American charges of discrimination leveled against the dominant society are exaggerated. However, when black immigrants experience racial discrimination themselves, they develop common interests with African Americans. More recently, efforts to recognize their commonalities have been made on both sides for mutual benefit and advancement. In June 2005, for instance, the African Catholic Ministry of the Roman Catholic Archdiocese in Indianapolis sponsored an event that brought together African Americans and Africans. A Celebration of the African Family Tree allowed both groups to learn about elements of each other's cultures and to recognize their common ancestry.[61] In cities across the country similar intiatives and events are occurring.

While it is true that at first Africans, like other immigrant groups, did not seek to challenge the status quo and were not necessarily politically active, in recent years African immigrants have championed political causes. In 1999, when Guinean immigrant Amadou Diallo was shot to death by New York City police officers, African immigrants joined African American groups in rallying and protesting the injustice. Likewise, African immigrants attempted to educate the African community regarding their rights in the United States. An African legal, human, and civil rights center was established in Washington, DC, in 1999 to educate and represent African immigrants. The center provides legal services to immigrants, aids Africans who find themselves homeless, and works with Africans seeking asylum in the United States.[62]

Formal organizations such as the Constituency for Africa (CFA) continue to serve as voices for the continent. Founded by the African American Melvin Foote, the CFA, like the Council on African Affairs in an earlier era, aims to "to educate Americans about Africa and African development issues." A former Peace Corps volunteer, Foote founded the organization in 1990 "to establish a network of organizations, groups and individuals committed to the progress and empowerment of Africa and African people worldwide. CFA's mission is to build public and private support for Africa, and to help shape a progressive U.S. policy towards Africa."[63] The significant African immigrant population in the United States has also contributed to this endeavor.

Cities across the United States are also reaching out to African immigrants. In 2006 the mayor of Washington, DC, and the city council established the Office on African Affairs in response to the calls of African activists. The Office on African Affairs provides "constituent services and information to African communities through programmatic activities and outreach materials; serves as a liaison between the African communities, District government agencies, and the Mayor; and provides briefings to the Mayor and District government agencies about the particular needs or interests of the African residents of the District of Columbia."[64] Citing the fast-growing population of African immigrants in the region, supporters highlighted the need for a service that would address issues of cultural isolation, inadequate resources, and lack of employment opportunities for Africans.[65] In September 2007 the office, co-sponsored by African businesses and other organizations, celebrated the contributions of African immigrants to the city with an event bringing together native Africans living in the Washington, DC, metropolitan area.

Despite greater integration into American society, African immigrants continue to maintain strong ties with their homelands, sending large-scale remittances back to the continent. Research shows that as the earning power of the diasporic Africans grows, the remittances increase. As the composition of the black population in the United States changes with the increasing number of African immigrants, Countee Cullen's question "What is Africa to me?" will be asked over and over again. The answer might have ramifications on larger issues such as allocation of resources (health, educational, social services), voting patterns, affirmative action, and many other policy issues.

On February 21, 2005, a *New York Times* headline proclaimed: "More Africans Enter U.S. Than in Days of Slavery." An earlier article revealed that "twice as many sub-Saharan Africans—about one million—have migrated to the United States in the last 30 years as during the entire era of the trans-Atlantic slave trade."[66] Interest in this large-scale migration by the *Times* and other news outlets indicates significant attention to the growing number of immigrants from Africa entering the United States. The phenomenon of African immigration has caught the attention of scholars, the media, and the public policy world. The "new" African immigration, one scholar noted, provides "a new interpretation of African-American history. . . . [The late twentieth and early twenty-first century black migration reveals] a new diversity, people coming with their languages, their cultures, their food."[67] By comparing this large African population to the native-born African American population, such pieces also have a potential for problematizing the relationship between African immigrants and African Americans, as discussions emerge about who can truly be defined as "African American," and what such a label signifies.

"We have this special bond.
We share a common loss."

When Barack Obama, a young senator from Illinois, threw his hat into the presidential race in 2008, there was a groundswell of support from different constituencies of African-descended populations all over the world. The Trinidadian Calypso singer Mighty Sparrow paid homage in song. Highlighting changes that would happen for the world with Obama's election, "Barack the Magnificent" posited the senator as a savior who would "stop the war, stop genocide in Darfur!" "No matter what," the singer urged, "get health care for who have not." Jamaican reggae artist Cocoa Tea implored: "African-American rise, And keep your eyes on the prize. 'Cause now none of them realize The black man is in their eyes." The African American Michael Franti sang an upbeat tune with Obama's own refrain of "Yes we can," exhorting listeners, "Remember, doesn't matter who you are, we are all one people." In Africa Zambian musicians Mutamula Mwale, Jay, Elijah, Mau, Sista D, Yvonne Mwale, Dambisa, Bee Man, Sebastian Mutale, and John Kabanga, inspired by Obama's words, came together to produce "Change We Can Believe." The Ghanaian Blakk Rasta's catchy refrain called listeners to "come make we talk about Barack Obama."[1]

Obama's campaign and election generated tremendous elation on the continent. His African father had, after all, studied in the United States, where he met his American wife. While Africans on the continent and black Americans in the United States touted him as the first African American president, dissenting voices proclaimed that Obama, while black, was not truly African American. During his campaign and subsequent election many Americans with ancestors who had been enslaved argued that Obama, a man with a white American mother and a Kenyan father, did not, and could not, represent their historical experiences. For him to be African American, they argued, his ancestors must have experienced the horrors of the slave trade and slavery.

Amid the euphoria of the first man of African descent elected president, few paid attention to such distinctions, but those opposing pronouncements raised an important issue regarding who is qualified to assume the label "African American." Running against Obama in a local election, Alan Keyes had declared: "Barack Obama and I have the same race—that is, physical characteristics. We are not from the same heritage. My ancestors toiled in slavery in this country. My consciousness, who I am as a person, has been shaped by my struggle, deeply emotional and deeply painful, with the reality of that heritage."[2] As we have seen, many black Americans eschew the term *African American* itself. Some saw support for Obama and his eventual election as another slap in the face. His parentage, many argued, seemed more palatable to white Americans than a black American's whose ancestors were formerly enslaved. Obama, after all, was raised largely by his white grandparents and had had little connection with his father. Nonetheless, he identified as a black American, and his wife, Michelle, was from the kind of background Keyes found acceptable. But for most African Americans, having the first black viable candidate for the White House overshadowed the desire or impulse to nitpick over Obama's heritage.

Notwithstanding the support Obama received from black Americans, the growing African immigrant population in the United States and the increasing number of African-descended people in the United States who are not directly tied to the country's history of slavery have prompted discussions about who can be authentically called "African American." It has provoked debates about affirmative action in college admissions and employment, access to privileges and social services, and raised questions as to whether or not African immigrants are entitled to the benefits and rewards of African American activism.

In the twenty-first century African immigrants are establishing a "diaspora in reverse." Once again, women and men with immediate and tangible links to Africa are coming to the United States—this time voluntarily. Sociologists and geographers are studying their settlement patterns, their immigrant ethos, their educational levels, and how they experience life in the United States. Immigrants perceive their status in the United States differently than do the descendants of enslaved Africans brought to the country centuries ago, and they are often unwilling to identify with African Americans. Stereotypes abound on both sides, as each group is reluctant to recognize commonalities and common cause. Nonetheless, encounters with the racial norms in the United States sometimes affords African immigrants insight into the experiences of black Americans.

African immigrants, because of their growing numbers, have also distinguished themselves from their African American counterparts in a variety of ways. What has this meant for thinking about links between African Americans and Africa? If the definition of an African American has expanded, the links, connections, identification, influence, involvement, and engagement with the continent have shifted once again. A more complex and nuanced relationship has emerged as Africa continues to play a significant role in the lives of African-descended people in the United States. Whether they have direct ties to the continent, as immigrants and their children do, or whether they are descendants of Africans brought to the country as a consequence of the transatlantic slave trade, Africa continues to loom large in the consciousness of blacks in the United States.

Although African Americans have sought a homeland in Africa, and some have settled on the continent, either temporarily or permanently, it continues to exist largely in the imagination of black Americans. They maintain an interest in Africa and in African affairs, traveling to the continent on heritage tours or, more recently, as a holiday destination. South Africa has proven a draw to many

African Americans. Nelson Mandela, who invoked pride and respect among diasporan blacks around the world, is key to understanding this interest in post-apartheid South Africa. With his release in 1990 after more than thirty years in prison, Mandela's insistence on reconciliation and rapprochement between whites and blacks resulted in a country largely governed by black South Africans, but from which its white citizens did not flee. South Africa managed to avoid civil war in the wake of a sometimes-violent liberation struggle. Perhaps for black Americans this semblance of racial unity is attractive, a vision of what their country might be.

The twenty-first century, with its technological innovations, social media, ease of travel, and other advancements, has provided avenues for people of African descent in the diaspora to have a more robust relationship with the continent. The growing immigrant population is transnational, moving back and forth with greater fluidity between Africa and the United States. Diaspora networks are created as Africans keep abreast of events in their countries of origin. Many see themselves as sojourners, hoping to return to their homelands, and have maintained strong ties to those places. African immigrants have contributed to fashion trends, pop culture, cuisine, art, culture, entertainment, media, and other forums, making the continent and its people a recognizable part of the landscape, particularly in urban cities in the Northeast. Stock stereotypes of Africa continue, but most African Americans have a deeper understanding of the continent and its people than their ancestors did.

There have been moments of tension between the two groups. African immigrants' access to opportunities gained through struggle has posed some challenges for the relationship between African Americans and Africans living in the United States. In 2004 the *New York Times*, with the sensationalist headline "Top Colleges Take More Blacks, but Which Ones?" reported on a forum at Harvard University at which noted scholars Lani Guinier and Henry Louis Gates Jr. pointed out that most black students at Ivy League schools in the United States were the children of black immigrants rather than the descendants of those with slave heritage from the United States. According to Guinier, "Many colleges rely on private networks that disproportionately benefit the children of African and West Indian immigrants who come from majority black countries and who arrived in the United States after

1965." The socioeconomic backgrounds of these immigrants, she argues, are privileged: "Like their wealthier white counterparts, many first- and second-generation immigrants of color test well because they retain a national identity free of America's racial caste system and enjoy material and cultural advantages, including professional or well-educated parents. They do not internalize the stigma of race and are thus less affected by the burden of 'stereotype threat,' the anxiety about confirming assumptions of intellectual inferiority that depresses test scores of highly motivated indigenous black Americans. Diversity produces a more interesting campus rainbow of students who benefited from a host of advantages assembled from birth."[3]

Over the years, similar criticisms have emerged about colleges favoring black immigrants at the expense of African Americans. Nevertheless, with the growing numbers of American-born children of African immigrants, there is a realization that Africans are here to stay, and that in the eyes of most Americans, as the immigration scholar George Sanchez, notes, "on the most basic level, when black people are observed on American streets, almost all Americans, even when they possess racist views, assume that who they are encountering are indeed United States citizens." Furthermore, the experiences of American-born children of African immigrants, particularly those with lower socioeconomic status, are similar to their African American counterparts. They do not escape racial profiling, discrimination, or violence.[4]

Black immigrants too are realizing that the racial hierarchy that has always operated in the country's history does not spare those directly from Africa. Like the Africans brought involuntarily to toil on plantations and farms in the American colonies, who brought elements of their cultures and backgrounds to the new land, so too do Africans coming in recent decades bring their cultural practices and customs. The differences are many. Most new African immigrants, as we have seen, typically come without coercion, and they often have a choice about where they will settle and with whom they will interact. Most have the opportunity to travel back to Africa, and some lead intercontinental lives. While long stays in the United States might result in more assimilation and loss of cultural practices, they are able to hold onto many aspects of their countries and communities.[5]

In this regard the descendants of Africans brought to the country enslaved are very different. While African Americans, now more than ever, have the opportunity to engage with the African continent in countless ways—travel and tourism, adoption of religious and cultural practices, names and dress, and migration—they remain Americans with African antecedents. For most black Americans the imagined Africa still exists. Growing interest in discovering their roots, made possible by DNA tests, however suspect, now allows for greater connection to specific locations on the continent—to Senegal, Mali, Guinea—and to specific ethnicities—Wolof or Vai. Some African nations acknowledge this, reaching out to their "kinfolk" in the diaspora to garner interest in aiding development. However, the "new African diaspora" with strong ties to their countries is a more significant market, if you will, for African governments to tap. What might this mean for native-born African Americans?

In 1990 Phillipe Wamba penned a memoir of his experiences as the child of an African American mother and a Congolese father. *Kinship* chronicles a life spent in the United States and Africa, trying to understand both worlds and himself. Wamba writes expressively of misunderstandings and apprehension, but also of moments of engagement and unity, reflecting that "all black people have been forced to contend with Africa and what it means to them. Some may conclude that it holds no importance to them, but all feel pressured to decide one way or another."[6] In the twenty-first century his words continue to ring true, as the two groups encounter each other in these "reverse" and "overlapping" diasporas.

What are the implications of these overlapping diasporas for dialogues and exchanges on race, racism, activism, and religion? The growing number of African immigrants is generating another conversation. Debates and discussion about who can embrace the label "African American," dialogues about cultural appropriation, and a fascination with Chimamanda Adichie, Ankara fabrics, and Akon have drawn attention to an African presence in the United States. Increasing transnationalism and the mobility affordable airfare provides allow them to keep their feet on the continent while embracing an American identity. They are augmenting the "African American" population in the United States and, like earlier Africans, are presenting their own vision (version?) of the continent—now in more precise ways. They speak for Nigeria, Ghana, or Sierra Leone, rather than for Africa writ large. They are Igbo, Mende, Wolof, or Yoruba. But they are also Afropolitans—"Africans of the world."[7]

The significant immigrant population has, arguably, allowed contemporary African Americans to connect in more tangible ways with Africa. The many African restaurants, churches, cultural associations, and institutions attract African Americans. Recent events, as we have seen, have encouraged common cause between the two groups. Intermarriages, rare when my parents met, are now commonplace. The children of these unions seamlessly straddle the two cultures. The American-born children of African immigrants have been more successful at understanding American society than their parents have, as evidenced in their increased participation in civic and political issues. Children born to African immigrants also understand their status differently, as they encounter African Americans in schools and face white Americans who view them as black Americans, regardless of their ethnic or national origin. As they face xenophobia and violence, racial and religious profiling (there is a significant Muslim component), African immigrants are acknowledging their commonality with black Americans and recognizing their shared aims.

Wamba concluded: "Anyone can claim Africa as a 'motherland,' but only black people are claimed by Africa so powerfully, whether we like it or not."[8] This was true of Africans brought forcibly to the United States, and it remains true of their descendants today, but today's competing claims for Africa may be marginalizing black Americans, whose ancestors were brought to America in chains.

African Americans have moved into the twenty-first century with many of the same struggles they have lived with since the seventeenth. While they have made tremendous strides in attaining citizenship and liberty, there is much to be done to achieve full acceptance and equality in the country to which they were forcibly brought. It has been interesting to observe African American responses to their condition in the United States. During the years of Barack Obama's presidency, black Americans expressed a tremendous amount of hope and optimism, particularly during his first term in office.

In recent years, however, with high-profile cases of aggression toward black citizens—the killing of Trayvon Martin, the deaths of

Michael Brown, Sandra Bland, and Eric Garner, among others, at the hands of police, and the mass shooting of black parishioners in a South Carolina church—African Americans, shocked and outraged, have organized in protest movements such as Black Lives Matter. Joining in these movements, African immigrants are increasingly recognizing that their status and plight are bound up with that of African Americans, regardless of whether they embrace or eschew politics and activism.

In 2016, seventeen years after her son was killed by police in New York City, Amadou Diallo's mother, Khadiatou, addressed the annual fund-raising event hosted by an organization she founded in her son's name to raise scholarship money for students of African descent. She co-hosted the event with David Dinkins, the former mayor of New York, and the former governor of New York, David Paterson, both African Americans. Diallo noted their connection, observing that "we have this special bond," and "we share a common loss." She lamented her son's loss but celebrated his desire to further his education. "It's almost like celebrating Amadou," Diallo remarked. "Picking him up from where he was in the vestibule with the 41 bullets, dusting him off and giving him back his story. His aspirations to go to college. His belief in the dream, the American dream."[9] This American dream is one that black Americans have struggled for centuries to attain. They have lost and regained hope in that dream, sometimes eschewing it by looking to Africa, but mostly fighting for it by remaining in the United States.

Africa has not emerged as an alternative in the discourse of black Americans as they face new challenges in this century. They continue to settle in Africa in small numbers and often cite reasons similar to their ancestors'. Jimmy Thorne, an African American living in Ghana, remarks: "Once you accept it as your home, why wouldn't you stay in your home? . . . This is where we come from originally, so maybe that's why we're here. Maybe it's divine providence."[10] But for most African Americans, "Africa is here."

Inasmuch as the continent has been present, or been a part of the conversation (or movement), it has been in the participation of African immigrants, alongside African Americans, in the protests and outrage over the killings that sparked Black Lives Matter. A generation of American-born children of African immigrants who, while socialized by African parents to think of themselves as Ethiopian, Nigerian, or Ghanaian, has assumed an African American identity. They are beneficiaries of the struggle for self-determination and opportunities fought for by Maria Stewart, Henry Highland Garnet, Bishop Turner, W. E. B. Du Bois, the Robesons, Pauli Murray, and many more. They have gained from civil rights legislation and other structural changes in American society that provided African American citizens with the chance to attain the same rights as their white counterparts. Affirmative action, fair housing legislation, and the Supreme Court decision in *Brown vs. Board of Education* have redressed some of the marginalization and discrimination black citizens faced for centuries. Voting rights laws have empowered African Americans, allowing them representation. Sadly, much remains to be done.

In a country still fraught with racial issues and where people of African descent are economically disadvantaged and constructed in negative ways, ties between African Americans and Africa are being created and strengthened in the United States on American soil. In this country many from the African continent worked and died. In today's America, in their quest to understand each other, both groups might wonder, as Phillis Wheatley did so long ago: "How like a Barbarian Should I look to the Natives." Perhaps the trick is to recognize that in different contexts, in different places, and in different times, in this America they have all been, or are still, "barbarians" and "natives," trying to speak each other's language. In order to do so, the "links in history" must be maintained.

Notes

Introduction

1. Amelia Blyden, "Hearing the Stone," unpublished memoir (2004), 13–14.
2. Isabel Wilkerson, "'African-American' Favored by Many of America's Blacks," *Special to the New York Times*, January 31, 1989, http://www. nytimes.com/1989/01/31/us/african-american-favored-by-many-of-america-s-blacks.html.
3. Quoted in Tunde Adeleke, *The Case against Afrocentrism* (Jackson: University Press of Mississippi, 2009), 120.
4. Frederick Douglass, "The Folly of Colonization," quoted in *Negro Social and Political Thought: 1850–1920*, ed. Howard Brotz (New York: Basic Books, 1966), 328, also at http://teachingamericanhistory.org/library/document/the-folly-of colonization. See also B. L. Martin, "From Negro to Black to African American: The Power of Names and Naming," *Political Science Quarterly* 106, no. 1 (1991): 83–107.
5. See Christopher Miller, *Blank Darkness: Africanist Discourse in French* (Chicago: University of Chicago Press, 1985); Gomez, "African Identity and Slavery in the Americas."
6. https://www.poetryfoundation.org/poems/45465/on-being-brought-from-africa-to-america.
7. Smith, *A Narrative of the Life and Adventures of Venture.*
8. Alexander, *African or American?* 51.
9. Alexander, *African or American?* 83. See also Eddie S. Glaude Jr., *Exodus! Religion, Race, and Nation in Early Nineteenth-Century Black America* (Chicago: University of Chicago Press, 2000), 127.
10. "*Anglo-African* Newspaper," in *Encyclopedia of African American History, 1619–1895: From the Colonial Period to the Age of Frederick Douglass*, ed. Paul Finkelman (New York: Oxford University Press, 2006), 71.
11. W. E. B. Du Bois, "The Name 'Negro,'" *The Crisis*, March 1928, 96–97.

12. Lerone Bennett Jr., "What's in a Name? Negro vs. Afro-American vs. Black," *Ebony*, November 1967, 48, 46, 47, http://www.virginia.edu/woodson/courses/aas102%20(spring%2001)/articles/names/bennett.htm.
13. Bennett, "What's in a Name?" 46.
14. Quoted in Wilkerson, "'African-American' Favored by Many of America's Blacks."
15. NBC, *Today Show*, "Morgan Freeman Says 'I'm Not African!'" *YouTube*, December 24, 2013, https://www.youtube.com/watch?v=CBSgaIUzfwU; see also John Peterson, "Morgan Freeman: Obama, Mandela, Batman and Me," *Guardian*, July 12, 2012, http://www.theguardian.com/film/2012/jul/12/morgan-freeman-obama-mandela-batman.
16. Ira Reid, *The Negro Immigrant: His Background, Characteristics and Social Adjustment, 1899–1937* (New York: AMS, 1939), 25.
17. Black Lives Matter website, https://blacklivesmatter.com/about/what-we-believe/. In an interview with the *Guardian* Garza observes: "We have said from the very beginning that our movement is about . . . the fact that there isn't much quality of life for black people in this country. Our conditions are pretty similar to conditions for black people around the world, which is how we know that it's not isolated—that it's intentional and that it's systematic." Elle Hunt, "Alicia Garza on the Beauty and the Burden of Black Lives Matter," *Guardian*, September 2, 2016, https://www.theguardian.com/us-news/2016/sep/02/alicia-garza-on-the-beauty-and-the-burden-of-black-lives-matter.
18. For a discussion of this, see C. J. La Roche and M. L. Blakey, "Seizing Intellectual Power: The Dialogue at the New York African Burial Ground," *Historical Archaeology* 31, no. 3 (1997): 84–106; and M. E. Mack and M. L. Blakey, "The New York African Burial Ground Project: Past Biases, Current Dilemmas, and Future Research Opportunities," *Historical Archaeology* 38, no. 1 (2004): 10–17.

Chapter One. "What is Africa to me?"

1. Countee Cullen, "Heritage," http://www.poemhunter.com/poem/heritage/.
2. Eddy L. Harris, *Native Stranger: A Black American's Journey into the Heart of Africa* (New York: Vintage Books, 1993), 312. Other perspectives on the relationship between African Americans and Africans in the same vein include Keith Richburg's indictment of Africa and its problems. Having covered the continent for many years, Richburg, though he acknowledges his African ancestry, concludes: "Thank God my ancestor got out, because, now I am not one of them. In short, Thank God that I am an American." Keith B. Richburg, *Out of America: A Black Man Confronts Africa* (New York: Basic Books, 1997), xviii.
3. Claude Clegg, *Africa and the American Imagination* (N.p.: Proquest Information and Learning, 2006, e-book).

4. Creolization here refers to the process by which people from the Old World (for our purposes, Africa) transformed in the New World. It is a process by which enslaved Africans created new lives and institutions in the Americas, whether language, religion, or cultural practices. It involved transformation and loss, but also resulted in creativity. There is a tremendous literature on creolization and some significant debates about its utility. See, for example, Sidney W. Mintz and Richard Price, *The Birth of African-American Culture: An Anthropological Perspective* (Boston: Beacon, 1992); Richard Price, "Créolisation, Creolization, and Créolité," *Small Axe*, March 1, 2017, 211–19, doi: https://doi.org/10.1215/07990537-3843962; James Sidbury and Jorge Cañizares-Esguerra, "Mapping Ethnogenesis in the Early Modern Atlantic," *William and Mary Quarterly* 68, no. 2 (2011): 181–208, doi:10.5309/willmaryquar.68.2.0181; David Buisseret and Steven G. Reinhardt, eds., *Creolization in the Americas* (College Station: Texas A&M Press, 2009); Robin Cohen and Paolo Toninato, eds., *The Creolization Reader: Studies in Mixed Identities and Cultures* (New York: Routledge, 2009).

5. Gomez, "African Identity and Slavery in the Americas," 111, 118.

6. See Isani, "'Gambia on My Soul,'" 65.

7. "Map: The Growing New Nation," *Africans in America*, part 3, 1998–99, https://www.pbs.org/wgbh/aia/part3/map3.html.

8. Psalm 68:31, *King James Bible*, https://www.kingjamesbibleonline.org/Psalms-68-31/.

9. There is a tremendous amount of literature on European and American representations of Africa in the nineteenth and twentieth centuries. See, for example, Hickey and Wylie, *An Enchanting Darkness*; Keim, *Mistaking Africa*; Hammond and Jablow, *The Africa That Never Was*; Pieterse, *White on Black*. The classic work on European images of Africa is, of course, Curtin, *The Image of Africa*.

10. Georg Wilhelm Friedrich Hegel, *The Philosophy of History*, trans. J. Sibree (Kitchener, Ontario: Batoche Books, 2001), 109, http://socserv2.socsci.mcmaster.ca/~econ/ugcm/3ll3/hegel/history.pdf.

11. "Dangers in Africa: M. Jules Boreill Tells of the Perils He Experienced during His Travels," *Rocky Mountain News*, January 5, 1890, 5; "Four Young Savages: Members of the Karco Tribe, of Africa, Sent to America to Be Educated," *Milwaukee Sentinel*, January 18, 1890, 2; "Cannibal Race Found in Africa: Arthur Sharp Returns from the Dark Continent," *News and Observer*, December 30, 1899, 6.

12. George Washington Williams, "History of the Twelfth Baptist Church," quoted in John H. Franklin, *George Washington Williams: A Biography* (Durham, NC: Duke University Press, 1998), 10.

13. Franklin, *George Washington Williams*, 10–11.

14. George Washington Williams, *History of the Negro Race in America from 1619 to 1880: As Negroes, as Slaves, as Soldiers, and as Citizens* (New York: G. P.

Putnam's Sons, 1883), vi, http://www.gutenberg.org/files/15735/15735-h/
15735-h.htm.

15. B. D. Dickinson. "Ancient Africa and the Early Black American Historians, 1883–1915," *American Quarterly* 36, no. 5 (1984): 687, doi:10.2307/
2712867.

16. George Washington Williams, *An Open Letter to His Serene Majesty Léo-
pold II, King of the Belgians and Sovereign of the Independent State of Congo,*
July 18, 1890, in *Barbara Harlow and Mia Carter, Archives of Empire* (Durham: Duke University Press, 2003), 772.

17. Adam Hochschild, *King Leopold's Ghost: A Story of Greed, Terror, and
Heroism in Colonial Africa* (Boston: Houghton Mifflin, 1999).

18. Franklin, *George Washington Williams,* xvii.

19. A useful perspective on African American historians and Africa is Bruce,
"Ancient Africa and the Early Black American Historians." Dickson argues that these early historians focused on ancient Africa "because it re-
solved the problem of a dual identity in ways that an appreciation of
modern Africa could not. Modern Africa was generally taken by black
and white people alike as a primitive, backward continent" (695).

20. W. E. B. Du Bois, *Black Folk Then and Now: An Essay in the History and Sociology of the Negro Race,* ed. Henry Louis Gates Jr. (Oxford: Oxford University Press, 2007), xxxi.

21. W. E. B. Du Bois, *The Negro* (Project Gutenberg, 2005), http://www.
gutenberg.org/files/15359/15359-h/15359-h.htm.

22. W. E. B. Du Bois, "The Concept of Race," in *The Oxford W. E. B. Du Bois
Reader,* ed. Eric J. Sundquist (Oxford: Oxford University Press, 1996), 87.

23. Jerry Gershenhorn, *Melville J. Herskovits and the Racial Politics of Knowledge* (Lincoln: University of Nebraska Press, 2004), 105.

24. Carter G. Woodson, *The Miseducation of the Negro* (Drewryville, VA:
Khalifah's Bookseller and Associates, 2006), https://devontekwatson.files.
wordpress.com/2013/10/miseducation-text.pdf.

25. Darlene Clark Hine, *The State of Afro-American History: Past, Present, and
Future* (Baton Rouge: Louisiana State University Press, 1986); John H.
Franklin, *From Slavery to Freedom: A History of African Americans* (New
York: McGraw-Hill, 2010).

26. J. Gershenhorn, "Not an Academic Affair: African American Scholars and
the Development of African Studies Programs in the United States,
1942–1960," *Journal of African American History* 94 (2009): 49.

27. "Native African Student Likes American Food," *Chicago Defender,*
November 23, 1940; "Says Minister Took His Wife; Given Divorce,"
Chicago Defender, January 13, 1923.

28. "African Student Visitor to City," *Chicago Defender,* January 3, 1931.

29. See J. H. Clarke, "Say Brother," *Essence,* June 1985, 9.

30. See J. H. Clarke, "African-American Historians and the Reclaiming of
African History," *Présence africaine,* n.s., no. 110 (1979): 29–48, http://

www.jstor.org/stable/24349918. In 1996 the filmmaker St. Clair Bourne made an interesting documentary of Clarke's life, showcasing his path to the study of African history, his high influence, and his intellectual legacy. See *John Henrik Clarke—A Great and Mighty Walk*, https://www.youtube.com/watch?v=njdQzyQnHeg.

31. For a discussion of J. A. Rogers's influence, see Asukile, "Joel Augustus Rogers." For a short biography and list of publications, see https://www.africanglobe.net/featured/rogers-historian-journalist-author/. Rogers published works with titles that served to illustrate the greatness of Africa. See *From Superman to Man* (New York: J. A. Rogers, 1917); *Africa's Gift to America: The Afro-American in the Making and Saving of the United States* (New York: J. A. Rogers, 1961); J. A. Rogers, *One Hundred Amazing Facts about the Negro* (New York: J. A. Rogers, 1934); *World's Great Men and Women of African Descent* (New York: J. A. Rogers, 1935); *Real Facts about Ethiopia* (New York: J. A. Rogers, 1936); *Your History: From the Beginning of Time to the Present* (Pittsburgh: Pittsburgh Courier, 1940); *Africa's Gift to America*, rev. ed. (New York: J. A. Rogers, 1961); *Five Negro Presidents* (New York: J. A. Rogers, 1965) His work, much of which was self-published, served to generate pride in their African ancestry among black Americans.

32. "Joel Augustus Rogers (1883–1966)," *The Crisis* 73, no. 4 (1966): 201. See also the entry on Joel Rogers in Leslie Alexander, ed., *Encyclopedia of African American History* (Santa Barbara, CA: ABC-CLIO, 2010), 2:249.

Chapter Two. "I tried to keep their voices in my head"

1. Lawrence Hill, *Someone Knows My Name: A Novel* (New York: Norton, 2008).

2. Sweet, "Defying Social Death," 255; Toyin Falola, "Social Institutions: Kinship Systems," in *Africa*, vol. 2, *African Cultures and Societies Before 1885*, ed. Toyin Falola (Durham, NC: Carolina Academic Press, 2000).

3. "Family," *Motherlandnigeria.com*, http://www.motherlandnigeria.com/proverbs.html#Family.

4. Chinua Achebe, *Things Fall Apart* (New York: Anchor Books, 2008), 3, 8.

5. See Becker, "We are Real Slaves, Real Ismkhan."

6. Maghreb, meaning "west" in Arabic, refers to the region in North Africa west of Egypt. See also "The Word Maghreb," *Maghreb Studies*, http://www.maghreb-studies-association.co.uk/en/allhome.html.

7. D. T. Niane, *Sundiata: An Epic of Old Mali* (New York: Pearson, 2006), 38.

8. Paul Halsall, "Ibn Battuta: Travels in Asia and Africa, 1325–1354," *Medieval Sourcebook*, last modified February 21, 2001, http://sourcebooks.fordham.edu/source/1354-ibnbattuta.asp.

9. See Thornton, "Elite Women in the Kingdom of Kongo," 460.

10. Wright, "'What Do You Mean There Were No Tribes in Africa?'" 418. Wright also discusses the difficulty of reconstructing the history of the slave trade in Niumi and the Gambia because of the country's citizens' knowledge of Alex Haley's *Roots*. He writes: "Today, the story of the Gambia-River slave trade in the minds of most Gambians is the story Haley told in *Roots*." Wright, "The Effect of Alex Haley's *Roots*."

11. Tishken, "Indigenous Religions." See also Boubacar Barry, *Senegambia and the Atlantic Slave Trade*, trans. Ayi Kwei Armah. (Cambridge: Cambridge University Press, 1998).

12. "Kongo Religion," *Overview of World Religions*, http://www.philtar.ac.uk/ encyclopedia/sub/kongo.html. See also Anthony Appiah and Henry Louis Gates Jr., eds., *Africana: The Encyclopedia of the African and African American Experience* (New York: Oxford University Press, 2005); Igor Kopytoff, "Ancestors as Elders in Africa," in *Perspectives on Africa: A Reader in Culture, History and Representation*, ed. Roy Richard Grinker, Stephen C. Lubkemann, and Christopher B. Steiner (Oxford: Wiley-Blackwell, 2010), 313–22.

13. See Ras Michael Brown, *African-Atlantic Cultures and the South Carolina Lowcountry* (Cambridge: Cambridge University Press, 2012), 90–126.

14. David Northrup, *Africa's Discovery of Europe, 1450–1850* (New York: Oxford University Press, 2014); Davidson, *West Africa Before the Colonial Era*.

15. There is significant amount of material on the early relationship between the Portuguese and the Kingdom of Kongo. See Basil Davidson, *The African Slave Trade*, rev. ed. (Boston: Little, Brown, 1980); John Thornton, *Africa and Africans in the Making of the Atlantic World, 1400–1800*, 2nd ed. (Cambridge: Cambridge University Press, 1998).

16. See George E. Brooks, *Eurafricans in Western Africa: Commerce, Social Status, Gender, and Religious Observance from the Sixteenth to the Eighteenth Century* (Athens: Ohio University Press, 2003).

17. Berlin, *Many Thousands Gone*.

18. Lovejoy, *Transformations in Slavery*; Lovejoy, *Ideology of Slavery in Africa*. See also Klein and Robertson, *Women and Slavery in Africa*.

19. See Jennifer Morgan, *Laboring Women: Reproduction and Gender in New World Slavery: Early American Studies* (Philadelphia: University of Pennsylvania Press, 2004), 50–68.

20. Lovejoy, *Transformations in Slavery*. How Africans resisted is convincingly shown in Sylviane Diouf, *Fighting the Slave Trade: West African Strategies* (Athens: Ohio University Press, 2003).

21. Smallwood, *Saltwater Slavery*, 35.

22. Hill, *Someone Knows*, 25.

23. Gomez, *Exchanging Our Country Marks*; Hall, *Slavery and African Ethnicities in the Americas*; Heywood and Thornton, *Central Africans*. While the 12–15 million estimate is generally accepted by scholars, lower and higher figures have been cited. One of the first scholars to cite numbers for Afri-

cans exported to the Americas was Phillip Curtin, who provided the number of 10 million. W. E. B Du Bois's doctoral thesis cited 100 million, but Curtin argued the number had not been scientifically calculated. Joseph Inikori has challenged Curtin's numbers, giving the higher number of 15 million exported. See Joseph Inikori, *Forced Migration: The Impact of the Export Slave Trade on African Societies* (London: Hutchinson, 1982), 20. A 1991 publication by the Nation of Islam, *The Secret Relation between Blacks and Jews*, cites a number of 600 million, which many scholars have challenged as ridiculously high. See, for example, Winthrop D. Jordan, "Slavery and the Jews," *Atlantic Monthly*, September 1995, 109–14. This is clearly a highly charged and political issue. We will, after all, never have an accurate number. However, from the perspective of those who were enslaved, whether the number was 10 million or 600 million, the effect was devastating and the consequences dire.

24. See Lovejoy, The *"Middle Passage."* See also Heywood and Thornton, *Central Africans*; Brown, *African-Atlantic Cultures*.

25. Cameron Monroe and Akinwumi Ogundiran, *Power and Landscape in Atlantic West Africa: Archaeological Perspectives* (New York: Cambridge University Press, 2012). See also Christopher R. Decorse, *An Archaeology of Elmina: Africans and Europeans on the Gold Coast, 1400–1900* (Washington, DC: Smithsonian Institution Press, 2001), 286; Christopher R. Decorse, ed., *West Africa during the Atlantic Slave Trade: Archaeological Perspectives* (London: Leicester University Press, 2001); C. R. DeCorse, "West African Archaeology and the Atlantic Slave Trade," *Slavery and Abolition* 12, no. 2 (1991): 92–96.

26. *The Biography of Mahommah Gardo Baquaqua: His Passage from Slavery to Freedom in Africa and America, Written and Revised from His Own Words by Samuel Moore, Esq.* (Detroit: George E. Pomeroy and Co. Tribune Office, 1854), 35.

27. Roy E. Finkenbine, "Belinda's Petition: Reparations for Slavery in Revolutionary Massachusetts," *William and Mary Quarterly* 64, no. 1 (January 2007): 95–104.

28. Equiano, *Interesting Narrative of the Life of Olaudah Equiano*. Literary scholar Vincent Carretta has questioned Equiano's African birth, suggesting that he might have been born in South Carolina. He does not assert this conclusively. Historians of Africa such as Paul Lovejoy have challenged Carretta's conclusion. In some respects Equiano's birthplace is not important, and we can read his description of the Middle Passage as representative of the experience of millions of Africans. See Vincent Carretta, *Equiano, the African: Biography of a Self-Made Man* (Athens: University of Georgia Press, 2005); and Paul E. Lovejoy, "Issues of Motivation—Vassa/Equiano and Carretta's Critique of the Evidence," *Slavery and Abolition* 28, no. 1 (2007): 121–25.

29. Hill, *Someone Knows*, 28.

30. *The Biography of Mahommah Gardo Baquaqua: His Passage from Slavery to Freedom in Africa and America*, ed. Robin Law and Paul E. Lovejoy (Princeton, NJ: Markus Wiener, 2003). Paul Lovejoy notes that in the 1650s it took the average ship 133 days to cross the Atlantic from Africa. In the early eighteenth century, it took 75–80 days. By the end of that century the trip was reduced to 50–65 days. Between 1820 and 1850 the time was further reduced, to 40–50 days. Better ship designs and technology account for the reduction in time. Paul E. Lovejoy, *The "Middle Passage": The Enforced Migration of Africans across the Atlantic* (Cambridge: ProQuest, 2006), http://gateway.proquest.com/openurl?url_ver=Z39.88-2004&res_dat=xri:bsc:&rft_dat=xri:bsc:ft:essay:22LOVE.

31. Rediker, *The Amistad Rebellion.* See also Arthur Abraham, *Amistad Revolt: An Historical Legacy of Sierra Leone and the United States* (Freetown, Sierra Leone: United States Information Service, 1987). Documents relating to the case can be found at the National Archives, https://www.archives.gov/education/lessons/amistad.

32. Hawthorne, " 'Being Now, as It Were, One Family,' " 55.

33. Alex Haley, *Roots: The Saga of an American Family* (New York: Doubleday, 1976), 226.

34. Smallwood, *Saltwater Slavery*, 101.

35. Smith, *A Narrative of the Life and Adventures of Venture.* See also Paul Lovejoy, "The African Background of Venture Smith," in *Venture Smith and the Business of Slavery and Freedom* (Amherst: University of Massachusetts Press, 2010), 35–55.

Chapter Three. "We, the African Members, form ourselves into a Society"

1. Smith, *A Narrative of the Life and Adventures of Venture.*

2. Peter H. Wood, "Strange New Land: 1502–1619," in *To Make Our World Anew: A History of African Americans*, ed. Robin D. G. Kelley and Earl Lewis (Oxford: Oxford University Press, 2000).

3. These first African "settlers" were likely casualties of a civil war in West Central Africa.

4. James H. Sweet, "African Identity and Slave Resistance in the Portuguese Atlantic in the Atlantic World and Virginia, 1550–1624," in *The Atlantic World and Virginia, 1550–1624*, ed. Peter C. Mancall (Chapel Hill: University of North Carolina Press, 2007), 246.

5. Sweet, "African Identity and Slave Resistance," 246–47.

6. Wood, "Strange New Land," 63–70. See text of the 1705 law, "An Act concerning Servants and Slaves," *Encyclopedia Virginia*, https://www.encyclopediavirginia.org/_An_act_concerning_Servants_and_Slaves_1705.

7. Peter Wood, *Part 1, The Terrible Transformation, 1450–1750*, The Africans in America, PBS Online, http://www.pbs.org/wgbh/aia/part1/title.html.

8. Berlin, "From Creole to African," 252.

9. Bennett, *Before the* Mayflower.

10. See, for example, "African Americans and the End of Slavery in Massachusetts," http://www.masshist.org/endofslavery/index.php?id=58.

11. Smith, *A Narrative of the Life and Adventures of Venture.*

12. Richard Allen, *The Life, Experience, and Gospel Labours of the Rt. Rev. Richard Allen: To Which Is Annexed the Rise and Progress of the African Methodist Episcopal Church in the United States of America; Containing a Narrative of the Yellow Fever in the Year of Our Lord 1793, with an Address to the People of Colour in the United States, 1833, Documenting the American South,* University Library, the University of North Carolina at Chapel Hill, 2000, https://docsouth.unc.edu/neh/allen/allen.html.

13. Higginbotham, *In the Matter of Color,* 163.

14. See Carney, *Black Rice.*

15. Gomez, "African Identity and Slavery in the Americas," 112.

16. Sweet, "Reimagining the African-Atlantic Archive," 153. See also Gomez, "African Identity and Slavery in the Americas," 113; Erskine Clarke, "'They Shun the Scrutiny of White Men': Reports on Religion from the Georgia Lowcountry and West Africa, 1834–1850," in *African American Life in the Georgia Lowcountry: The Atlantic World and the Gullah Geechee,* ed. Philip Morgan (Athens: University of Georgia Press, 2010); Sterling Stuckey, *Slave Culture: Nationalist Theory and the Foundations of Black America* (New York: Oxford University Press, 1987); Douglas Chambers, "Igboes," in *The New Encyclopedia of Southern Culture,* vol. 6, *Ethnicity,* ed. Ray Celeste (Chapel Hill: University of North Carolina Press, 2007).

17. Berlin, "Atlantic Creoles," 266. Berlin designates "Atlantic creoles" as "those who by experience or choice, as well as by birth, became part of a new culture that emerged along the Atlantic littoral—in Africa, Europe, or the Americas—beginning in the 16th century. ... The term 'Atlantic creole' is designed to capture the cultural transformation that sometimes preceded generational change and sometimes was unaffected by it" (254). James Sweet takes issue with the "Atlantic Creoles" narrative, arguing that it tends to "exaggerate European impacts in Africa" ("Reimagining the African-Atlantic Archive," 149). John Thornton has persuasively argued that many Central Africans brought to the United States, because of their long contact with Europeans, were acculturated to European ways. See Thornton, "The African Experience of the '20 and Odd Negroes.'"

18. Equiano, *Interesting Narrative of the Life of Olaudah Equiano.*

19. For a good discussion of what Africans brought to the Americas, see Gomez, *Exchanging Our Country Marks;* see also Gomez, "African Identity and Slavery in the Americas"; Hall, *Slavery and African Ethnicities in the Americas;* and Margaret Washington Creel, *A Peculiar People: Slave Religion and Community-Culture among the Gullahs* (New York: New York University Press, 1988).

20. Brenda E. Stevenson, *Life in Black and White: Family and Community in the Slave South* (New York: Oxford University Press, 1996), 160. See also Sweet, "Defying Social Death"; Roberts, "African-Virginian Extended Kin," 36; John Blassingame, *The Slave Community* (New York: Oxford University Press, 1972).
21. See Joseph Holloway, ed., *Africanisms in American Culture* (Bloomington: Indiana University Press, 2005); David Dalby, ed., *African Language Review*, vol. 9 (London: Frank Cass, 1972).
22. Stuckey, *Slave Culture*, 7–9.
23. Wright, *African Americans in the Colonial Era*.
24. "Map: The Growing New Nation," *Africans in America*, part 3, 1998–99, https://www.pbs.org/wgbh/aia/part3/map3.html.
25. Wright, *African Americans in the Colonial Era*, 123.
26. Herbert Aptheker, ed., *A Documentary History of the Negro People in the United States* (New York: Citadel, 1965), 1:27.
27. Shane White, "Slavery in the North," *OAH Magazine of History* 17, no. 3 (2003): 17–21. See also Donald R. Wright, "Recent Literature on Slavery in Colonial North America." *OAH Magazine of History* 17, no. 3 (2003): 5–9; Erik R. Seeman, "Reassessing the 'Sankofa Symbol' in New York's African Burial Ground," *William and Mary Quarterly* 67, no. 1 (2010): 101–22. See also Erik R. Seeman, *Death in the New World: Cross-Cultural Encounters, 1492–1800* (Philadelphia: University of Pennsylvania Press, 2010).
28. Hodges, *Root and Branch*. See also Marshall, "Powerful and Righteous"; Timothy J. McMillan, "Black Magic: Witchcraft, Race, and Resistance in Colonial New England," *Journal of Black Studies* 25, no. 1 (1994): 103.
29. White, "Slavery in the North," 20.
30. Alexander, *African or American?* On Prince Hall, see Miller, *The Search for a Black Nationality*, 4.
31. Aptheker, *A Documentary History*, 1:17–18, 38.
32. "Museum of African American History, Boston and Nantucket," http://www.afroammuseum.org/site14.html.
33. David Walker, *Walker's Appeal, in Four Articles; Together with a Preamble, to the Coloured Citizens of the World, but in Particular, and Very Expressly, to Those of the United States of America, Written in Boston, State of Massachusetts, September 28, 1829* (Chapel Hill: University of North Carolina, 2014), 81, http://docsouth.unc.edu/nc/walker/menu.html.
34. Thomas Jefferson, *Notes on the State of Virginia* (Philadelphia: Prichard & Hall, 1788), cited in *Documenting the American South*, University Library, the University of North Carolina at Chapel Hill, http://docsouth.unc.edu/southlit/jefferson/jefferson.html.
35. Maria Stewart, "An Address Delivered at the African Masonic Hall, Boston, February 27, 1833," cited in Richard Newman, Patrick Rael, and Philip Lapsansky, eds., *Pamphlets of Protest: An Anthology of Early African-*

American Protest Literature, 1790–1860 (New York: Routledge, 2001), 123. See also Stewart, *Meditations from the Pen of Mrs. Maria W. Stewart.*

36. Alexander, *African or American?* 51.
37. Walker, *Walker's Appeal,* 65.
38. Aptheker, *A Documentary History,* 1:40, 44.
39. Alexander, *African or American?* 21, 51.

Chapter Four. "It is the will of GOD for you to come into the possessions of your ancestors"

1. Some accounts of the Erskine family story refer to Martha Gains as his mother, but I believe she was his wife's mother.
2. "Captain Sherman to Thomas James, President of the Pennsylvania Colonization Society, June 4, 1830," *African Repository* 6, no. 6 (1830).
3. Smallwood, *Saltwater Slavery,* 33–64.
4. Alexander, *African or American?*
5. See Miller, *The Search for a Black Nationality,* ch. 1.
6. Herbert Aptheker, ed., *A Documentary History of the Negro People in the United States,* vol. 1, *Colonial Times through the Civil War* (New York: Citadel, 1969), 7–8, also quoted in Horton and Horton, *Hard Road to Freedom,* 62.
7. "The Boston Plan," *Africans in America,* part 2, http://www.pbs.org/wgbh/aia/part2/2h59t.html.
8. "Lord Dunmore's Proclamation, November 7, 1775," *NCpedia,* https://www.ncpedia.org/media/image/lord-dunmore-proclamation-1775.
9. Pybus, *Epic Journeys of Freedom,* 205.
10. David George, *An Account of the Life of Mr. David George from Sierra Leone in Africa Given by Himself in a Conversation with Brother Rippon of London, and Brother Pearce of Birmingham* (Louisville, KY: Southern Baptist Theological Seminary Library, 1980), 473–84. Also cited in *Black Loyalists: Our History, Our People,* http://blackloyalist.com/cdc/documents/diaries/george_a_life.htm. See also the entry on David George in Carretta, *Unchained Voices.* It is worth noting how George's description of his first glimpse of Africa reverses the usual "trope" of seeing the Statue of Liberty in other American immigration stories. Brooks, *The Silver Bluff Church.* On George's life in Sierra Leone, see Fyfe, *History of Sierra Leone,* 69–101. See also "David George," in *Black Loyalists: Our History, Our People,* http://www.blackpast.org/gah/george-david-1742–1810#sthash.IuAbPlww.dpuf.
11. Quoted in C. Pybus, "'One Militant Saint': The Much Traveled Life of Mary Perth," *Journal of Colonialism and Colonial History* 9, no. 3 (2008): 1, http://proxygw.wrlc.org/login?url=http://search.proquest.com/docview/210670741?accountid=11243. See also Mary Louise Clifford, *From Slavery to Freetown: Black Loyalists After the American Revolution* (Jefferson, NC: McFarland, 1999); Adrienne Shadd, "The Lord Seemed to say 'Go':

Women and the Underground Railroad Movement," in *We're Rooted Here and They Can't Pull Us Up: Essays in African Canadian Women's History*, ed. Peggy Bristow (Buffalo, NY: University of Toronto Press, 1994); Fyfe, *History of Sierra Leone*, 85.

12. "Memoirs of the Life of Boston King," *Methodist Magazine*, May 1798, http://antislavery.eserver.org/narratives/boston_king/bostonkingproof.pdf/.

13. Miller, *The Search for a Black Nationality*.

14. T. Perronet Thompson to Castlereagh, November 2, 1808, Despatch 4, re: State of the Colony and Its Inhabitants, CO 267/24, Public Records Office, Kew Gardens, London.

15. Quoted in Pybus, "One Militant Saint," 1.

16. "Cuffe to John James and Alexander Wilson, 1809," in *Captain Paul Cuffe's Logs and Letters, 1808–1817: A Black Quaker's "Voice from within the Veil*," ed. Rosalind Cobb Wiggins (Washington, DC: Howard University Press, 1996), 80.

17. Quoted in Miller, *The Search for a Black Nationality*, 56. On Cuffe, see Lamont D. Thomas, *Paul Cuffe: Black Entrepreneur and Pan-Africanist* (Urbana: University of Illinois Press, 1988), ch. 13.

18. Quoted in Jackson, *Let This Voice Be Heard*, 307.

19. *Freedom's Journal*, June 13, 1828, extracted from African American Newspapers collection. See also James and Russwurm, *Struggles of John Brown Russwurm*. See also George Apperson, "George M. Erskine, Slave, Presbyterian, Missionary," *Presbyterian Voice*, December 2001, http://www.synodoflivingwaters.com/the_voice/2001/10erskine.html.

20. "The Rev. George M. Erskine," *African Repository* 5, no. 1 (1829): 30. See Nemata Blyden, "Early Black Atlantic Identities," in *Back to Africa*, vol. 2, *The Ideology and Practice of the African Returnee Phenomenon from the Caribbean and North America*, ed. Kwesi Kwaa Prah, CASAS book series 92 (Cape Town: Centre for Advanced Studies of African Society, 2012).

21. See "Africa and America," *African Repository* 46, no. 7 (1868), with extract from *Calvinistic Magazine*, printed in 1829, that claimed the family's return allowed her to "return in company with an enlightened and Christian offspring." David Nelson, James Gallaher, and Frederick Ross, "An Interesting Sight," *Calvinistic Magazine* 3, no. 2 (1829).

22. "Letter of the Rev. George M. Erskine," *African Repository* 6, no. 4 (1830): 121.

23. Finkenbine, *Sources of the African-American Past*, 37.

24. Abraham Camp, "Free Illinois Black, July 1818 Letter," in Aptheker, *A Documentary History*, 1:72.

25. "Letter of the Rev. George M. Erskine," 121.

26. "A Large Expedition for Liberia," *African Repository* 42, no. 12 (1866): 374.

27. Queen Victoria's journals, July 16, 1892, Windsor Castle, RA VIC/MAIN/QVJ (W) (Princess Beatrice's copies). Martha married twice. Her

first husband was Zion (Sion) Harris, who traveled on the same ship from America to Liberia. After Harris died, she married Mr. Ricks.

28. "Mr. Ellsworth's Appeal," *African Repository* 18, no. 9 (1842): 218.

29. Diana Skipwith, "James to Sally Cocke, March 6, 1843," in Wiley, *Slaves No More*, 43.

30. See Daniel Coker, *Journal of Daniel Coker, a Descendant of Africa, from the Time of Leaving New York, in the Ship* Elizabeth, *Capt. Sebor, on a Voyage for Sherbro, in Africa, in Company with Three Agents, and about Ninety Persons of Colour: The Rev. Samuel Bacon, John B. Bankson, Samuel S. Crozer, Agents; With an Appendix* (Baltimore, MD: Edward J. Coale, in aid of the funds of the Maryland Auxiliary Colonization Society; John D. Toy, printer, 1820), 17, 22. See also Daniel Coker, *A Dialogue between a Virginian and an African Minister* (Baltimore, MD: Benjamin Edes for Joseph James, 1810). The full pamphlet is also included in Richard Newman, Patrick Rael, and Philip Lapsansky, eds., *Pamphlets of Protest: An Anthology of Early African-American Protest Literature, 1790–1860* (New York: Routledge, 2001). For Coker to Lockes, see See Blyden, "Edward Jones"; Debra Newman Ham entry in *Encyclopedia of African American History, 1619–1895: From the Colonial Period to the Age of Frederick Douglass*, ed. Paul Finkelman (New York: Oxford University Press, 2006), 308–10.

31. See Davidson Nicol, "The Life and Times of Edward Jones," unpublished manuscript, 1994, used by permission of the Nicol Family; Powers, *Black Charlestonians*, 57. See also Edward Jones, "Amherst College Class of 1826," from the Amherst College Biographical Record, Centennial Edition (1821–1921), Amherst College, 1927, also at http://www3.amherst.edu/~rjyanco94/genealogy/acbiorecord/1826.html#jones-e. "Amherst College Class of 1826"; Blyden, "Edward Jones"; Hugh Hawkins, "Edward Jones: First American Negro College Graduate?" *School and Society* 89, no. 2198 (1961); Hawkins, "Edward Jones, Marginal Man"; C. G. Contee, "The Reverend Edward Jones, Missionary-Educator to Sierra Leone and 'First' Afro-American College Graduate, 1808?–1865," *Negro History Bulletin* 38, no. 1 (1975); Harold Wade Jr., *Black Men of Amherst* (Amherst, MA: Amherst College Press, 1976); Davidson Nicol, "The Jones Family of Charleston, London and Africa," in *Sierra Leone Studies at Birmingham, Proceedings of the Fifth Birmingham Sierra Leone Studies Symposium*, ed. Adam Jones, Peter K. Mitchell, and Margaret Peil (Birmingham, UK: University of Birmingham, 1990); Michael Crowder, "From Amherst to Fourah Bay: Principal Edward Jones," in *Two Hundred Years of Inter-cultural Evolution and Perspectives for the Future: Bicentenary of Sierra Leone Symposium* (Fourah Bay: University of Sierra Leone, 1987); Fyfe, *History of Sierra Leone*, 387. See also Nicol, "The Life and Times of Edward Jones"; Hawkins, "Edward Jones, Marginal Man," 244. Why Jones chose to look to Africa at this time is unclear, but it is likely that because of laws in South Carolina that prevented blacks who left the state from returning, Jones could not go back home and therefore

may have chosen Africa as an alternative. It seems Jones went to Liberia first and then on to Sierra Leone. This is logical given the interest of the Mission School in Liberia. Hugh Hawkins suggests that the Church Missionary Society, already established in Sierra Leone, may have enticed Jones from the American missionary establishment.

32. Quoted in Wheatley, *Complete Writings*, 159.

33. For an interesting discussion of the differences, see Ousmane K. Power-Greene, *Against Wind and Tide: The African American Struggle against the Colonization Movement* (New York: New York University Press, 2014). For more recent perspectives and debates on the American Colonization Society, the emigration movement, and opposition to it, see Tomek, *Colonization and Its Discontents*; Beverly C. Tomek and Matthew J. Hetrick, eds., *New Directions in the Study of African American Recolonization* (Gainesville: University Press of Florida, 2017).

34. In his *Appeal* David Walker made reference to the Ohio case in his criticism of colonization: "Do the colonizationists think to send us off without first being reconciled to us? Do they think to bundle us up like brutes and send us off, as they did our brethren of the State of Ohio?" David Walker, *Walker's Appeal, in Four Articles; Together with a Preamble, to the Coloured Citizens of the World, but in Particular, and Very Expressly, to Those of the United States of America, Written in Boston, State of Massachusetts, September 28, 1829* (Chapel Hill: University of North Carolina, 2014), 77, http://docsouth.unc.edu/nc/walker/menu.html.

35. Quoted in Alexander, *African or American?* 76. The quote is from the Reverend Peter Williams Jr. from a speech made on Independence Day 1830.

36. Alexander, *African or American?* 79.

37. Thomas Jennings, "Free New York Black, 1828," in Alexander, *African or American?* 83.

38. Walker, *Walker's Appeal.*

39. Walker, *Walker's Appeal*, 62, 77.

40. Frederick Douglas, "Colonization," *North Star*, January 26, 1849, http://utc.iath.virginia.edu/abolitn/abar03at.html.

41. Henry Highland Garnet, "Address Delivered before the National Convention of Colored Citizens, Buffalo, New York, August 16, 1843," in *Walker's Appeal, with a Brief Sketch of His Life. And Also Garnet's Address to the Slaves of the United States of America* (New York: J. H. Tobitt, 1848), 89–97.

42. "Words from the People; African Civilization Society," letter to the editor from A. A. Constantine, corresponding secretary, *New York Times*, April 17, 1860. J. T. Holly was Bishop James Theodore Holly, another proponent of emigration.

43. Kenneth Barnes, *Journey of Hope: The Back-to-Africa Movement in Arkansas in the Late 1800s* (Chapel Hill: University of North Carolina Press,

2004), 102–3. A series of unflattering editorials in the *New York Age* and *New York Freeman* attacked "Dr. Blyden" in the belief that he was the impostor. In May 1891 Blyden's son responded to one such editorial, contradicting "this malicious assertion," and assuring readers his father was in Africa, not in an Arkansas jail. "He Is Not the Fire Brand," *New York Age*, August 15, 1891.

44. Bernard K. Duffy and Richard W. Leeman, *The Will of a People: A Critical Anthology of Great African American Speeches* (Carbondale: Southern Illinois University Press, 2012), 94. A good treatment of the late nineteenth- and early twentieth-century emigration movement is Redkey, *Black Exodus*.

45. Grant, *The Way It Was in the South*, 386.

46. "Colonization and Emigration," in *In Motion: The African-American Migration Experience* (New York: Schomburg Center for Research in Black Culture, 2005), http://www.inmotionaame.org/home.cfm.

47. *The Crisis*, July 1915, 132. See also PBS, "Henry McNeal Turner"; Redkey, "Bishop Turner's African Dream."

Chapter Five. "Africa is their country. They should claim it."

1. Alexander Crummell, "The Progress and Prospects of the Republic of Liberia: Delivered at the Annual Meeting of the New York State Colonization Society, May 9, 1861," in *The Future of Africa: Sermons, Addresses Delivered in Liberia* (New York: Negro Universities Press, 1969), 134, https://archive.org/details/futureafricabeio1crumgoog.

2. Simon Greenleaf, *The Independent Republic of Liberia: Its Constitution and Declaration of Independence: Address of the Colonists to the Free People of Color in the United States, with Other Documents: Issued Chiefly for the Use of the Free People of Color* (Philadelphia: Pennsylvania Colonization Society, 1848). See also "Liberian Declaration of Independence," *The Liberian Constitutions*, http://onliberia.org/con_declaration.htm.

3. John H. Bracey Jr., August Meier, and Elliott Rudwick, eds., *Black Nationalism in America* (Indianapolis: Bobbs-Merrill, 1970), xxvii.

4. Martin R. Delany, "Political Destiny of the Colored Race, on the American Continent," in *Proceedings of the National Emigration Convention of Colored People, Held at Cleveland, Ohio, August 24, 1854* (Pittsburgh: A. A. Anderson, 1854), http://uncpress.unc.edu/browse/page/471.

5. Anna Julia Cooper, "A Voice from the South by a Black Woman of the South," in *Documenting the American South*, University Library, the University of North Carolina at Chapel Hill, 1998, 30, http://docsouth.unc.edu/church/cooper/cooper.html.

6. Although Delany lobbied to serve as United States representative to Liberia, he was never appointed. In 1871 J. K. Milton Turner was appointed consul general to Liberia, where he presented his credentials to President

Edward James Roye, an emigrant from Ohio. See Skinner, *African Americans and U.S. Policy toward Africa*, 69.

7. Miller, *The Search for a Black Nationality*, 4. The belief that New World blacks could serve as examples of the benefits of Christianity and Western culture was perpetuated in the nineteenth century. It was a common argument among humanitarians in Europe and America, and New World blacks themselves internalized it. This was a notion that fell in with nineteenth-century European missionary and imperial ideas that exposure to Western values and education was best for Africans. Throughout the nineteenth century, American blacks articulated these ideas, with variations. Once black Americans were in Africa, many of their preconceptions and opinions changed, and their responses to the Africans they encountered varied. See also Magubane, *The Ties That Bind*, 23.

8. Greenleaf, *The Independent Republic of Liberia*. See also "Liberian Declaration of Independence."

9. Quoted in Horton and Horton, *Hard Road to Freedom*, 102.

10. Quoted in Killingray, "The Black Atlantic Missionary Movement," 6. Half of that number were women, mostly unmarried (22).

11. Williams, *Black Americans and the Evangelization of Africa*, 110. Sylvia Jacobs argues that American missions at this time had two goals—to evangelize among peoples they considered heathen and to develop social institutions, such as schools, hospitals, and agriculture, in order to achieve Westernization in Africa. See "The Historical Role of Afro-Americans in American Missionary Efforts in Africa," in Jacobs, *Black Americans and the Missionary Movement in Africa*.

12. See Alexander, *African or American?* ch. 2, for discussion of black activism in New York. Crummell's father, Boston, was a member of the African Society in New York, and also of the Haytian Emigration Society.

13. Otey Scruggs, "Alexander Crummell," in *Dictionary of American Negro Biography*, ed. Rayford W. Logan and Michael R. Winston (New York: Norton, 1982), 15.

14. Alexander Crummell, *The Relations and Duties of Free Colored Men in America to Africa* (Champaign, IL: Hartford, 1861), https://archive.org/details/relationsdutiesoooocrum.

15. John Wesley and Edward Bowen, eds., *Africa and the American Negro: Addresses and Proceedings of the Congress on Africa: Held under the Auspices of the Stewart Missionary Foundation for Africa of Gammon Theological Seminary in Connection with the Cotton States and International Exposition, December 13–15, 1895* (1895), in *Documenting the American South*, University Library, the University of North Carolina at Chapel Hill, 2001, http://docsouth.unc.edu/church/bowen/bowen.html.

16. Amanda Smith, *An Autobiography: The Story of the Lord's Dealings with Mrs. Amanda Smith the Colored Evangelist; Containing an Account of Her Life Work of Faith, and Her Travels in America, England, Ireland, Scotland,*

India, and Africa, as an Independent Missionary (1893), in *Documenting the American South*, Academic Affairs Library, University of North Carolina at Chapel Hill, 1990, http://docsouth.unc.edu/neh/smitham/smith.html. See also Sandy Martin, "Spelman's Emma B. Delaney and the African Mission," in *This Far by Faith: Readings in African-American Women's Religious Biography*, ed. Judith Weisenfeld and Richard Newman (New York: Routledge, 1996), 225; S. D. Martin, "Spelman's Emma B. Delaney and the African Mission," *Journal of Religious Thought* 41, no. 1 (1984): 22; Spelman College, *Spelman Messenger*, May 1896, 89, http://digitalcommons.auctr.edu/scmessenger/89; Spelman College, *Spelman Messenger*, December 1900, 124, http://digitalcommons.auctr.edu/scmessenger/124. See also Brandi Hughes, "Reconstruction's Revival: The Foreign Mission Board of the National Baptist Convention and the Roots of Black Populist Diplomacy," in *African Americans in U.S. Foreign Policy: From the Era of Frederick Douglass to the Age of Obama*, ed. Linda Heywood, Allison Blakely, Charles Stith, and Joshua C. Yesnowitz (Chicago: University of Illinois Press, 2015), 83–108, http://www.jstor.org.proxygw.wrlc.org/stable/10.5406/j.ctt6wr5pv.9. For more recent work, see Y. Pierce, "Leaving Husband, Home, and Baby and All: African American Women and Nineteenth-Century Global Missions," *Journal of World Christianity* 6, no. 2 (2016): 277–90. For an interesting discussion of the relationship between African American and indigenous African women, see Joanna Tenneh Diggs, "The Role of Women in National Development in Liberia, 1800–1900" (PhD diss., University of Illinois, 1989). According to Diggs, African American and indigenous women interacted in religion and education as well as through trade, employment, and intermarriage. Nevertheless, she argues, integration was never complete. African American women eschewed agriculture and heavy labor and often utilized indigenous women for labor purposes (ch. 4). For the difficulties encountered by African American missionaries, see Betty Collier-Thomas, *Jesus, Jobs, and Justice: African American Women and Religion* (New York: Knopf, 2010), ch. 4; Jacobs, "African-American Women Missionaries," 384. See also Jacobs, "Give a Thought to Africa"; Jacobs, "Three African American Women Missionaries," 320.

17. Hughes, "Reconstruction's Revival," 87.
18. See Pagan Kennedy, *Black Livingstone: A True Tale of Adventure in the Nineteenth-Century Congo* (Santa Fe, NM: Santa Fe Writers Project, 2013). On Sheppard's activism against Belgian colonialism, see Adam Hochschild, *King Leopold's Ghost: A Story of Greed, Terror, and Heroism in Colonial Africa* (Boston: Houghton Mifflin, 1999). Scholars such as Alain Locke were influenced by the exposure to African art afforded by Sheppard's collection of African art. See H. G. Cureau, "William H. Sheppard: Missionary to the Congo, and Collector of African Art," *Journal of Negro History* 67, no. 4 (1982): 340–52.

19. Williams, "Ethnic Relations of African Students," 229–31; Collier-Thomas, *Jesus, Jobs, and Justice*, 228. See also Martin, "Spelman's Emma B. Delaney and the African Mission."

20. Sylvia Jacobs, *The African Nexus: Black American Perspectives on the European Partitioning of Africa, 1880–1920* (Westport, CO: Greenwood, 1981), 67–79.

21. Quoted in Jeanette Eileen Jones, *In Search of Brightest Africa: Reimagining the Dark Continent in American Culture, 1884–1936* (Athens: University of Georgia Press, 2010), 85.

22. T. Thomas Fortune, quoted in Jones, *In Search of Brightest Africa*, 38. See also Aldridge, "Becoming American," 38; Donald F. Roth, "The 'Black Man's Burden': The Racial Background of Afro-American Missionaries and Africa," in Jacobs, *Black Americans and the Missionary Movement in Africa*, 24; Wesley and Bowen, *Africa and the American Negro*; W. L. Williams, "Black Journalism's Opinions about Africa during the Late Nineteenth Century," *Phylon* 34, no. 3 (1973): 224–35.

23. Wesley and Bowen, *Africa and the American Negro*; Henry McNeal Turner, "Our Sentiments," *Voice of Mission* 5, no. 6 (1897).

24. Darlene Clark Hine, William C. Hine, and Stanley Harrold, "Lynchings in the United States," in *African Americans: A Concise History*, vol. 2, *1889–1932* (Upper Saddle River, NJ: Prentice Hall, 2004), 243.

25. Harvard Sitkoff, *Struggle for Black Equality, 1954–1992* (New York: Hill & Wang, 1993), 4.

26. John Hope Franklin and Isidore Starr, eds., *The Negro in Twentieth Century America: A Reader on the Struggle for Civil Rights* (New York: Vintage Books, 1967); Ray Stannard Baker, *Following the Color Line: An Account of Negro Citizenship in the American Democracy* (New York: Doubleday, Page, 1908).

27. W. E. B Du Bois, "Segregation in the North," *The Crisis*, April 1934, 115–17.

28. Langley, "Chief Sam's African Movement," 165. See also Robert Hill, ed., *Pan African Biography* (Los Angeles: Crossroads/African Studies Center, 1987); David Chang, *The Color of the Land* (Chapel Hill: University of North Carolina Press, 2010); William E. Bittle and Gilbert Geis, *The Longest Way Home: Chief Alfred C. Sam's Back-to-Africa Movement* (Detroit: Wayne State University Press, 1964).

29. Quoted in Langley, "Chief Sam's African Movement," 173. See also "African 'Paradise' Lure for Negroes," *New York Times*, February 11, 1914, http://query.nytimes.com/mem/archive-free/pdf?res=990DE1D61F3BE633A25752C1A9649C946596D6CF.

30. Franklin and Starr, *The Negro in Twentieth Century America*.

31. Quoted in Leon Litwack, *Trouble in Mind* (New York: Knopf, 1998), 486.

32. James Meriwether, *Proudly We Can Be Africans: Black Americans and Africa, 1935–1961* (Chapel Hill: University of North Carolina Press, 2002), 19.

33. Emory Warren Ross Papers, Burke Library at Union Theological Seminary, Columbia University, New York.

34. Meriwether, *Proudly We Can Be Africans*, 19.

35. W. E. B. Du Bois, "On Being Ashamed of Oneself," in Eric J. Sundquist, ed., *The Oxford W. E. B. Du Bois Reader* (New York: Oxford University Press, 1996), 76.

36. "Negro Protectorate in Africa Proposed," *Baltimore Sun*, January 22, 1919.

37. Meriwether, *Proudly We Can Be Africans*, 21–22.

38. Quoted in Paula Giddings, *When and Where I Enter: The Impact of Black Women on Race and Sex in America* (New York: Harper Collins, 2006), 195.

39. See Robert Hill, ed., *The Marcus Garvey and Universal Negro Improvement Association Papers*, vol. 9, *Africa for the Africans, June 1921–1922* (Los Angeles: University of California Press, 1995); Robert Hill, ed., *The Marcus Garvey and Universal Negro Improvement Association Papers*, vol. 10, *Africa for Africans, 1923–1945* (Los Angeles: University of California Press, 2006).

40. See Colin Grant, *Negro with a Hat: The Rise and Fall of Marcus Garvey* (New York: Oxford University Press, 2010), 244; Ula Taylor, *The Veiled Garvey: The Life and Times of Amy Jacques Garvey* (Chapel Hill: University of North Carolina Press, 2002), 110. Records show Marke entering the country in 1920 and 1922. For an interesting analysis of Garvey's influence and impact in South Africa, see Robert Trent Vinson, *The Americans Are Coming! Dreams of African American Liberation in Segregationist South Africa* (Athens: Ohio University Press, 2011).

41. Quoted in Howard Brotz, ed., *Negro Social and Political Thought, 1850–1920: Representative Texts* (New York: Basic Books, 1923), 568.

42. "Protests Alien Bill: Booker T. Washington Says It's Unfair to His Race," *Washington Post*, January 15, 1915.

43. Andrew Zimmerman, *Alabama in Africa: Booker T. Washington, the German Empire, and the Globalization of the New South* (Princeton, NJ: Princeton University Press, 2010).

44. On Washington's influence on Africans, see Louis Harlan, *Booker T. Washington: The Making of a Black Leader, 1856–1901* (New York: Oxford University Press, 1972).

45. Williams, "Ethnic Relations of African Students." See also Nemata Blyden, "Relationships among Blacks in Diaspora: African and Caribbean Immigrants and American-Born Blacks," in *Africans in Global Migration: Searching for Promised Lands*, ed. John A. Arthur, Joseph Takougang, and Thomas Owusu (Lanham, MD: Lexington Books, 2012), 161–74.

46. See Ralston, "American Episodes in the Making of an African Leader," 75. See also Steven Gish, *Alfred B. Xuma: African, American, South African* (New York: New York University Press, 2000). Dube received high school training at Oberlin and did a theology degree at Brooklyn

Theological Seminary in New York City in the late 1890s. He was certainly influenced by Washington. See Heather Hughes, *The First President: A Life of John L. Dube, Founding President of the ANC* (Auckland Park, South Africa: Jacana Media, 2011). William Manning Marable, "African Nationalist: The Life of John Langalibalele Dube" (PhD diss., University of Maryland, 1976); Hunt Davis, "John L. Dube: A South African Exponent of Booker T. Washington," *Journal of African Studies* 2, no. 4 (1975). Manning Marable rather strongly argues that Dube's American experience "established the intellectual rationale for his educational and political thought for the rest of his adult life." See also R. T. Vinson and R. Edgar, "Zulus Abroad: Cultural Representations and Educational Experiences of Zulus in America, 1880–1945," *Journal of African Studies* 33, no. 1 (2007): 43–62.

47. See Edwin W. Smith, *Aggrey of Africa: A Study in Black and White* (New York: Doubleday, Doran, 1929). See also S. M. Jacobs, "James Emman Kwegyir Aggrey: An African Intellectual in the United States," *Journal of Negro History* 81, no. 1 (1996): 47–61; Williams, "Ethnic Relations of African Students." Aggrey was the sole black member of the Phelps Stokes Fund's commission sent to assess education in Africa.

48. James Aggrey Papers, box 147–3, folder 21, Moorland-Spingarn Research Center, Howard University, Washington, DC.

49. "Rev. Orishatukeh Faduma" *American Missionary* 57, no. 1 (1904): 16.

50. Orishatukeh Faduma, "The African Movement: The Perils of Pioneering—A Parallel," *Sierra Leone Weekly News*, September 11, 1915, quoted in Langley, "Chief Sam's African Movement," 176. See also Moses Nathaniel Moore Jr., "Orishatukeh Faduma: An Intellectual Biography of a Liberal Evangelical Pan-Africanist, 1857–1946" (PhD diss., Union Theological Seminary, 1987), 260. Faduma spent a period of eight years in Sierra Leone on and off after he left, opening a school in the colony.

51. See Simbini Mamba Nkomo, "The African Student Union," in Pamphlet, *The Student World. Negro Students in Africa, America, and Europe: April 1923*, James Aggrey Papers, folder 13: Writings by "The Native Students of Africa" Staff.

52. Rina Okonkwo, "Orishatukeh Faduma: A Man of Two Worlds," *Journal of Negro History* 68, no. 1 (1983): 26.

53. Quoted in Alfred Xuma, *Charlotte Manye (Mrs. Maxeke): "What an Educated African Girl Can Do,"* ed. Dovie King Clarke (Alice, Lovedale, South Africa: Women's Parent Mite Missionary Society of the A.M.E. Church, 1930), 1, http://www.historicalpapers.wits.ac.za/inventories/inv_pdfo/AD2186/AD2186-Ha2-01-jpeg.pdf. See also N. Masilela, "The 'Black Atlantic' and African Modernity to South Africa," *Research in African Literatures* 27, no. 4 (1996): 88–96; and April, "Theorising Women." For other laudatory perspectives on Manye, see Daluxolo Molantoa, "What They Said about Missionary School Pioneer Dr. Charlotte Maxeke,"

Gateways to a New World—Profiles of Eminent Missionary Education Schools in South Africa, January 29, 2016, https://gatewaystoanewworld.word-press.com/2016/01/29/what-they-said-about-dr-charlotte-maxeke/. Also on Charlotte Manye, see Zubeida Jaffer, *Beauty of the Heart: The Life and Times of Charlotte Maxeke* (Bloemfontein, South Africa; Sun, 2016). See also Veit Erlmann, *African Stars: Studies in Black South African Performance* (Chicago: University of Chicago Press, 1991), 21–53.

54. Williams, "Ethnic Relations of African Students," 232; The *Baptist Home Mission Monthly,* an organ of the American Baptist Home Mission Society, published several articles on African American female missionaries and young African women brought to the United States to be educated. An article on some of these young women, including Yongebloed, Clark, and Rattray, offered their Congolese names. Interestingly, the missionary who sponsored one of them, Nora Gordon, was also given the Congolese name Sita. *Baptist Home Mission Monthly, Volume 17–18* (Ann Arbor: University of Michigan and American Baptist Home Mission Society, 1895), 389–400. Included with the article was a picture of four young women captioned "Vunga, Zinga, Nkebani and Sita." Collier-Thomas, *Jesus, Jobs, and Justice,* 228. Suluka's husband was Dr. Andrew Holmes from Fort Valley, Georgia.

55. Gareth Griffiths, "Coming to America: 'African Princes' in America, 1886 to the Present Day," in *Literature, the Visual Arts and Globalization in Africa and Its Diaspora,* ed. Lokangaka Losambe and Maureen Eke (Trenton, NJ: African World Press, 2011), 149. See also Felix Ekechi, "Christianity," in *Africa,* vol. 2, *African Cultures and Societies Before 1885,* ed. Felix Ekechi (Durham, NC: Carolina Academic Press, 2000); Adebayo Oyebade, "Euro-African Relations to 1885," in *Africa,* vol. 1, *African History Before 1885,* ed. Toyin Falola (Durham, NC: Carolina Academic Press, 2000), 82.

56. "Hampton Graduating Class," *America Archives,* http://www.accessgenealogy.com/native/schools/hampton2/graduating_class_1884.htm. See also Griffiths, *"Coming to America,"* 149.

57. Jabez Ayodele Langley, quoting Kobina Sekyi in *The Parting of the Ways* (1922?), located in J. A. Langley, "Garveyism and African Nationalism," *Race & Class* 11, no. 2 (1969): 157, 166.

58. Quoted in Ibrahim Sundiata, *Brothers and Strangers: Black Zion, Black Slavery, 1914–1940* (Durham, NC: Duke University Press, 2003), 37.

59. Berman, "American Influence on African Education," 13.

60. "Aggrey to Rose, October 24, 1920," James Aggrey Papers.

61. T. S. Gale, "Segregation in British West Africa," *Cahiers d'études africaines* 20, no. 80 (1980): 495–507.

62. Shepperson, "Notes on Negro American Influences on the Emergence of African Nationalism," 304. Sol Plaatje came on a speaking tour and had exchanges with Robert Russa Moton, Washington's successor at Tuskegee.

See Brian Willan, *Sol Plaatje: A Biography* (Braamfontein, South Africa: Ravan, 1984). See also Robert Hill and Gregory Pirio, "'Africa for Africans': The Garvey Movement in South Africa, 1920–1940," in *The Politics of Race, Class and Nationalism in 20th Century South Africa*, ed. Shula Marks and Stanley Trapido (Los Angeles: The Regents of the University of California, 1987); Vinson, *The Americans are Coming!*; Adam Ewing, *The Age of Garvey: How Jamaican Activist Created a Mass Movement and Changed Global Black Politics* (Princeton, NJ: Princeton University Press, 2014). While this book is mainly concerned with African Americans and their views/relationship and representation of Africa, it is worth noting that Africans too understood, and understand, the experiences of African Americans in particular ways.

Chapter Six. "My Africa, Motherland of the Negro peoples!"

1. "2000 Parade in Harlem's Protest to Ethiopian Invasion," *Baltimore Afro American*, May 11, 1935.
2. C. Fyfe, "Race, Empire and the Historians," *Race & Class* 33, no. 4 (1992): 26. See also C. Fyfe, "Using Race as an Instrument of Policy: A Historical View," *Race & Class* 36, no. 2 (1994): 69–77.
3. See Nemata Blyden, *West Indians in West Africa: A Diaspora in Reverse* (Rochester, NY: University of Rochester Press, 2000).
4. See Kevin Shillington, *A History of Africa* (New York: Palgrave Macmillan, 2012), 362; Robert William July, *The Origins of Modern African Thought: Its Development in West Africa during the Nineteenth and Twentieth Centuries* (New York: F. A. Praeger, 1968); Philip Serge Zachernuk, *Colonial Subjects: An African Intelligentsia and Atlantic Ideas* (Charlottesville, VA: University Press of Virginia, 2000).
5. Marc Matera, "Black Internationalism and African and Caribbean Intellectuals in London, 1919–1950" (PhD diss., Rutgers University, 2008), 105.
6. Ibrahim Sundiata, *Brothers and Strangers: Black Zion, Black Slavery, 1914–1940* (Durham, NC: Duke University Press, 2003).
7. Selassie's name before he became king was Ras Tafari. He would later inspire Jamaicans to found Rastafarianism in the early 1930s. Another interesting connection to Ethiopia is the settlement at Shashemane in Ethiopia by Rastafarians from the U.S. and the Caribbean.
8. William R. Scott, *The Sons of Sheba's Race: African-Americans and the Italo-Ethiopian War, 1935–1941* (Bloomington: Indiana University Press, 1993). See also E. O. Erhagbe and E. A. Ifidon, "African-Americans and the Italo-Ethiopian Crisis, 1935–1936: The Practical Dimension of Pan-Africanism," *Aethiopica: International Journal of Ethiopian and Eritrean Studies* 11 (2008); Robinson, "The African Diaspora and the Italo-Ethiopian Crisis," 61; Joseph E. Harris, *African-American Reactions to War*

in Ethiopia, 1936–1941 (Baton Rouge: Louisiana State University Press, 1994).

9. "From the Press of a Nation," *The Crisis* 42, no. 8 (1935): 214. Extract from the *Daily Worker* in "Rally to Support of Abyssinian Masses," *Chicago Defender,* January 5, 1935. The *Daily Worker* was a Communist paper and a white commentator could have just as well written this statement, although it was likely an African American. The newspaper was not particularly black in its staff or outlook. Regardless of its author, it expressed the sentiments of many African Americans, whether they were Communist or not. It is interesting to note that while the Communist Party had black members, it was silent on the Soviet Union's continued sale of oil to Italy, an act that contributed to Italy's ability to subdue and occupy Ethiopia.

10. Quoted in Robinson, "The African Diaspora," 27, 63. *Chicago Defender,* July 22, 1935. For Mrs. Thompson's observations, see "Why Go to Ethiopia," *Chicago Defender,* August 17, 1935.

11. See Keisha N. Blain, "Teaching Black Internationalism and Americanah," *Blog of the American Studies Journal,* January 27, 2015, https://amsjournal. wordpress.com/2015/01/27/teaching-black-internationalism-and-americanah/. There is a rich literature on black internationalism. See especially Michael O. West, William G. Martin, and Fanon Che Wilkins, eds., *From Toussaint to Tupac: The Black International since the Age of Revolution* (Chapel Hill: University of North Carolina Press, 2009); Minkah Makalani, *In the Cause of Freedom: Radical Black Internationalism from Harlem to London, 1917–1939* (Chapel Hill: University of North Carolina Press, 2011); Brent Hayes Edwards, *The Practice of Diaspora: Literature, Translation, and the Rise of Black Internationalist* (Cambridge, MA: Harvard University Press, 2003); Roderick Bush, *The End of White World Supremacy: Black Internationalism and the Problem of the Color Line* (Philadelphia: Temple University Press, 2009). More recently, scholars are paying more attention to black women's internationalism. See Mary G. Rolinson, "Mabel Murphy Smythe: Black Women and Internationalism," in *Georgia Women: Their Lives and Times,* ed. Ann Short Chirhart and Kathleen Clark (Athens: University of Georgia Press, 2014); Dayo F. Gore, "From Communist Politics to Black Power: The Visionary Politics and Transnational Solidarities of Victoria 'Vicki' Ama Garvin," in *Want to Start a Revolution? Radical Women in the Black Freedom Struggle* (New York: New York University, 2009); Gerald Horne, *Race Woman: The Lives of Shirley Graham Du Bois* (New York: New York University Press, 2000); Barbara Ransby, *Eslanda: The Large and Unconventional Life of Mrs. Paul Robeson* (New Haven, CT: Yale University Press, 2013); Yevette Richards, *Maida Springer: Pan-Africanist and International Labor Leader* (Pittsburgh: University of Pittsburgh Press, 2000); Y. Richards, "African and African-American Labor Leaders in the Struggle over International Affiliation," *International Journal of African Historical*

Studies 31, no. 2 (1998): 301–34. See also K. N. Blain, "'We Want to Set the World on Fire': Black Nationalist Women and Diasporic Politics in the New Negro World, 1940–1944," *Journal of Social History* 49, no. 1 (2015): 194–212.

12. Harvard Sitkoff, *Struggle for Black Equality, 1954–1980* (New York: Hill & Wang, 1981), 4.

13. See W. E. B. Du Bois, "Segregation in the North," *The Crisis*, April 1934, 115–16.

14. W. E. B. Du Bois, "Pan-Africa and New Racial Philosophy" (1933), in *A Documentary History of the Negro People in the United States*, vol. 3, *From the Beginning of the New Deal to the End of the Second World War, 1933–1945* (New York: Citadel, 1975), 47.

15. Jones, *In Search of Brightest Africa*, 22.

16. S. Delgado-Tall, "The New Negro Movement and the African Heritage in a Pan-Africanist Perspective," *Journal of Black Studies* 31, no. 3, (2001): 288–310. See also Trudier, "The Image of Africa in the Literature of the Harlem Renaissance."

17. See Shane Graham and John Walters, eds., *Langston Hughes and the South African Drum Generation* (New York: Palgrave Macmillan, 2010).

18. J. C. Parker, "'Made-in-America Revolutions'? The 'Black University' and the American Role in the Decolonization of the Black Atlantic," *Journal of American History* 96, no. 3 (2009): 732. Alain Locke, "Apropos of Africa," in *The Works of Alain Locke*, ed. Charles Molesworth (New York: Oxford University Press, 2012).

19. Quoted in Dorothy Hunton, *Alphaeus Hunton: The Unsung Valiant* (Richmond Hill, NY: D. K. Hunton, 1986), 60–62. See also Rayford W. Logan, *The African Mandates in World Politics* (Washington, DC: Public Affairs, 1949); Alioune Diop and John A. Davis, *Africa Seen by American Negroes* (Paris: Presence Africaine, 1958).

20. Langston Hughes, *The Big Sea: An Autobiography*, (Hill & Wang, 1964), 10–11. See also Arnold Rampersand, *The Life of Langston Hughes* (Oxford: Oxford University Press, 2002). On Bunche, see Robert R. Edgar, ed., *An African American in South Africa: The Travel Notes of Ralph J. Bunche, 28 September 1937–1 January 1938* (Athens: Ohio University Press, 1992). More broadly, see Cheryl Fish and Farah J. Griffin, eds., *Stranger in the Village: Two Centuries of African American Travel Writing* (Boston: Beacon, 1998).

21. Hughes (1940), quoted in Delgado-Tall, "The New Negro Movement," 290–91.

22. "Africa Not Fatherland of Negroes, NAACP Tells Bilbo," July 12, 1945, NAACP Papers, 1940–55, General Office File, Africa (Frederick, MD: University Publications of America, 1992).

23. Darlene Clark Hine, William C. Hine, and Stanley Harrold, eds., *African Americans: A Concise History*, vol. 2, *1889–1932* (Hoboken, NJ: Pearson, 2013), 359.

24. See K. Dunn, "Lights ... Camera ... Africa: Images of Africa and Africans in Western Popular Films in the 1930s," *African Studies Review* 39, no. 1 (1996): 149.

25. Quoted in Paul Robeson and Philip Foner, *Paul Robeson Speaks: Writings, Speeches, Interviews, 1918–1974* (Secaucus, NJ: Citadel, 1978), 351. Original citation from Robeson, "Here's My Story," *Freedom*, June 1953. With respect to learning languages and studying culture, Robeson wrote in 1935: "Meanwhile in my music, my plays, my films, I want to carry always this central idea—to be African." Quoted in J. H. Clarke, "Paul Robeson: The Artist as Activist and Social Thinker," *Présence Africaine*, no. 107 (1978): 230.

26. Quoted in Paul Robeson Jr., *The Undiscovered Paul Robeson: Quest for Freedom, 1939–1976* (Hoboken, NJ: John Wiley & Sons, 2010), 209. This statement was made in 1934 at the League of Colored Peoples Conference.

27. See David Henry Anthony III, *Max Yergan: Race Man, Internationalist, Cold Warrior* (New York: New York University Press, 2006).

28. Paul Robeson to Walter White, May 22, 1945, NAACP Papers, 1940–55, General Office File, Africa.

29. Eslanda Robeson, *African Journey* (New York: John Day, 1945), 9.

30. Robeson, *African Journey*, 90, 187. See Barbara Ransby, "Eslanda Robeson and Cold War Politics," *Race & Class* 54, no. 4 (2013): 104–9; and for a more comprehensive biography of Eslanda Robeson's life and politics, see Ransby, *Eslanda*. See also M. Mahon, "Eslanda Goode Robeson's *African Journey:* The Politics of Identification and Representation in the African Diaspora," *Souls: A Critical Journal of Black Politics, Culture, and Society* 8, no. 3 (2006).

31. E. F. Frazier, "Ethnic Family Patterns: The Negro Family in the United States," *American Journal of Sociology* 53, no. 6 (1948): 435.

32. Richards, *Maida Springer*, 5.

33. James Meriwether, *Proudly We Can Be Africans: Black Americans and Africa, 1935–1961* (Chapel Hill: University of North Carolina Press, 2002), 204.

34. However, some, like Randolph, Maida Springer, and Pauli Murray, were vocal and loud on the subject in the 1950s, carrying on long after CAA voices fell silent. Anti-Communism and anticolonialism could exist side by side, often reinforcing each other. While Communist anticolonialism got crushed, other variants survived. See E. Arnesen, "Civil Rights and the Cold War at Home: Postwar Activism, Anticommunism, and the Decline of the Left," *American Communist History* 11, no. 1 (2012). In subsequent years the Justice Department and the FBI harassed the CAA. Whether Yergan aided them or not is unclear.

35. See Nnamdi Azikiwe, *Zik: A Selection of Speeches from Nnamdi Azikiwe, Governor-General of the Federation of Nigeria, Formerly President of the Nigerian Senate, Formerly Premier of the Eastern Region of Nigeria* (Cambridge: Cambridge University Press, 1961), http://www.blackpast.

org/1959-nnamdi-azikiwe-addresses-national-association-advancement-colored-people-organizations-50th-ann#sthash.nr9VVfxC.dpuf.

36. Penny M. Von Eschen, *Race against Empire: Black Americans and Anticolonialism, 1937–1957* (Ithaca, NY: Cornell University Press, 1997), 102, 118, 125, 146.

37. Paul Robeson and Max Yergan were signatories to an appeal calling for an end to the oppression of Africans in South Africa. Council on African Affairs, *An Urgent Call for Immediate Protest against Racial Injustice and the Brutal Smashing of the African Mine Workers' Strike in the Union of South Africa*, 1946, W. E. B. Du Bois Papers (MS 312), Special Collections and University Archives, University of Massachusetts Amherst Libraries, http://credo.library.umass.edu/view/full/mums312-b109-i424. For the conference, see Meriwether, *Proudly We Can Be Africans*, 138. The conference is also mentioned in a report put out by the CAA. See Council on African Affairs, *Spotlight on Africa*, May 18, 1954, W. E. B. Du Bois Papers (MS 312), Special Collections and University Archives, University of Massachusetts Amherst Libraries.

38. Channing Tobias, "To Our Friends in Africa," March 21, 1947, MRL 1: Emory Warren Ross Papers, series 2, box 9, folder 8, Burke Library at Union Theological Seminary, Columbia University, New York.

39. Claude Barnett and Etta Moten, "A West African Journey," September 1, 1947, 19, 25, MRL 1: Emory Warren Ross Papers, series 2, box 9, folder 8, Burke Library at Union Theological Seminary, Columbia University, New York.

40. Barnett and Moten, "A West African Journey," 31.

41. International Committee on Christian Literature for Africa, 1934–1954, MRL 1, Emory Warren Ross Papers, series 2, box 8, folder 3, Burke Library at Union Theological Seminary, Columbia University, New York. The Barnett manuscript can be found in the Emory Warren Ross Papers, 1877–1972. Missionary Research Library Archives, section 1, Emory Warren Ross Papers; Phelps Stokes Fund, 1944–1961, Emory Warren Ross Papers, series 2, box 9, folder 8; International Committee on Christian Literature for Africa, 1934–1954, MRL 1, Emory Warren Ross Papers, series 2, box 8, folder 3, 25, 28.

42. Barnett to W. E. F. Ward, September 6, 1947, in Phelps Stokes Fund, 1944–1961, MRL 1, Emory Warren Ross Papers, 1877–1972, series 2, box 9, folder 8.

43. Enclosure in Emory Warren Ross Papers. Pamphlet put out by Charles Pearson Publishers.

44. "Princess Wins Suit against Fisk U.: Autobiography Judged Hers; Charged President Made Copy of Book," *Baltimore Afro-American*, February 10, 1945.

45. Africans formed their first organizations in the early twentieth century. In June 1919 the *Chicago Defender* "big weekend edition" reported on a

"convention composed of native Africans." The students, "in attendance at various colleges throughout the city," met to discuss a variety of topics, including missionary work and their role in it. The article noted that many of the students "expect to return to their native land soon and engage in work beneficial to their people there." "Native African Students Hold Council," *Chicago Defender,* June 14, 1919.

46. "We Make Our Bow," in *African Interpreter,* February 1943, 4, NAACP Papers, 1940–55, General Office File, Africa (Frederick, MD: University Publications of America, 1992).

47. "We Make Our Bow," 4.

48. Generic letter of invitation addressed to "Dear Friend" from Warren Marr II, provisional chairman of the organization, May 13, 1958, NAACP Papers, Africa, Sierra Leone, 1958–1961.

49. "African Chieftainess and Aide Here," *New York Times,* May 21, 1958, 8.

50. Asadata Dafora Papers, folder 1/6: Programs, 1931–1959, Schomburg Center for Research in Black Culture, New York Public Library. African Americans were integral members of Dafora's troupe. Often billed in his programs with African names, some argued that they sought authenticity. For example, Frances Atkins took the name Musu Esami. In the 1960s it became common practice for African Americans to take African names. See Julia L. Foulkes, *Modern Bodies: Dance and American Modernism from Martha Graham to Alvin Ailey* (Chapel Hill: University of North Carolina Press, 2002).

51. "Kingsley Mbadiwe to Mary McLeod Bethune, November 17, 1944," African Academy of Arts and Research folder, Mary McLeod Bethune Papers: The Bethune Foundation Collection, part 3: subject files, 1939–1955, *ProQuest History Vault: The Black Freedom Struggle in the 20th Century: Organizational Records and Personal Papers.*

52. Paula Giddings, *Where and When I Enter: The Impact of Black Women on Race and Sex in America* (New York: Harper Collins, 1984), ch. 12.

53. Letter of invitation from Joseph Acquah to Bethune, July 17, 1950, "A Proposed College to Be Erected in West Africa to Be Supported by Americans of African Descent,"4, in Mary McLeod Bethune Papers: The Bethune Foundation Collection, part 3: subject files, 1939–1955, *ProQuest History Vault: The Black Freedom Struggle in the 20th Century: Organizational Records and Personal Papers.*

54. Bethune to Mr. J. Chukwuka Ezenekwe, November 29, 1954, Mary McLeod Bethune Papers: The Bethune Foundation Collection, part 3: subject files, 1939–1955, *ProQuest History Vault: The Black Freedom Struggle in the 20th Century: Organizational Records and Personal Papers.*

55. Henrietta Peters to Sallie Stewart, July 9, 1930, Sallie W. Stewart Correspondence, 1930–1931, *Records of the National Association of Colored Women's Clubs, 1895–1992, part 1: Minutes of National Conventions, Publications, and President's Office Correspondence, ProQuest History Vault: The Black*

Freedom Struggle in the 20th Century: Organizational Records and Personal Papers.

56. Elliott Skinner, "Afro-Americans in Search of Africa: The Scholars' Dilemma," in *Transformation and Resiliency in Africa*, ed. Pearl Robinson and Elliott Skinner (Washington, DC: Howard University Press, 1983). See also Skinner, *African Americans and US Policy toward Africa*; Martin Staniland, "African-Americans and Africa," in *American Intellectuals and African Nationalists* (New Haven, CT: Yale University Press, 1991); Jones, *In Search of Brightest Africa.*

57. See Meriwether, *Proudly We Can Be Africans*; McCray to Barnett, November 18, 1946, Claude A. Barnett Papers: The Associated Negro Press, 1918–1967, part 3: Subject Files on Black Americans, series G: Philanthropic and Social Organizations, 1925–1966, *ProQuest History Vault: The Black Freedom Struggle in the 20th Century: Organizational Records and Personal Papers*. McCray, a labor activist and co-founder with Edith Sampson of the Chicago-based Afro World Fellowship, would later become involved in the labor movement in Africa. Long a Pan-Africanist, he took pride in his African ancestry, and would follow through with his call for diasporan blacks to help develop Africa by moving to newly independent Ghana. See Yevette Richards, "The Activism of George McCray," in *Black Power beyond Borders: The Global Dimensions of the Black Power Movement*, ed. Nico Slate (New York: Palgrave Macmillian, 2012).

58. See Brenda Gayle Plummer, *In Search of Power: African Americans in the Era of Decolonization, 1956–1974* (Cambridge: Cambridge University Press, 2012), 38.

Chapter Seven. "I wanted to see this Africa"

1. Richard Wright, *Black Power* (New York: Harper Collins, 1954), 9.

2. Since Richard Wright made his journey, other African Americans and diasporan blacks have also gone in search of their African heritage, or to discover why they were not, in fact, connected to Africa. See Sadiya Hartman, *Lose Your Mother: A Journey along the Atlantic Slave Route* (New York: Farrar, Straus & Giroux, 2007); and Caryl Phillips, *The Atlantic Sound* (New York: Vintage Books, 2000), among others.

3. Wright, *Black Power*, 12.

4. Richard Wright, *Native Son* (New York: Harper & Row, 1940), 35. For an interesting perspective on Wright's views on Africa, see C. O. Ogunyemi, "Richard Wright and Africa," *International Fiction Review* 7, no. 1 (1980); "Trader Horn Trailer," *YouTube*, March 16, 2017, https://www.youtube.com/watch?v=dxXM8Movro8.

5. African Americans and Africans had also cooperated at the founding of the United Nations in 1945. See Carol Anderson, *Eyes off the Prize: The UN and the African American Struggle for Human Rights, 1944–1955* (New

York: Cambridge University Press, 2004); M. Sherwood, "There Is No Deal for the Blackman in San Francisco," *International Journal of African Historical Studies* 29, no. 1 (1996): 71–94.

6. James Meriwether, *Proudly We Can Be Africans: Black Americans and Africa, 1935–1961* (Chapel Hill: University of North Carolina Press, 2002). See also Ebere Nwaubani, *The United States and Decolonization in West Africa, 1950–1960* (Rochester: University of Rochester Press, 2001).

7. S. C. Drake, "The American Negro's Relation to Africa," *Africa Today* 14, no. 6 (1967): 12–15.

8. Wright, *Black Power,* 66.

9. Kevin Gaines, *American Africans in Ghana* (Chapel Hill: University of North Carolina Press, 2008), 110; Rosalind Rosenberg, *Jane Crow: The Life of Pauli Murray* (New York: Oxford University Press, 2017), 235–36.

10. Pauli Murray, interview by Genna Rae McNeil, February 13, 1976, *Series G: Southern Women, Southern Oral History Program Collection,* http://docsouth.unc.edu/sohp/html_use/G-0044.html.

11. A. Wyse, "The Sierra Leone Branch of the National Congress of British West Africa, 1918–1946," *International Journal of African Historical Studies* 18, no. 4 (1985): 675–98.

12. *The Autobiography of Kwame Nkrumah* (Edinburgh: Thomas Nelson and Sons, 1957), 42; see also ch. 3.

13. Meriwether, *Proudly We Can Be Africans,* 173.

14. "Salute from Harlem," *Ghana Today,* August 20,1958, https://play.google.com/books/reader?id=GsEqAAAAMAAJ&printsec=frontcover&output=reader&hl=en&pg=GBS.PA346 and https://play.google.com/books/reader?id=GsEqAAAAMAAJ&printsec=frontcover&output=reader&hl=en&pg=GBS.PA339. See also Gaines, *American Africans in Ghana.*

15. "On the Tour with Thomasina Norfold," *Amsterdam News,* November 14, 1959, quoted in Brenda Gayle Plummer, *In Search of Power: African Americans in the Era of Decolonization, 1956–1974* (Cambridge: Cambridge University Press, 2013), 34; Evelyn Cunningham, "Guinea's President Toura's Visit Evokes: New U.S. Look at Africa," *Pittsburgh Courier,* November 14, 1959, 3.

16. News release entitled "Mrs. Robeson Denounces McCarthy Quiz," *Associated Negro Press* (ANP) files with ANP byline. Barbara Ransby writes about Eslanda's testimony before McCarthy in "Eslanda Robeson and Cold War Politics," *Race & Class* 54, no. 4 (2013): 104–9.

17. Seon is the mother of comedian Dave Chappelle. George Kibala Bauer, "How many of you know Dave Chappelle's mother worked for Patrice Lumumba?" May 19, 2015, http://africasacountry.com/2015/05/how-many-of-you-know-dave-chappelles-mother-worked-for-patrice-lumumba/. Seon would later work for Africare: see http://www.thehistorymakers.org/biography/yvonne-seon-39.

18. "UN Riot Symbol of Black Unrest," *Chicago Defender,* March 4, 1961. See also P. E. Joseph, "Dashikis and Democracy: Black Studies, Student Ac-

tivism, and the Black Power Movement," *Journal of African American History* 88, no. 2 (2003): 182–203. James Hicks was a longtime journalist for the *Amsterdam News,* an African American newspaper. He was the first black journalist to report on United Nations news. See Wolfgang Saxon, "James Hicks, 70, Journalist; Ex-*Amsterdam News* Editor," *New York Times,* January 22, 1986, http://www.nytimes.com/1986/01/22/obituaries/james-hicks-70-journalist-ex-amsterdam-news-editor.html.

19. Nnamdi Azikiwe, "Nnamdi Azikiwe Addresses the NAACP Convention on the Organization's 50th Anniversary," 1959, http://www.blackpast. org/1959-nnamdi-azikiwe-addresses-national-association-advancement-colored-people-organizations-50th-ann#sthash.nr9VVfxC.dpuf. See also Nnamdi Azikiwe, *Zik: A Selection from the Speeches of Nnamdi Azikiwe, Governor-General of the Federation of Nigeria, Formerly President of the Nigerian Senate, Formerly Premier of the Eastern Region of Nigeria* (Cambridge: Cambridge University Press, 1961).

20. Brenda Gayle Plummer, *In Search of Power: African Americans in the Era of Decolonization, 1956–1974* (Cambridge: Cambridge University Press, 2013), 4.

21. Cunningham, "Guinea's President Toura's Visit," 3.

22. L. F. Palmer Jr., "Violence Fails to Halt 'Sit-In,'" *Daily Defender,* March 23, 1960, 9, http://proxygw.wrlc.org/login?url=https://search.proquest. com/docview/493789234?accountid=11243.

23. Gaines, *American Africans in Ghana,* 5.

24. Kevin Gaines, "African-American Expatriates in Ghana," *Souls* (1999): 66.

25. Martin Luther King Jr., "Birth of a New Nation" (sermon delivered at Dexter Avenue Baptist Church, Montgomery, AL, April 7, 1957).

26. Gaines, *American Africans in Ghana,* 170.

27. F. C. Wilkins, "The Making of Black Internationalists: SNCC and Africa Before the Launching of Black Power, 1960–1965," *Journal of African American History* 92, no. 4 (2007): 471.

28. Wilkins, "The Making of Black Internationalists," 490n61.

29. Quoted in Wilkins, "The Making of Black Internationalists," 480. See also R. J. Hayes, "A Free Black Mind Is a Concealed Weapon: Institutions and Social Movements in the African Diaspora," *Souls: A Critical Journal of Black Politics, Culture, and Society* 9, no. 3 (2007): 223–34.

30. "Nigerian and U.S. Negro Artists Blend Tales at AMSAC Festival in Lagos," *Ebony,* March 1962, 84.

31. Quoted in Wilkins, "The Making of Black Internationalists," 484.

32. Meriwether, *Proudly We Can Be Africans,* 151.

33. "Nigerian and U.S. Negro Artists Blend Tales," 89.

34. Gaines, *American Africans in Ghana,* 190–94. See also Maya Angelou, *All God's Children Need Traveling Shoes* (New York: Random House, 1986); James T. Campbell, *Middle Passages: African American Journeys to Africa, 1787–2005* (New York: Penguin Books, 2007).

35. Angelou, *All God's Children Need Traveling Shoes,* 195–96.

36. Angelou, *All God's Children Need Traveling Shoes*, 206–7.

37. Campbell, *Middle Passages*, 348.

38. Maya Angelou, "Africa," *AfroPoets Famous Black Writers*, http://www.afropoets.net/mayaangelou21.html, and "America," https://genius.com/Maya-angelou-america-annotated. Both poems are also included in Maya Angelou, *The Complete Poetry* (New York: Random House, 2015).

39. Meriwether, *Proudly We Can Be Africans*, 205. See also Gaines, *American Africans in Ghana*, 206.

40. "African Liberation Support Committee," *African Activist Archive*, http://africanactivist.msu.edu/organization.php?name=African+Liberation+Support+Committee.

41. Randall Robinson, *Defending the Spirit: A Black Life in America* (New York: Penguin, 1998), 96.

42. Robinson writes: "In the 1970s, African Americans who wanted to do policy work on Africa hitched their wagons to Congressman Diggs' star." Robinson, *Defending the Spirit*, 95. Robinson later became disenchanted, and left the United States to settle in Saint Kitts. See Randall Robinson, *Quitting America: The Departure of a Black Man from His Native Land* (New York: Dutton Adult, 2004).

43. See James B. Stewart, "Amandla! The Sullivan Principles and the Battle to End Apartheid in South Africa, 1975–1987," *Journal of African American History* 96, no. 1 (2011): 62–89, doi:10.5323/jafriamerhist.96.1.0062. See also Leon Sullivan, *The (Sullivan) Statement of Principles (Fourth Amplification)* (Philadelphia: International Council for Equality of Opportunity Principles, 1984).

44. See David Clark Scott, "The Sullivan Principles: A Code of Conduct for US Companies in South Africa," *Christian Science Monitor*, April 1, 1986, https://www.csmonitor.com/1986/0401/africa1.html.

45. Quoted in Joe Logan, "Harry Belafonte's 30-Year Labor of Love for Africa," *Chicago Tribune*, August 15, 1985, http://articles.chicagotribune.com/1985-08-15/features/8502230384_1_harry-belafonte-usa-for-africa-delegation-golden-nugget-casino-hotel.

46. Nelson Bangston, Elizabeth Lanis, Phyllis Suskid, and Peter Weiss, "Special Session of the Executive Board of the American Committee on Africa," *African American Archivist*, August 27, 1957, http://kora.matrix.msu.edu/files/50/304/32-130-246B-84-PW%20ACOA%20EB%209-27-57%200pt.pdf.

47. "Flier for the Free South Africa Movement Rally, December 20, 1884," *African Activist Archive*, http://kora.matrix.msu.edu/files/50/304/32-130-1A24-84-Free_SA_dec20_1984.pdf. Sylvia Hill is an academic at the University of the District of Columbia. A formative experience for her was attending the Sixth Pan-Africanist Congress in Dar es Salaam in 1974. See "Free South Africa Movement," *African American Archivist*, http://africanactivist.msu.edu/organization.php?name=Free%20South%20Africa%20Movement.

48. "Oprah's Mission to Empower Women and Girls in South Africa," http://www.impactingourfuture.com/news/oprahs-mission-to-empower-women-

and-girls-in-south-africa. See also Andrew Meldrum Henley-on-Klip, "'Their Story Is My Story': Oprah Opens $40m School for South African Girls," *Guardian*, January 3, 2007. On African Americans and the anti-apartheid movement, the author consulted Nesbitt, *Race for Sanctions*. See also "U.S. Activists and Politicians Campaign at South African Embassy for End to Apartheid, 1984–1985," *Global Nonviolent Action Database*, http://nvdatabase.swarthmore.edu/content/us-activists-and-politicians-cam-paign-south-african-embassy-end-apartheid-1984–1985. Gerald Horne has argued, however, that the NAACP distanced itself from the African National Congress of South Africa during the anti-apartheid movement in the United States, perceiving the ANC as Communist. See G. Horne, "Looking Forward/Looking Backward: The Black Constituency for Africa Past & Present," *Black Scholar* 29, no. 1 (2015): 31.

49. "Maya Angelou Writes Poem in Honour of Nelson Mandela," *Guardian*, December 7, 2013, https://www.theguardian.com/world/2013/dec/07/maya-angelou-poem-nelson-mandela. See also Harriet Staff, "Maya Angelou Presents a Tribute Poem on Behalf of the American People to Nelson Mandela," Poetry Foundation, December 12, 2013, https://www.poetryfoundation.org/harriet/2013/12/maya-angelou-presents-a-tribute-poem-on-behalf-of-the-american-people-to-nelson-mandela.

50. For an analysis of hip-hop as black nationalism, see J. L. Decker, "The State of Rap: Time and Place in Hip Hop Nationalism," *Social Text* 34 (1993): 53–84.

51. August Wilson, quoted in Alex Poinsett, "August Wilson: Hottest New Playwright," *Ebony*, November 1987, 74.

52. Quoted in Shannon, "Framing African American Cultural Identity," 29. See also Bissiri, "Aspects of Africanness in August Wilson's Drama."

53. Horne, "Looking Forward/Looking Backward," 33.

54. Joseph Takougang, "Contemporary African Immigrants to the United States," *Ìrìnkèrindò* 2 (December 2003), http://search.proquest.com/docview/37876203/.

55. David Crary, "Africans in U.S. Caught between Worlds," *USA Today*, June 16, 2007.

56. Monica Anderson, "African Immigrant Population in U.S. Steadily Climbs," *Pew Research Center*, February 14, 2017, http://www.pewresearch.org/fact-tank/2017/02/14/african-immigrant-population-in-u-s-steadily-climbs/.

57. Y. K. Djamba, "African Immigrants in the United States: A Socio-demo-graphic Profile in Comparison to Native Blacks," *African and Asian Studies* 34, no. 2 (1999): 210–15; Elizabeth M. Grieco, "The Foreign Born from Mexico in the United States: 1960–2000," in *The Hispanic Challenge? What We Know about Latino Migration*, ed. P. Strum and A. Selee (Washington, DC: Woodrow Wilson International Center for Scholars, 2004), 7–15.

58. J. E. Benson, "Exploring the Racial Identities of Black Immigrants in the United States," *Sociological Forum* 21, no. 2 (2006): 221. See also Festus E. Obiakor and Patrick A. Grant, eds., *Foreign-Born African Americans: Silenced Voices in the Discourse on Race* (New York: Nova Saence, 2002); L. Freeman, "Does Spatial Assimilation Work for Black Immigrants in the United States?" *Urban Studies* 39, no. 11 (2002).

59. Chimamanda Ngozi Adichie, *Americanah* (New York: Anchor Books, 2013), 17, 70, 331–32, 410.

60. Jemima Pierre, "Interrogating Blackness: Race and Identity Formation in the African Diaspora," *Transforming Anthropology* 11, no. 1 (2002): 51–53.

61. K. K. Apraku, *African Émigrés in the US* (New York: Praeger, 1991); Brandon A. Perry, "Historic Celebration to Build Bridges among Local Residents and African Immigrants," *Indianapolis Recorder*, June 3, 2005.

62. S. Iwarere, "D.C. Based Center Reaches out to African Immigrants," *Washington Informer* 40, no. 41 (2004).

63. "President's Bio," *Constituency for Africa*, http://www.cfa-network.org/business-services-presidents-bio.

64. "Washington DC, Mayor's Office on African Affairs," *Office on African Affairs*, www.oaa.dc.gov.

65. Yolanda Woodlee, "Activists Call for African Affairs Office," *Washington Post*, December 29, 2005.

66. Felicia Lee, "Black Migration, Both Slave and Free," *New York Times*, February 2 2005.

67. Lee, "Black Migration."

Epilogue

1. "Michelle Obama: 'The Blood of Africa Runs through My Veins," *Washington Post*, July 30, 2014, https://www.washingtonpost.com/posttv/national/michelle-obama-the-blood-of-africa-runs-through-my-veins/2014/07/30/949a485c-182e-11e4-88f7-96ed767bb747_video.html; Hannah E. Adewumi, "Zambian Musicians Sing Obama Lyrics in 'Change We Can Believe In': Obama Inauguration Speech Inspires Song," June 25, 2009, http://iipdigital.usembassy.gov/st/english/article/2009/06/20090625120207sztiwomodo.3060266.html#ixzz4bc84uEgL; Blakk Rasta, Barack Obama, https://www.youtube.com/watch?v=L85YFopyPHo. When President Obama, visited Ghana in 2009 the composition served as sort of a theme song of his visit. Tata Kinge, "Musician Tata Kinge's Tribute to U.S. President Barack Obama," December 18, 2012, BBC World Service video, http://www.bbc.co.uk/programmes/p012s8jx; Sebastien Berger, "Kenya Declares National Holiday in Celebration of Barack Obama's Presidential Victory," *Telegraph*, November 5, 2008, http://www.telegraph.co.uk/news/worldnews/barackobama/3385610/Kenya-declares-national-holiday-in-celebration-of-Barack-Obamas-presidential-victory.html; Ofeibea Quist-Arcton, "Africa

Celebrates Barack Obama's Victory," *NPR*, November 5, 2008, http://www.npr.org/templates/story/story.php?storyId=96643771.

2. Violet S. Johnson, "When Blackness Stings: African and Afro-Caribbean Immigrants, Race, and Racism in Late Twentieth Century America," *Journal of American Ethnic History* 36, no. 1 (2016): 31–62.

3. Sara Rimer and Karen W. Arenson, "Top Colleges Take More Blacks, but Which Ones?" *New York Times*, June 24, 2004; Lani Guinier, "Our Preference for the Privileged," *Boston Globe*, July 9, 2004, http://archive.boston.com/news/globe/editorial_opinion/oped/articles/2004/07/09/our_preference_for_the_privileged?pg=full.

4. G. J. Sanchez, "Race, Nation and Culture in Recent Immigration Studies," *Journal of American Ethnic History* 18, no. 4 (1999): 72

5. It is important to note that there has been a significant population of African refugees in the United States. Liberians, Eritreans, Ethiopians, and Somalians have often arrived fleeing wars, famine, repression, drought, and so on. These men and women have often not come voluntarily.

6. Phillipe Wamba, *Kinship: A Family's Journey in Africa and America* (New York: Penguin Putnam, 2000), 328.

7. *Afropolitan* was a term coined by the writer Taiye Selasi to describe what she calls the "newest generation of African emigrants," the children of postcolonial African immigrants seeking better opportunities in metropolitan cities in the United States and Europe. Taiye Selasi, "Bye-Bye Babar," *LIP Magazine*, March 3, 2005, http://thelip.robertsharp.co.uk/?p=76. For a discussion of the Afropolitan phenomenon, see C. Eze, "'We, Afropolitans,'" *Journal of African Cultural Studies* 28, no. 1 (2015): 114–19; E. Dabiri, "'Why I Am (Still) Not an Afropolitan,'" *Journal of African Cultural Studies* 28, no. 1 (2016): 104–8; S. Balakrishnan, "The Afropolitan Idea: New Perspectives on Cosmopolitanism in African Studies," *History Compass* 15, no. 2 (2017). Horne argues, "Solidarity across the Atlantic must be based on more than common melanin content, for although this is not an irrelevant concern, solidarity must also be based on a common struggle." G. Horne, "Looking Forward/Looking Backward: The Black Constituency for Africa Past & Present," *Black Scholar* 29, no. 1 (2015): 32.

8. Wamba, *Kinship*, 328.

9. Rich Schapiro, "Amadou Diallo's Mother Finally Finds Peace 17 Years After Son's Slaying by NYPD," *New York Daily News*, February 4, 2006, http://www.nydailynews.com/new-york/amadou-diallo-mother-finally-peace-nypd-shooting-article-1.2519647.

10. Chris Stein, "Back to Africa? For Some African-Americans, the Answer Is Yes," *Christian Science Monitor*, April 4, 2014, https://www.csmonitor.com/World/2014/0404/Back-to-Africa-For-some-African-Americans-the-answer-is-yes. Stein cites an estimated three thousand black Americans living in Ghana.

Bibliography

Abraham, Arthur. *An Introduction to the Precolonial History of the Mende of Sierra Leone.* Lewiston, NY: Edwin Mellen, 2003.

Abraham, Arthur, and John Warner Barber. *The Amistad Revolt: Struggle for Freedom.* Charleston, SC: Nabu, 2012.

Aldridge, Daniel W., III, ed. *Becoming American: The African American Quest for Civil Rights, 1861–1976.* The American History Series, vol. 34. Hoboken, NJ: Wiley, 2011.

Alexander, Leslie M. *African or American? Black Identity and Political Activism in New York City, 1784–1861.* Champaign: University of Illinois Press, 2011.

Anderson, Eric. "Black Émigrés: The Emergence of Nineteenth-Century United States Black Nationalism in Response to Haitian Emigration, 1816–1840." *49th Parallel: An Interdisciplinary Journal of North American Studies* 1 (1999): 1–8. http://artsweb.bham.ac.uk/49thparallel/backissues/issue1/emigres.htm.

Angell, Stephen Ward. *Bishop Henry McNeal Turner and African-American Religion in the South.* Knoxville: University of Tennessee Press, 1992.

April, Thomaza. "Theorising Women: The Intellectual Contributions of Charlotte Maxeke to the Struggle for Liberation in South Africa" (PhD diss., University of the Western Cape, 2012).

Bacon, Margaret Hope, and Emma J. Lepsansky-Werner, eds. *Back to Africa: Benjamin Coates and the Colonization Movement in the America, 1848–1880.* Philadelphia: Pennsylvania State University Press, 2006.

Becker, Cynthia. "We Are Real Slaves, Real Ismkhan: Memories of the Trans-Saharan Slave Trade of the Tafilalet of South-eastern Morocco." *Journal of North African Studies* 7, no. 4 (2002): 97–121.

Bell, Howard Holman, ed. *Minutes of the Proceedings of the National Negro Conventions, 1830–1864.* New York: Arno, 1969.

Bennett, Lerone, Jr. *Before the* Mayflower: *A History of Black America.* Chicago: Chicago Johnson, 2007.

Berlin, Ira. "From Creole to African: Atlantic Creoles and the Origins of African-American Society in Mainland North America." *William and Mary Quarterly* 53, no. 2 (1996): 251–88.

———. *Many Thousands Gone: The First Two Centuries of Slavery in North America.* Cambridge, MA: Harvard University Press, 1998.

Berman, Edward J. "American Influence on African Education: The Role of the Phelps-Stokes Fund's Education Commissions." *Comparative Education Review* 15, no. 2 (1971): 132–45.

Bissiri, Amadou. "Aspects of Africanness in August Wilson's Drama: Reading *The Piano Lesson* through Wole Soyinka's Drama," *African American Review* 30, no. 1 (Spring 1996): 99–113.

Blackett, Richard. "Martin R. Delany and Robert Campbell: Black Americans in Search of an African Colony." *Journal of Negro History* 62, no. 1 (1977): 1–25.

Blyden, Nemata. "Edward Jones: An African American in Sierra Leone." In *Moving On: Black Loyalists in the Afro-Atlantic World,* edited by John W. Pulis. New York: Garland, 1999.

Brooks, Walter H. *The Silver Bluff Church: A History of Negro Baptist Churches in America.* Washington, DC: R. L. Pendleton, 1910.

Campbell, James T. *Songs of Zion: The African Methodist Episcopal Church in the United States and South Africa.* New York: Oxford University Press, 1995.

Campbell, Robert. *A Pilgrimage to My Motherland: An Account of a Journey among the Egbas and Yorubas of Central Africa in 1859–1860.* New York: Thomas Hamilton, 1861.

Campbell, Robert, and M. R. Delany. *Search for a Place: Black Separatism and Africa, 1860.* Ann Arbor: University of Michigan Press, 1969.

Carey, Matthew. *Letters on the Colonization Society.* Philadelphia: L. Johnson, 1834.

Carney, Judith. *Black Rice: The African Origins of Rice Cultivation in the Americas.* Cambridge, MA: Harvard University Press, 2001.

Carretta, Vincent, ed. *Unchained Voices: An Anthology of Black Authors in the English-Speaking World of the Eighteenth Century.* Lexington: University Press of Kentucky, 2004.

Clarke, John Henrik. "African-American Historians and the Reclaiming of African History." *Présence africaine,* n.s., no. 110 (1979): 29–48.

Cohen, Lara Langer, and Jordan Alexander Stein, eds. *Early African American Print Culture.* Philadelphia: University of Pennsylvania Press, 2014.

Constantine, A. A. "Letter to the Editor from A. A. Constantine, Corresponding Secretary." *New York Times Words from the People: African Civilization Society,* April 17, 1860.

Curtin, Phillip D. *The Image of Africa: British Ideas and Action, 1780–1850.* Vol. 1. Madison: University of Wisconsin Press, 1973.

Davidson, Basil. *West Africa Before the Colonial Era: A History to 1850*. New York: Longman, 1998.

Delany, Martin Robison. *The Condition, Elevation, Emigration, and Destiny of the Colored People in the United States*. New York: Arno, 1968.

Dickson, Bruce D. "Ancient Africa and the Early Black American Historians, 1883–1915." *American Quarterly* 36, no. 5 (1984): 684–99.

Dixon, Chris. *African America and Haiti: Emigration and Black Nationalism in the Nineteenth Century*. Westport, CO: Greenwood, 2000.

Dorsey, Bruce Allen. "A Gendered History of African Colonization in the Antebellum United States." *Journal of Social History* 34, no. 1 (2000): 77–103.

Duffy, Bernard K., and Richard W. Leeman, eds. *The Will of the People: A Critical Anthology of Great African American Speeches*. Carbondale: Southern Illinois University Press, 2012.

Dunn, Elwood D., and Svend E. Holsoe, eds. *Historical Dictionary of Liberia*. Metuchen, NJ: Scarecrow, 1985.

Equiano, Olaudah. *Interesting Narrative of the Life of Olaudah Equiano*. Edited by Robert J. Allison. Boston: Bedford Books of St. Martin's, 1995.

Fields-Black, Edda L. *Deep Roots: Rice Farmers in West Africa and the African Diaspora*. Bloomington: Indiana University Press, 2008.

———. "Untangling the Many Roots of West African Mangrove Rice Farming: Rice Technology in the Rio Nunez Region, Earliest Times to c. 1800." *Journal of African History* 49, no. 1 (2008): 1–21.

Finkenbine, Roy E. *Sources of the African-American Past: Primary Sources in American History*. New York: Longman, 1997.

Freeman, Frederick. *Yaradee: A Plea for Africa, in Familiar Conversations on the Subject of Slavery and Colonization*. New York: Negro University Press, 1969.

Fyfe, Christopher. *A History of Sierra Leone*. London: Oxford University Press, 1962.

———. "The Sierra Leone Press in the Nineteenth Century." *Sierra Leone Studies*, n.s., 8 (1957): 226–36.

Garrison, William Lloyd. *Thoughts on African Colonization*. New York: Arno, 1968.

Gomez, Michael A. "African Identity and Slavery in the Americas." *Radical History Review* 75 (1999): 111–20.

———. *Exchanging Our Country Marks: The Transformation of African Identities in the Colonial and Antebellum South*. Chapel Hill: University of North Carolina Press, 1998.

Grant, Donald L. *The Way It Was in the South: The Black Experience in Georgia*. Athens: University of Georgia Press, 2001.

Gruesser, John Cullen. *The Empire Abroad and the Empire at Home: African American Literature and the Era of Overseas Expansion*. Athens: University of Georgia Press, 2012.

Hall, Gwendolyn M. *Slavery and African Ethnicities in the Americas: Restoring the Links*. Chapel Hill: University of North Carolina Press, 2005.

Hammond, Dorothy, and Alta Jablow. *The Africa That Never Was: Four Centuries of British Writing about Africa*. Prospect Heights, IL: Waveland, 1970.

Harrell, Willie J. *Origins of the African American Jeremiad*. Jefferson, NC: McFarland, 2011.

Harris, Joseph, ed. *Global Dimensions of the African Diaspora*. Washington, DC: Howard University Press, 1982.

Hawkins, Hugh. "Edward Jones, Marginal Man." In *Black Apostles at Home and Abroad: Afro-Americans and the Christian Mission from the Revolution to Reconstruction*, edited by David W. Willis and Richard Newman. Boston: G. K. Hall, 1982.

Hawthorne, Walter. "'Being Now, as It Were, One Family': Shipmate Bonding on the Slave Vessel *Emilia*, in Rio de Janeiro and Throughout the Atlantic World." *Luso-Brazilian Review* 45, no. 1 (2008): 53–77.

———. *Planting Rice and Harvesting Slaves: Transformation along the Guinea-Bissau Coast, 1400–1900*. Portsmouth, NH: Heinemann, 2003.

Hawthorne, Walter, and José L. Nafafé, "The Historical Roots of Multicultural Unity along the Upper Guinea Coast and Guinea-Bissau." *Social Dynamics* 42, no. 1 (2016): 31–45.

Heywood, Linda M., and John K. Thornton, eds. *Central Africans, Atlantic Creoles, and the Making of the Foundation of the Americas, 1585–1660*. New York: Cambridge University Press, 2007.

Hickey, Dennis, and Kenneth C. Wylie. *An Enchanting Darkness: The American Vision of Africa in the Twentieth Century*. East Lansing: Michigan State University Press, 1993.

Higginbotham, Leon A., Jr. *In the Matter of Color: Race and the American Legal Process: The Colonial Period*. New York: Oxford University Press, 1978.

Hodges, Graham. *Root and Branch: African Americans in New York and East Jersey, 1613–1863*. Chapel Hill: North Carolina University Press, 1999.

Horton, James Oliver, and Lois E. Horton. *Hard Road to Freedom: The Story of African America*. New Brunswick, NJ: Rutgers University Press, 2001.

Isani, Mukhtar Ali. "'Gambia on My Soul': Africa and the African in the Writings of Phillis Wheatley." *MELUS* 6, no. 1 (1979): 64–72.

Jackson, Maurice. *Let This Voice Be Heard: Anthony Benezet, Father of Atlantic Abolitionism*. Philadelphia: University of Pennsylvania Press, 2009.

Jacobs, Sylvia M. "African-American Women Missionaries and European Imperialism in Southern Africa, 1888–1920." *Women's Studies International Forum* 13, no. 94 (1990): 381–94.

———, ed. *Black Americans and the Missionary Movement in Africa*. Westport, CO: Greenwood, 1982.

———. "Give a Thought to Africa: Black Women Missionaries in South Africa." In *Western Women and Imperialism: Complicity and Resistance*, edited by Nupur Chaudhur and Margaret Strobels. Bloomington: Indiana University Press, 1992.

———. "Three African Women Missionaries in the Congo, 1887–1899: The Confluence of Race, Culture, Identity and Nationality." In *Competing Kingdoms: Women, Mission, Nation, and the American Protestant Empire, 1812–1960*, edited by Barbara Reeves-Ellington, Kathryn Kish Sklar, and Connie A. Shemo. Durham, NC: Duke University Press, 2010.

James, Winston, and John Brown Russwurm. *Struggles of John Brown Russwurm: The Life and Writings of a Pan-Africanist Pioneer, 1799–1851*. New York: New York University Press, 2010.

Jenkins, David. *Black Zion: The Return of Afro-Americans and the West Indians to Africa*. London: Wildwood House, 1975.

Johnson, Charles S. *Bitter Canaan: The Story of the Negro Republic*. New Brunswick, NJ: Transaction Books, 1987.

Jones, Jeannette Eileen. *In Search of Brightest Africa: Reimagining the Dark Continent in American Culture, 1884–1936*. Athens: University of Georgia Press, 2010.

Keim, Curtis A. *Mistaking Africa: Curiosities and Inventions of the American Mind*. Boulder, CO: Westview, 2009.

Killingray, David. "The Black Atlantic Missionary Movement and Africa, 1780s–1920s." *Journal of Religion in Africa* 33, no. 1 (2003): 3–31.

Klein, Martin A., and Claire C. Robertson. *Women and Slavery in Africa*. Madison: University of Wisconsin Press, 1983.

Kocher, Kurt Lee. "A Duty to America and Africa: A History of the Independent African Colonization Movement in Pennsylvania." *Pennsylvania History* 51, no. 2 (1984): 118–53.

Langley, J. Ayo. "Chief Sam's African Movement and Race Consciousness in West Africa." *Phylon* 32, no. 2 (1971): 164–78.

Lawrence, Benjamin Nicholas. *Amistad's Orphans: An Atlantic Story of Children, Slavery, and Smuggling*. New Haven, CT: Yale University Press, 2014.

Levecq, Christine. "What Is Africa to Me Now? The Politics of Unhappy Returns." *Journeys* 16, no. 2 (2015): 79–100.

Littlefield, Daniel C. *Rice and Slaves: Ethnicity and the Slave Trade in Colonial South Carolina*. Baton Rouge: Louisiana State University Press, 1981.

Litwack, Leon F. *North of Slavery: The Negro in the Free States, 1790–1860*. Chicago: University of Chicago Press, 1961.

Lovejoy, Paul, ed. *Ideology of Slavery in Africa*. Beverly Hills, CA: Sage, 1981.

———. *The "Middle Passage": The Enforced Migration of Africans across the Atlantic*. Cambridge: ProQuest LLC, 2006.

———. *Transformations in Slavery: A History of Slavery in Africa*. New York: Cambridge University Press, 2012.

MacMillan, Timothy J. "Black Magic: Witchcraft, Race and Resistance in Colonial New England," *Journal of Black Studies* 25, no. 1 (1994): 99–117.

Magubane, Bernard. *The Ties That Bind: African American Consciousness of Africa*. Trenton, NJ: Africa World Press, 1987.

Markwei, Matei. "The Rev. Daniel Coker of Sierra Leone." *Sierra Leone Bulletin of Religion* 7, no. 2 (1965): 41–48.

Marshall, Kenneth E. "Powerful and Righteous: The Transatlantic Survival and Cultural Resistance of an Enslaved African Family in Eighteenth-Century New Jersey." *Journal of American Ethnic History* 23, no. 2 (2004): 23–49.

McDaniel, Antonio. *Swing Low, Sweet Chariot: The Mortality Cost of Colonizing Liberia in the Nineteenth Century*. Chicago: University of Chicago Press, 1995.

Mehlinger, Louis R. "The Attitude of the Free Negro toward African Colonization." In *Not a Slave! Free People of Color in Antebellum America, 1790–1860*, edited by Lacy Shaw. New York: American Heritage Custom, 1995.

Miller, Floyd John. *The Search for a Black Nationality: Black Emigration and Colonization, 1787–1863*. Urbana: University of Illinois Press, 1975.

Miller, Randall, ed. *Letters of a Slave Family*. Ithaca, NY: Cornell University Press, 1978.

Moses, Wilson J. *Afrotopia: The Roots of African American Popular History*. Cambridge: Cambridge University Press, 1998.

———. *Alexander Crummell: A Study of Civilization and Discontent*. Amherst: University of Massachusetts Press, 1992.

Nash, Gary B. *Forging Freedom: The Formation of Philadelphia's Black Community, 1720–1840*. Cambridge, MA: Harvard University Press, 1988.

Nesbitt, Francis Njubi. *Race for Sanctions: African Americans against Apartheid, 1946–1994*. Bloomington: Indiana University Press, 2004.

Newman, Richard, and David W. Wills. *Black Apostles at Home and Abroad: Afro-Americans and the Christian Mission from the Revolution to Reconstruction*. Boston: G. K. Hall, 1982.

Ntongela, Masilela. "The 'Black Atlantic' and African Modernity to South Africa." *Research in African Literatures* 27, no. 4 (1996): 88–96.

PBS. "Henry McNeal Turner." *This Far by Faith: African-American Spiritual Journeys*, last modified 2003. http://www.pbs.org/thisfarbyfaith/people/henry_mcneal_turner.html.

Pieterse, Jan Nederveen. *White on Black: Images of Africa and Blacks in Western Popular Culture*. New Haven, CT: Yale University Press, 1992.

Powers, Bernard Edward. *Black Charlestonians: A Social History, 1833–1869*. Fayetteville: University of Arkansas Press, 1994.

Pybus, Cassandra. *Epic Journeys of Freedom: Runaway Slaves of the American Revolution and Their Global Quest for Liberty*. Boston: Beacon, 2006.

Ralston, Richard D. "American Episodes in the Making of an African Leader: A Case of Alfred B. Xuma (1893–1962)." *International Journal of African Historical Studies* 6, no. 1 (1973): 72–93.

Rediker, Marcus. *The Amistad Rebellion: An Atlantic Odyssey of Slavery and Freedom*. New York: Penguin Books, 2013.

Redkey, Edwin S. "Bishop Turner's African Dream." *Journal of American History* 54, no. 2 (n.d.): 271–90.

———. *Black Exodus: Black Nationalist and Back-to-Africa Movements, 1890–1910*. New Haven, CT: Yale University Press, 1969.

———, ed. *Respect Black: The Writings and Speeches of Henry McNeal Turner*. New York: Arno, 1971.

Reif, Michelle. "Thinking Locally, Acting Globally: The International Agenda of African American Clubwomen, 1880–1940." *Journal of African American History* 89, no. 3 (2004): 203–22.

Rigsby, Gregory. *Alexander Crummell: Pioneer of the Nineteenth-Century Pan-African Thought*. New York: Greenwood, 1987.

Rina, Okonkwo. "Orishatukeh Faduma: A Man of Two Worlds." *Journal of Negro History* 68, no. 1 (1983): 24–36.

Roberts, Kevin. "African-Virginian Extended Kin: The Prevalence of West African Family Forms among Slaves in Virginia, 1740–1870." MA thesis, Virginia Polytechnic Institute and State University, 1999.

Robinson, Cedric K. "The African Diaspora and the Italo-Ethiopian Crisis." *Race & Class* 27 (1985): 51–65.

Saillant, John, ed. "Circular Addressed to the Colored Brethren and Friends in America: An Unpublished Essay by Lott Cary, Sent from Liberia to Virginia, 1827." *Virginia Magazine of History and Biography* 104, no. 4 (1996): 481–504.

Sanneh, Lamin. *Abolitionists Abroad: American Blacks and the Making of Modern West Africa*. Cambridge, MA: Harvard University Press, 2001.

Seifman, Elif. "The United Colonization Societies of New York and Pennsylvania and the Establishment of the African Colony of Bassa Cove." *Pennsylvania History* 35, no. 1 (1968): 23–44.

Shannon, Sandra G. "Framing African American Cultural Identity: The Bookends Plays in August Wilson's 10-Play Cycle." *College Literature* 36, no. 2 (Spring 2009): 26–39.

Shepperson, George. "Notes on Negro American Influences on the Emergence of African Nationalism." *Journal of African History* 1, no. 2 (1960): 299–312.

Skinner, Elliott P. *African Americans and US Policy toward Africa, 1850–1924: In Defense of Black Nationality*. Washington, DC: Howard University Press, 1994.

Smallwood, Stephanie E. *Saltwater Slavery: A Middle Passage from Africa to American Diaspora*. Cambridge, MA: Harvard University Press, 2007.

Smith, James Wesley. *Sojourners in Search of Freedom: The Settlement of Liberia by Black Americans*. Lanham, MD: University Press of America, 1987.

Smith, Venture. *A Narrative of the Life and Adventures of Venture, a Native of Africa: But Resident above Sixty Years in the United States of America, Related by Himself.* Chapel Hill: University of North Carolina Press Academic Affairs Library, 2000.

Staudenraus, P. J. *The African Colonization Movement, 1816–1865.* New York: Columbia University Press, 1961.

Stewart, Maria W. *Meditations from the Pen of Mrs. Maria W. Stewart (Widow of the Late James W. Stewart), Now Matron of the Freedman's Hospital, and Presented in 1832 to the First African Baptist Church and Society of Boston, Mass.* Washington, DC: Enterprise, 1879.

Sweet, James H. "Defying Social Death: The Multiple Configurations of African Slave Family in the Atlantic World." *William and Mary Quarterly* 70, no. 2 (2013): 251–72.

———. "Reimagining the African-Atlantic Archive: Method, Concept, Epistemology, Ontology." *Journal of African History* 55, no. 2 (2007): 147–59.

Thabiti, Asukile. "Joel Augustus Rogers: Black International Journalism, Archival Research and Black Print Culture." *Journal of African American History* 95, nos. 3–4 (2010): 322–47.

Thornton, John K. "The African Experience of the '20 and Odd Negroes' Arriving in Virginia in 1619." *William and Mary Quarterly* 55, no. 3 (1998): 421–34.

———. "Elite Women in the Kingdom of Kongo: Historical Perspectives on Women's Political Power." *Journal of African History* 47, no. 3 (2006): 437–60.

Tillet, Salamishah. "In the Shadow of the Castle: (Trans)Nationalism, African American Tourism, and Gorée Island." *Research in African Literature* 40, no. 4 (2009): 122–41.

Tishken, Joel E. "Indigenous Religions." In *Africa,* vol. 2, *African Cultures and Societies Before 1885,* edited by Toyin Falola. Durham, NC: Carolina Academic Press, 2000.

Tomek, Beverly C. *Colonization and Its Discontents: Emancipation, Emigration, and Antislavery in Antebellum Pennsylvania.* New York: New York University Press, 2012.

Trudier, Harris. "The Image of Africa in the Literature of the Harlem Renaissance." In *Freedom's Story.* TeacherServe, National Humanities Center. http://nationalhumanitiescenter.org/tserve/freedom/1917beyond/essays/harlem.htm.

Tunde, Adeleke. *UnAfrican Americans: Nineteenth-Century Black Nationalists and the Civilizing Mission.* Lexington: University Press of Kentucky, 1998.

Uche, Kalu O. "Ebony Kinship: Americo-Liberians, Sierra Leone Creoles and the Indigenous African Populations, 1820–1900: A Comparative Analysis." PhD diss., Howard University, 1974.

Wheatley, Phillis. *Phillis Wheatley: Complete Writings.* Edited by Vincent Carretta. New York: Penguin Classics, 2001.

Wiley, Bell Irvin, ed. *Slaves No More: Letters from Liberia, 1833–1869.* Lexington: University Press of Kentucky, 1980.

Williams, Samuel. *Four Years in Liberia: A Sketch of the Life of Rev. Samuel Williams.* New York: Arno, 1969.

Williams, Walter L. *Black Americans and the Evangelization of Africa, 1877–1900.* Madison: University of Wisconsin Press, 1982.

———. "Ethnic Relations of African Students in the United States with Black Americans, 1870–1900." *Journal of Negro History* 65, no. 3 (1980): 228–49.

Winch, Julie. *Philadelphia's Black Elite: Activism, Accommodation, and the Struggle for Autonomy, 1787–1848.* Philadelphia: Temple University Press, 1988.

Wood, Peter. *Black Majority: Negroes in Colonial South Carolina from 1670 through the Stono Rebellion.* New York: Knopf, 1974.

Woodson, Carter G. *A Century of Negro Migration.* New York: Russell & Russell, 1969.

Wright, Donald R. *African Americans in the Colonial Era: From African Origins through the American Revolution.* Wheeling, IL: Harlan Davidson, 2000.

———. "The Effect of Alex Haley's *Roots* on How Gambians Remember the Atlantic Slave Trade." *History in Africa* 38 (2011): 295–318.

———. "'What Do You Mean There Were No Tribes in Africa?' Thoughts on Boundaries—and Related Matters—in Precolonial Africa." *History in Africa* 26 (1999): 409–26.

Index

An italicized page number indicates a figure.